ROMNEY

ROMNEY

****

A Political Biography
on Mitt Romney's Dad

by

DAN ANGEL

ISBN: 1-4783-9337-8
ISBN-13: 9781478393375

To

Pat

Foreword

ONE of the astonishing things about American politics is the narrow base from which it selects its candidates for major political office. Lawyers, a smattering of men with academic backgrounds and those who have been long active in government constitute the overwhelming percentage of candidates for top office. Although industry and commerce absorb by far the majority of our population, all too rarely does the leader of one of our companies seek elected position. This is an unfortunate loss of talent because these men have wrestled with so many of the very problems with which modern government executives must cope: human relations, selection of able assistants, budgets in the millions, mammoth construction projects, long-range planning and the need for imaginative approaches to new problems. While executives of large corporations are frequently in top administrative positions in government, the number who have been asked or have volunteered to go before the people asking for their votes is small. Wendell Willkie, John Volpe and Charles Percy are some of the better known, but no one has made the transition from captain of industry to successful candidate and political leader with more brilliance than George Romney.

For those who are worried that the United States is becoming a country of specialists, of men knowing more and more about less and less, George Romney's varied career gives reason for new hope. Farm helper, carpenter, lather, stenographer, tariff specialist, lobbyist, industrial association representative, auto builder, constitutional-convention leader and governor—all of these George Romney has been, and in each of them he has been a success. From each job he has learned lessons which he has applied to later work. Further, throughout his career, he has demonstrated a capacity for growth, in that he constantly improves in each task he undertakes. His whole life has been marked by a refusal to be stuck in a narrow rut, and he has displayed a spirit of adventure, a responsiveness to challenge and a willingness to take a chance.

Among his personal characteristics are a constantly inquisitive mind and a deeply ingrained sense of service that undoubtedly stem from his family heritage and his religion. Coupled with the above, he has an extraordinary amount of energy resulting from his keeping in top physical condition, a rocklike personal integrity and a deep faith in the abilities, initiative and decency of the American citizen.

With its dramatically increasing population and its political philosophy that government has an obligation to assist in solving problems that previously were ignored or were left to the private sector, the United States is undergoing an intensive re-examination of its governmental structure. Increasingly, it is becoming apparent that leaving decision-making to Washington is too slow, too expensive and too inefficient. Attempts to have Washington share this process with individual cities have not brought any more satisfactory results. The solution lies in vigorous, responsive, innovative and responsible state governments. George Romney has been in the vanguard of the effort to make state government realize its maximum potential of service to the people. He led the effort to give Michigan a constitution that permits the chief executive to actually run the affairs of the state, and that places responsibility squarely on the governor's shoulders. He successfully had enacted state fiscal reforms so that a governor would have the finances to do his job correctly. And he has shown a keen understanding that the number-one domestic problem of our nation today is to make our cities liveable. To help achieve this, George Romney has dramatically increased state aid to local governments, increased by 55 percent state aid to local schools, pushed support for local colleges, fought for stronger civil rights, better water- and air- pollution control, doubled rehabilitation facilities for delinquents, launched a comprehensive attack against mental retardation and strengthened community mental-health facilities. Above all, he has kept his eye on the principal solution for the eradication of poverty, namely, the availability of more and better jobs through the encouragement of industry to locate and expand within his state. The effort to improve our cities has had no more competent champion than George Romney.

As a political figure, Governor Romney has met the acid test— he wins. Not only has he successively increased his own plurality in what was previously a Democratic state; he has also demonstrated that his brand of politics appeals to the Independents, 75 percent of whom voted for him in 1966, and even to Democrats, 25 percent of whom gave him their votes. His further attraction as a candidate is that his coattails are long, as demonstrated by his sweeping into office with him a United States senator, five new congressmen and control of both branches of the legislature.

The Republican party, but even more the nation, has reason to be grateful that a man of George Romney's ability, energy and integrity is willing to come forward to serve the people. His is the leadership we need on the national level.

JOHN H. CHAFEE
Governor of Rhode Island

State House
Providence, Rhode Island
August 3, 1967

Preface

THE date was September 14, 1962, and a young M.A. candidate from Wayne State University was in Gaylord, Michigan, listening to an automobile executive turned political candidate. George Romney was speaking to a group of television and radio broadcasters. I was hearing him for the first time, and the speech seemed to carry a special message for me: "The world of ideas is not a precise world. It is subject to constant interpretation and reinterpretation. You can't see through and determine the length of an idea like you can an automobile. It takes a lot more time to test the performance of an idea about better government than to test the performance of a car. Yet the basic decisions about what kind of state and what kind of nation we will have in the future are made on the evaluation of ideas—of political concepts. And the response of the people—the making of those basic decisions about the future —depends on how well, how fully and how accurately the ideas of political candidates are communicated . . . and it is essential that everyone associated with public communication make these political viewpoints known accurately and extensively."

That last line seemed to reach out and grab at me, for I was to make my living teaching communications. Here, then, was my Ph.D. thesis, whether George Romney won or lost. He won; and in March, 1964—on Good Friday—I secured his permission to work somewhere in that year's campaign. In my first interview with him he scribbled in a book I had brought with me: "I appreciate the interest you are taking in my history. Success to you in your analysis. I'll be very interested in your conclusions."

That fall I was named Lenore Romney's personal escort and

later the Governor's press-car driver. Both positions gave me maximum exposure to Romney while not really putting me in the position of a Romney subject. It meant spending three nights at the Romney home in East Lansing. For two months everywhere the Governor went I followed. It was exciting and educational.

After the 1964 election I went to interview Lenore Romney at her home. We discussed the campaign, my recent visit to Salt Lake City, our weeks of travel together. Then she looked at me earnestly and said, "Dan, I've gotten a letter from a publisher who wants a book on my husband. Now, I don't have much time. I was wondering if you might be interested . . ."

That was about two years ago. However, this book is the product of four years of intensive study, and based on interviews with more than a hundred state and national political leaders, 110 scrapbooks collected from five Michigan dailies, library files, articles in periodicals, and travels from coast to coast.

A number of people have given me freely of their time and energy. I wish to express my gratitude to Governor George Romney, members of his family, friends, and past instructors for much heretofore unpublished information: his wife, Lenore; his brothers Charles, Maurice, and Miles; his sister Meryl; his stepmother, Amy Romney; his Uncle Junius Romney; Gerald Smith; Clarence Neslen; Vadal Peterson; David Kennedy; and Marion G. Romney.

American Motors executives deserving a large measure of gratitude include Edward L. Cushman, Howard E. Hallas, and John A. Conde.

Political personalities to whom I am indebted are Dwight D. Eisenhower, Governor William Scranton, Senator Everett Dirksen, Representative Gerald Ford, Judge John B. Swainson, Democratic National Committeeman Neil Staebler, Democratic State Chairman Zolton A. Ferency, Republican State Chairman Elly Peterson, Secretary of State James M. Hare, Lt. Governor William Milliken, Deputy Attorney General Leon Cohan, Republican Vice-Chairman William McLaughlin, New York National Committeeman George Hinman, F. Clifton White, Paul D. Bagwell, Clarence W. Lock, and August Scholle.

Members of the press to whom I am under obligation include

Phillip Lee, Albert Sander, James Brooks, Robert H. Longstaff, Richard Barnes, Robert Popa, Robert Blair, Roscoe Drummond, Robert Novak, and Arthur Edson.

Members of the Governor's campaign and regular staff who were helpful include Charles Harmon, Richard L. Milliman, Albert Applegate, Donald Faber, George Trumbull, Jr., Arthur Elliott, Jr., John Dempsey, Walter DeVries, Thomas Hart, Walker Graham, John Morrison, John Byington, Glen Bachelder, George Walker, Shirley Quinn, Isabel Saxton, and Elsie Candey.

Among others I am indebted to Thomas Mahoney, Creighton D. Holden, Ronda S. Fields, Douglas Hufnagle, Betsey Johnston, Pamala Mount, Donna Lundquist, Charles Sheffer, Olga Kolodica, Lila Colby, Morgan Oates, U.S. Representative Marvin Esch, Professor Willis F. Dunbar, Professor F. Cleaver Bald, and Professor George H. Mayer.

Special thanks are offered to my mother and father, who labored to make my collection of Romney clippings the most complete in existence; and to my wife, who during the first year of our marriage was too long a paper widow.

D. D. A.

Albion College
Albion, Michigan
May 15, 1967

Contents

Foreword by Gov. John H. Chafee
Preface

1	The Morning After	3
2	The Makings of a President?	12
3	Michigan Before Romney	29
4	The Political Prelude	46
5	Get Michigan on the Move	69
6	Keep Michigan on the Move	93
7	The Action Team	120
8	Measuring Political Success	147
9	Romney the Man	176
10	Romney's Image of America	194
11	The Path to the White House	211
	Notes	249
	Index	261

ROMNEY

1

The Morning After

IT was 9 A.M. on November the ninth. The phone at Detroit Republican headquarters rang. It rang a second time and kept ringing. Yesterday a secretary would have snatched it up and vibrantly announced, "It's a Republican year." But now the phone was unattended.

On the fourteenth floor of Detroit's Statler Hilton Hotel there was little more activity. The whole floor—and most of the thirteenth —had been set aside for the Romney election-night activities. Last night had been off limits to everyone not in the upper echelons of Romney's favor. But this morning there was no guard stationed at the elevators. No Romney aide stood by to screen out unauthorized personnel admittances. Even the theater ropes blocking off the presidential suite had been cast aside. The only spark of life at this end of the hallway was in 1416, where George Romney was getting ready for his 11 A.M. press conference.

Down the hall in 1402 (the information center of the night before) only four tired bodies could be seen: Isabel Saxton, capable and friendly Romney secretarial aide; Neil Bykerk and Jay Kennedy, two of the Governor's four bodyguards; and Leroy Augustine, GOP candidate for the State Board of Education. Isabel was still on duty, even though she had manned the observation post most of the night. Jay and Neil were keeping awake by fiddling with the big-screen television, while Leroy sat sleepy-eyed but content in a straight-backed chair just inside the door. He unexpectedly had been pulled into office with the full thrust of the Romney Revolution. So there he sat, smoking a cigarette in a euphoric daze, admitting that the only reason he wasn't in bed was that he didn't want to miss one minute of his victory!

Three littered banquet tables in the room bespoke the previous night's activities: overflowing ashtrays, dirty coffee cups, reams of scribble-laden paper, balloons bearing the "Romney-Milliken-Griffin—Action Team" inscription, and a small cardboard box bereft of its red pins that marked the wearers as Romney confidants. A UPI teletyper now rattled off these words: "MICHIGAN HOUSE RESULTS 56–54 REPUBLICAN . . . MICHIGAN SENATE RESULTS 20–18 REPUBLICAN." (At that early hour the UPI ticker was wrong on one count: the House ended in a 55–55 tie.)

Twelve stories down, the nearly empty mezzanine testified to the tremendous Republican victory. Although the hotel crews were busy trying to restore order, the three large rooms remained a shambles. All day Tuesday television and camera men from across the nation and the three major Detroit video stations had labored, preparing to witness the Romney landslide that pollsters had been proclaiming for months. By 4 P.M. they were ready.

The mezzanine was made up of three large rooms and a huge lobby. The communications room was the first on the right after leaving the elevator. There green cloths draped several banquet tables. Lining the left wall were a battery of pay phones, three house phones, two tables of typewriters, four television monitors, and all sorts of electrical devices.

Romney was expected to deliver his victory speech in Room 2, where a forty-foot platform had been erected. Three television monitors were evenly spaced across the stage, and ropes tapered off to the entrance to the communications room. A marble floor spanned the twenty feet from the victory platform to the press platform. Here six television cameras and a number of newsreel cameras sat idly by while a few photographers and reporters picked their way gingerly through the network of wires covering the floor.

Off to the left of the video room was the Action Team Cabaret. Three television monitors had been positioned here, too, but the atmosphere was purely social. There were six four-place and two eight-place tables, with extra chairs lining the walls. Two more tables were laden with glasses, water, and ice. Large pictures of

Romney and Griffin (the GOP senatorial nominee) draped every corner, and each table had been liberally supplied with blue-and-white Romney buttons. The organ that would later play victory music stood mute.

Time dragged for the mass-media men. They chitchatted, they smoked, they sat staring into space—waiting for the man of the hour. Suddenly something like an electric current spread through the room: "Romney—George Romney is on his way!" In moments the mobile units were dispatched to the southeast door of the Statler Hilton. There a small crowd had already begun to form, and it grew larger with each passing minute. People stood shoulder to shoulder, heedless of the cold and rain.

At 8:21 Romney's white Rambler Ambassador glided into view. Spontaneous applause and shouts of joyous welcome filled the night air. A spotlight found the right front door of the car as the Governor, dressed in a dark-blue overcoat, blue suit, and dark elephant-image tie, stepped out. A broad smile spread his lips, and his eyes sparkled. He was relaxed and in high spirits. A five-piece band struck up a chorus of "Hail to the Victors." The crowd immediately began to clap in time with the music, but Romney would have none of it. Not yet. Humbly acknowledging the genuinely expressed sentiments of the band of supporters, he and his wife Lenore, made their way through the host of reporters blocking the hotel entrance. He paused to make a brief remark about Charles Percy's expected win in Illinois. "I'm delighted that Percy is ahead. He's an excellent man. I've known him for years. He'll do a good job in the Senate."

Across the street at the Tuller Hotel, Democrats sensed early that the evening was not going to be a jubilant one. They went through the motions, but the winning spirit was all but crushed as early as 8 P.M., when the Michigan polls closed. G. Mennen Williams, the Democratic senatorial candidate, arrived at 8:35. When informed that several computerized vote profiles had given the election to his opponent Robert Griffin, he replied stiffly, "I don't know how you can predict who won before some of the voters have marked their ballots." He was not yielding an inch. If the grand old man of the Michigan Democratic party was going to lose, it would not be to a calculating machine! Williams had scarcely finished speaking when Zolton Ferency, the quick-witted Democratic gubernatorial candidate, arrived. The indicated Romney landslide left him surprisingly unruffled, for at 9 P.M., with less than 1 per cent of Detroit's heavy Democratic votes in, he led Romney 342–277. But it was the last time he would lead.

At 9:15 Romney and his Action Team invaded Room 1334 of the Statler, the gubernatorial hospitality suite, and he proceeded to glad-hand everybody in sight while accepting victory wishes from close friends and aides. He even took time to thank a young admirer for a gift he had received that morning while voting in Bloomfield Hills. The gift was a red brick inscribed: "The Cornerstone of Total American Progress—1968." By 10 P.M., with 18 per cent of the vote showing Romney ahead of Ferency by a 281,639 to 192,117 margin, CBS had stationed a television camera along with newscaster Joe Weaver by the mezzanine elevator in order to interview Romney at the moment of victory. The speculators were about two hours early. Yet there they stood, fixedly waiting in a crowd that jammed the whole lobby. Meanwhile the hot television lights would flick on and off with every false alarm while several hotel guests utilizing the elevator got a small dose of stage fright.

At 10:15 Charles Harmon (the Governor's young and articulate press secretary) and Walter DeVries came down to try to quiet the noisy crowd. Harmon mounted the victory podium in the video room and announced that Romney would not make an appearance "until they got more results." Then DeVries, an influential and normally aggressive political adviser, said rather diffidently, "We expect the Governor to get about 60 per cent of the vote and Senator Griffin to compile a plurality of about 53 per cent on the basis of our Data Control Center Computations." The announcement was greeted with another chorus of "Hail to the Victors" struck up by a ten-piece band from Berkley High School wearing white T shirts inscribed "ZAP POW ROMNEY TEAM WOW!" The boys marched in a circle in the lobby and played until they were exhausted.

By 11 P.M. a "spontaneous" demonstration was brewing in the video room. On both sides of the large victory platform professionally painted signs began to crop up: "AUTO DEALERS FOR ROMNEY," "OSTEOPATHS FOR ROMNEY," "BOWLING PROPRIETORS FOR ROMNEY," "FARMERS FOR ROMNEY," "DOCTORS FOR ROMNEY," "ARCHITECTS FOR ROMNEY," "LABOR FOR ROMNEY." Other placards in the blue and white campaign colors proclaimed simply, "ROMNEY IS GREAT IN 1968!"

At 11:25 P.M. over at the Tuller Hotel, Zolton Ferency made his way downstairs and conceded his defeat. At the announcement the Statler Hilton lobby went wild. But the deafening clamor quickly subsided as the crowd listened to Ferency's words. Flanked by his wife and two sons and casually smoking a cigarette, Zolton "Happy Warrior" Ferency struck a serious note: "I am most happy that the Democratic incumbents in high administrative posts, Frank Kelley [attorney general] and James Hare [secretary of state] are apparently being returned to office . . . But most of all I want to thank you most gratefully. . . .

"I want to say that I pledge my personal cooperation and support to George Romney, and I congratulate him on his victory, and I intend to support every measure calculated to further the interests of the people of the state of Michigan and give my support whenever I can in good conscience; and I know you will do the same. [*Loud applause*] The Happy Warrior is about to become the Happy Worrier. . . ." [*Laughter*]

Only minutes later G. Mennen "Soapy" Williams, Michigan's Mr. Democrat, walked with composure toward the same platform. As a thirty-seven-year-old neophyte in 1948 he was elected governor, then reelected five times, for a national record of six consecutive terms. He was talked about as a vice-presidential nominee in 1960, and had served as Assistant Secretary of State for African Affairs for five long years under Presidents Kennedy and Johnson. He had changed the great Republican fortress of Michigan into a Democratic stronghold. He was a six-foot-three giant who owned the hearts of a multitude of Michiganites. Yet tonight his spark was gone; Soapy had lost his lather. Accompanied by his bright-eyed wife, Nancy, who couldn't stop the tears, he began slowly, deliberately, "The people of Michigan have chosen Robert Griffin to be their senator. . . ."

The Statler Hilton lobby erupted. Women screamed, men made strange sounds, and young ladies planted kisses on everybody within reach. Republicans had not only elected George Romney by the largest plurality in the history of the state, they had defeated Mr. Democrat.

Williams continued, "I wish him every success in carrying out the duties of his high office . . ." but no one seemed to care what he had to say. The steady drone rose to hysteria and subsided only to arise anew from the moment Williams made his first utterance. Besides carrying in Griffin, Romney had provided enough coat-tail strength for five new GOP congressmen, five state senators, and eighteen state representatives. It was truly a Romney Revolution!

Everywhere there were shouts of "We want Romney!" "We want Romney!" Finally their king came forth, smiling, waving, clasping every hand. He beamed broadly, and not even the roar of the crowd could cover his deep and warm chuckle. Reporters who had been polite to one another only minutes earlier became short-tempered as they pushed and pressed to get near Romney. Whereas they had been covering only a state officer moments earlier, they now had no doubts that this man would be a presidential contender two years later. Apparently the crowd was of the same opinion, for the Governor approached the podium to cries of "Romney is great in Sixty-eight!" "Romney is great in Sixty-eight!" He smiled even more broadly, then struck the "hear no evil" pose. The crowd groaned with delight but immediately responded with respectful silence.

"This is a great day for us and for the people of Michigan," Romney began jovially. "We're most grateful for the outpouring of support that has come to us from all parts of our great state. The people have given us a mandate by their votes to continue our work for a better, more vital Michigan that will achieve total progress for all the people of this state." The crowd loved it, even though they had heard it hundreds of times in the past four years.

"Now we accept that mandate with a deep sense of humility," he said, "and we owe so much to so many people that I can't begin to recognize even a fraction of them. Three months ago we said that this would not be a one-man campaign or a two-man campaign but a team campaign and a team victory. And that's exactly what it is! [*Thundering applause*] There are thousands upon thousands of good citizens across this state who have contributed to this victory. This result was made possible by Republicans, Democrats, and Independents who recognized that this Republican team is free from the domination of any special-interest group. [*Prolonged applause*] Serving all the people of Michigan is our single purpose, and we expect to use every ounce of our energy to achieve total progress.

"Now I want to take this opportunity to thank each of you for your vote and your support. Certainly the outstanding result of this campaign has been the victory of Senator Robert Griffin. [*More applause*] What a terrific campaign he's waged! A man really has to have something on the ball to start out a three-to-one underdog and then wind up on top! [*Enthusiastic agreement*] You know, I've always said that a competitor is a man who starts in a revolving door behind you and comes out ahead of you . . . and that's what Bob Griffin has done! [*Shouts of approval*] He's shown the people of Michigan that he has the qualities to be a great United States senator and I know he'll do just that.

"Now, obviously we wouldn't be celebrating here tonight without the help of our wives, Lenore, Marge [Mrs. Griffin], and Helen [Mrs. Milliken]. Had they been on the ballot instead of us, the victory would be bigger! (*Laughter*) Now the task before us is to continue Michigan's progress. Just as we've recorded major accomplishments in the past in helping Michigan once again be a leader among the states, so too we have great plans for the future—"

"Sixty-eight," someone in the crowd blurted out, and the others responded with gusto. "Romney! Romney! Romney!" others yelled as the band struck a fanfare. "Charge!"

The Governor was pleased. "We have plans [*long pause*] for Michigan," he grinningly continued. "We intend to keep Michigan rolling. We intend to do exactly what we've been doing and what has been a major theme of this campaign. We're going to serve every single citizen of Michigan on an equal basis without commitment to any special-interest group or any power group. One of the greatest things about this victory is that the Republican party in Michigan is a people's party controlled by its citizen members!

"Now, finally, let me say this for Lenore and myself. When I think we've been privileged to be a part of the life of this great state and its people for thirty years and that the people of Michigan have again entrusted us with the heaviest responsibility and highest honor they can bestow, and when I think that we've been given the privilege of living in the land of the free with its responsibilities and its opportunities and its inspired universal principles that hold out hope to men and women everywhere, the least we can do is to work for you and all the people of this state with our hearts, our minds, and our spirits." At that point there was a further tribute of silence as the emotions of a great leader and his followers meshed. Finally a middle-aged man sang out, "We love you"; and no words could better have spelled out the sentiments of those present.

Now young Senator Robert Griffin made his way to the center of the platform. "To George and Lenore Romney go our heartfelt thanks for wonderfully effective support throughout this campaign. Governor Romney's tremendous victory is a mighty tribute to his inspiring leadership, and it's no wonder that the eyes of the nation are upon him tonight."

"So are the eyes of Texas," someone astutely observed, to the delight of the crowd—and the Governor.

In a matter of moments the Governor and his party started their exit while the organ blasted out "Stouthearted Men" (a Romney favorite since his missionary days in England), then broke into "Happy Days Are Here Again." This was a direct slam at Zolton Ferency. (It was his campaign theme song.) The crowd flowed in the direction Romney took from the platform as camera men began taking down their equipment and correspondents dashed frantically toward the communications room to write or phone in their reports. Tomorrow morning the world would know that George Romney was in a position to shoot for the top. . . .

At exactly the scheduled 11 A.M. on November 9, the subject of presidential speculation arrived for his post-election press conference. The marble floor from television cameras to speaker's platform was now neatly lined with four rows of straight-backed chairs for press reporters. And as George Romney, Lieutenant Governor Bill Milliken, Senator Bob Griffin, and Lenore Romney entered, a chorus of supporters broke into "Happy Birthday to You." It was Lenore Romney's fifty-eighth birthday.

Conscious of his new-found fame, Romney, eschewing free-styled commentary this morning, read almost every word. "The results in Michigan are sensational," he began. "We exceeded our most optimistic expectations." When his brief statement was finished and he opened the forum for questions, a reporter asked him about his plans for 1968. Romney read his comment. "I'm highly complimented so many people are thinking about me in that connection, but I've made no decision." Had he spoken to any other party leaders? another reporter wanted to know. Yes, he had talked with New York's newly reelected Governor Nelson Rockefeller, Massachusetts' new Negro Senator Ed Brooke, Chuck Percy and Mark Hatfield, the newly elected senators from Illinois and Oregon, and John Lindsay, mayor of New York City, "to name just a few." Had he spoken with Ronald Reagan, new governor of California? Yes. Did Reagan call him or did he call Reagan? Reagan called him. Was that significant? No. "If he hadn't have called me, I would have called him," Romney said with a deep chuckle, evidently enjoying the cat-and-mouse game.

The significance of it was that Reagan had made only one call that night . . . to George Romney. Could this mean that Reagan was in Romney's corner? Was Reagan ready to discuss party unity with Romney and with no one else? Did Reagan want a shot at the vice-presidency?

2

The Makings of a President?

SHORTLY before announcing for the governorship of Michigan in February, 1962, George Romney seemed only amused when his name was mentioned for a presidential nomination. "Are they really talking about me—a farm boy, born in Mexico?" he would say.[1] Recently the possibility of his seeking the nomination has taken on a much more serious tone.

Let us suppose that George Romney will declare for the GOP presidential nomination in 1968. Would his Mexican birth be an obstacle?

The Constitution of the United States states, Article II, Section 1, paragraph 4:

> No person except a natural born citizen, or a citizen of the United States at the time of the adoption of this Constitution, shall be eligible to the office of President; neither shall any person be eligible to that office who shall not have attained the age of thirty-five years, and been fourteen years a resident within the United States.

That seems clear enough; yet the phrase "natural born citizen" brings up the old argument of literal versus essential interpretation of the Constitution that has been with us since 1787. Perhaps the best commentary on the subject is that of Professor Edward S. Corwin of Princeton University in his book *The President, Office and Powers*. He cites two legal principles: by the first, the term natural-born citizen is restricted to those born *on the soil* of a country, but by the second, a person born of American *parentage* is eligible. The problem becomes more complex when legal grounds are found for the support of each. The Fourteenth Amendment favors the first principle, while the first Congress of the United

States declared that "the children of citizens of the United States that may be born beyond the sea, or outside the limits of the United States, shall be considered as natural born citizens. . . ."[2]

Political scientist Russell Kirk maintained, in 1963, that Governor Romney was a "naturalized," not a "natural born citizen," and concluded that, under the Constitution, Romney might be unable to take office.[3] But Romney enthusiasts can take heart. First, Corwin boldly states that "should the American people ever choose for President a person born abroad of American parents, it is highly improbable that any other constitutional agency would venture to challenge their decision."[4] Second, neither George Washington, John Adams, Thomas Jefferson, James Madison, James Monroe, John Quincy Adams, nor Andrew Jackson met with the on-the-soil principle. These presidents were born on what now is American soil but was British soil at time of birth. Third, Herbert Clark Hoover, our thirty-first President, may have set a precedent. Hoover had not been fourteen years a resident of this country immediately before taking office in 1928.[5] Fourth, Romney's Mexican roots might well be blamed on this nation's persecution of the Mormons.

The Church of Jesus Christ of Latter-Day Saints was founded in New York State on April 6, 1830, by twenty-six-year-old Joseph Smith, Jr. In 1823, Smith testified that Moroni, a heavenly messenger, appeared in response to prayer and revealed that there were golden plates hidden near the Smith home. Four years later, after being tempted and tried, Smith was presented with these plates, translated them, and produced the *Book of Mormon*. According to Thomas F. O'Dea the volume is "the record of the aboriginal inhabitants of the Western Hemisphere and covers a period of a thousand years, from 600 B.C. to 400 A.D."[6] The Mormons (as they are commonly known) believe in modern revelation. This means that they accept both the Old and the New Testaments (when translated correctly), the *Book of Mormon* (as revealed to Joseph Smith), the *Doctrine and Covenants* (a collection of revelations from the presidents of the church), and *The Pearl of Great Price* (which renders additional writings of Moses and Abraham).

The Saints (another nickname) believe in personal revelations for assistance in their daily lives but maintain that only the church president, or "prophet, seer and revelator," may have revelations that are to guide the entire church. Joseph Smith had a number of divine revelations that were to cause immediate strain. One such God-given command was that the Mormons should retreat from secular society and build a Zion (heavenly city) on earth. This they attempted to do in New York, Missouri, Illinois, Utah, and finally in Mexico. The quest was a stormy one, and one of which George Romney is a product.

Leaving New York after unsuccessfully attempting to bring a dead child back to life, Smith revealed that Missouri was to be "the land of promise and the place for the city of Zion."[7] Smith was wrong; instead, Missouri was to be the setting for the first "Mormon War." Missourians resented the Mormons' boasts of their divine right to the land, their thrift and ingenuity, and their friendly attitude toward the Indians. They resented also their abolitionist bent and feared that their own land might be exploited by the "fanatics." A riot broke out in August, 1838, when Gentiles (non-Mormons) tried to keep Mormons from voting, and on October 26, Governor Boggs proclaimed that "the Mormons must be exterminated or driven from the state." His words were all the Gentiles needed. In the Haun's Mill Massacre, seventeen Mormons were killed. Outnumbered five to one, the Mormons submitted to a degrading truce, their leaders were jailed, and "the gathered" moved to Illinois.

What happened in Hancock County, Illinois, looked like the second act of the same play on a larger stage. The more than eight thousand Mormons were welcomed with open arms. In December, 1840, the state legislature granted to the new Mormon city a charter of such latitude that Nauvoo was very nearly a separate city-state. Much of this early friendliness was based on public sympathy aroused by the unjust "Missouri persecution." Nauvoo prospered, and the swampland-based Zion became the largest city in Illinois. The Mormons constructed a temple, organized the Nauvoo Legion, and planned a university. Converts began coming from the British Isles, and the Mormons controlled the balance of power between the Whigs and Democrats. Consequently they were courted by both parties. When, however, Joseph Smith became a candidate for the presidency of the United States in 1844, both parties were alienated.

While all this was going on, Smith had a series of seven revelations that withdrew the Saints from the mainstream of Bible-belt Christianity. The most notorious revelation sanctioned the practice of polygamy by high-ranking officials of the church. This practice was viewed as downright immorality by Gentiles and created serious apostasy among Smith's followers. William Law, one of his two counselors, decided that Smith was a "fallen prophet." In June, 1844, Law and his followers published a paper, the *Nauvoo Expositor*, that exposed polygamy publicly and set forth resolutions for the basis of a new church. They rejected the "vicious principles of Joseph Smith" as presented in his revelations. Smith had the press destroyed.

Law sought safety at Carthage and took his argument to court, charging Smith with rioting. It was a case of civil-rights violation until Smith organized troops to defend the city against mob threats. Some labeled this last maneuver treason. Governor Ford asked Smith to surrender, promising him personal safety. The guarantee was a poor one. Smith was murdered in his Carthage cell.

The martyrdom of the leader only provided new impetus to the movement. The senior member of the Council of the Twelve Apostles, Brigham Young, took charge of the main body of Saints.

In the winter of 1846 the Saints were expelled from Illinois and exchanged enemies: instead of other men they fought the elements over the thousand-mile trek to the Great Salt Lake. Beginning at winter quarters on the west bank of the Missouri on April 7, 1847, and traveling by foot, horse, and covered wagon, Brigham Young's party of more than a hundred arrived in Utah on July 24, now celebrated as Pioneer Day. By 1870 more than eighty thousand Saints had traveled the thousand-mile trail, and today nearly six thousand unmarked graves lie along that route.

At last, by the nature of the desert terrain the Saints were separated from the secular world and allowed to build their Zion. Surviving an invasion of crickets in 1848 that threatened starvation, the Saints made the desert bloom through irrigation. In 1849 the U.S. Congress was petitioned for the Provisional Government of the State of Deseret (taken from the *Book of Mormon* and meaning "honeybee"). Statehood was denied—a big reason being the "immorality of plural marriages"—but Utah Territory was recognized in 1850, and Brigham Young became territorial governor.

Later, when President Buchanan received a written report that Young had destroyed the records of the Utah Supreme Court, he replaced Young with a Gentile governor, Alfred Cumming, and dispatched twenty-five hundred troops. The Saints, remembering Missouri and Illinois, felt this was open aggression. Brigham Young declared that it was time to "fight for freedom" and, if necessary, "to separate from the federal Union." The "Utah War" ended without serious harm when Cumming reported that the Supreme Court records were in order.

This issue was scarcely resolved when the question of polygamy again started to fan the flames of hostility. On August 28, 1852, the suppressed polygamy revelation was formally publicized in a special issue of the *Deseret News*. This acknowledgment, coupled with the rising proportion of Gentile settlers as mining became profitable and the railroad was completed, resulted in the Morrill (Anti-Bigamy) Law in 1862, which punished polygamy in the Territories; but it was not enforced in Utah.

Since polygamy was a divine revelation to the Saints, they regarded the practice as perfectly moral, although no demand was made by the church that a person take more than one spouse; in fact, more than 95 per cent of the Saints were monogamous. Before the church repealed its polygamy revelation in 1890, many of the practitioners of polygamy had fled to Canada or Mexico to avoid imprisonment.[8]

In 1882, Vermont Senator George Edmunds succeeded in getting a more stringent law passed. When in 1885 the Supreme Court upheld its constitutionality, Miles Park Romney, the Governor's four-wived grandfather, was reduced from a respected citizen to a criminal in a matter of minutes. He had no choice but to flee from St. Johns, Arizona. Mexico was close, offered economic opportunity, and the Saints had already established a colony in Mexico City. President Díaz welcomed the Mormons and sold them enough land to establish ten colonies in Sonora and Chihuahua.

Gaskell Romney, the Governor's father, was then fourteen. On February 20, 1895, he claimed Anna Amelia Pratt for his wife in Colonia Juárez, one of the larger Saint colonies. The couple settled in Colonia Dublan, near Chihuahua, and Gaskell became the owner of a farm, a lumber yard, and a sash-and-door factory. Six boys were born to the Romneys, three before Michigan's Governor: Gaskell Maurice (1897), Douglas Pratt (1899), and Miles Pratt (1903). George Wilcken, their fourth son, was born July 8, 1907, when both parents were American citizens. (Only a dozen of the more than four thousand colonists secured Mexican citizenship.)

The Mormon colonies prospered in farming and ranching, again arousing the envy of their neighbors—this time the Mexicans. The Mormons were driven out of Mexico by Pancho Villa when Romney was five and became what the Governor labels "the first displaced persons of the twentieth century." Anna, Miles, Douglas, Maurice, George, and Lawrence (born in 1910) were aboard a train that reached El Paso in August of 1912. Gaskell Romney rejoined his refugee family a few weeks before the birth of the sixth and last son, Charles Wilcken.

That September the Romneys moved to Los Angeles looking for work. Gaskell became a carpenter, and his destined-for-fame son attended kindergarten. Here he was taunted unmercifully by classmates who sneeringly called him, "Mexican!" One day, instead of remaining silent, he said, "Look, if a kitten were born in a barn, would that make it a horse?" The logic of this seemed to knock some of the sass out of his classmates.[9]

In the fall of 1913 the Gaskell Romneys moved to Oakley, Idaho. The farm venture lasted three years and revolved around the then not so popular Idaho potato. Weather conditions played havoc with the best farm planning, and potato prices plunged. Romney recalls that potato prices "got down to twenty-five cents a hundred pounds—and you couldn't sell them. We ate potatoes for breakfast, lunch and dinner. Some of my brothers still can't eat potatoes."[10]

In 1916 Gaskell Romney moved his family to Salt Lake City, Utah, and once again took to construction work for his livelihood. George was only nine, and at times could be very imaginative. His stepmother Amy tells of the time his mother took his elder brother Miles to California with her for a convention. Young George did not go. A few days after the pair had returned from the trip, young Romney's Sunday-school teacher remarked to Amy, "I'm so thrilled about George. He's always been so quiet! But today he opened up and told us all about his trip to California and all about the train!" "He had not meant to be dishonest," Amy is quick to add. "He had listened to Miles in such detail that he had made the experience his own." It was around this time that his younger brother Charles could get a rise out of him by saying, "I'm the only Romney who can ever be president, because I was born in this country." "That's not so," George would reply. "My mother and father were citizens, and I can so be president!"[11]

In the fall of 1917 the Romneys moved to Rexburg, Idaho. Here young Romney was to have his first jobs peeling tomatoes, thinning sugar beets, and shocking wheat. Here Gaskell Romney experienced such success through his building projects that the Rexburg Home Builders of which he was a director merged with two other companies to form the Rexburg Building and Loan Company. By 1921, however, farm prices collapsed and housing construction slowed to a snail's pace. The elder Romney went broke for the fourth time. About the only good news that year was George's graduation from Washington Grade School as valedictorian. His address, prepared without the aid of his parents, was delivered to an audience of eleven hundred; he recalls that "it was a short talk, but it seemed like a long speech at the time."

Later that summer the family moved back to Salt Lake City, where Romney's schooling included training at Roosevelt Junior High School and at the Latter-Day Saints High School and Junior College. To enter the college a youth under twenty-one needed fifteen units of work (a unit representing "the successful study in any subject pursued through an academic year of thirty-six weeks.")[12] In order to stay eligible for basketball, Romney took one unit in American history at the high school in the fall of 1925 while studying English, political science, public speaking, and ethics at the junior college.

In Salt Lake City, Gaskell again began a construction business and employed his sons as part-time helpers. The boys shingled roofs, put down floors, and became expert lathers. Miles and George became so efficient that friends called them the lightning lathers (they could nail on three thousand laths a day). Sometimes young Charles would tag along. When this happened, brotherly friction developed. "George and I used to have disagreements on how we would work on a house," Charles recalls. "George used to try to be the boss, and I didn't take to that too well."

Such spats were not altogether uncommon. In a family with six brothers there must be moments of disagreement. Romney's only sister Meryl relates that "George and Miles would lock the bedroom door and go at it verbally and physically." The father once threatened to settle the argument by putting a cold pipe in the middle of the bed so that the boys could not argue over who was on whose side.

Family life revolved around church activities, and Gaskell Romney, a bishop, was well liked and respected by his family. Meryl recalls her father as "someone you felt free to talk to, warmhearted, and one who always saw the light side." Brother Charles saw his father as one who "didn't give us money, but always provided ways for us to earn it. He was a real pal to his children." Amy Romney, George's step-mother and aunt, painted him as "a great storyteller always with a joke on hand." Once when the elder Romney was having a meeting at his home at seven in the evening, a guest arrived at seven-fifteen. "Are you still meeting at seven?" the guest asked. "Yes," replied Gaskell, "we will meet at seven if it takes until eight to do it!" Romney recalls that his father "taught by example." He was the sort of man who walked four miles through the snow one money-tight

Christmas Eve to bring smiles of joy to his children's faces with two shiny new sleds.

The Governor remembers his mother as one who "encouraged me in reading and read a great deal herself." He says that she "was certainly one who put considerable emphasis on truth and good morality," and a smile breaks across his rugged features when he fondly remembers getting a licking for not telling the truth, when, in fact, he really did! His brother Charles said that their mother was "one who counseled the children." He vividly recalls getting a lecture on responsibility once when he was late and says, "I'm sure George was the recipient of the same kind of treatment." After her death several stories that she wrote were published in a church magazine. Both parents died of heart attacks.

Romney's father took every opportunity to teach his boys a lesson from daily activities, and the carpentry trade was one such training ground. Once George was left alone to lathe a home and suddenly discovered that he was out of material. He called home and said that he did not have enough lathes. His father assured him that there were enough there, and the younger Romney replied, "Oh, no. There are only pieces." His father told him that there was "no economy in waste" and that if he had used the smaller pieces instead of long piece after long piece, he would have had enough. George finished the job in small pieces!

As a student Romney was "well liked by everybody at the high school" according to Gerald Smith, a classmate. Others recalled him as "clean-cut," "wholesome," and "very determined." Vadal Peterson, his high-school basketball and football coach, remembers him vividly: "He was clean as a pin. I never heard him say one vulgar or immoral thing about anybody. You know, you'll hear that sort of thing in the locker room, but that's one thing he'd never participate in."

And Romney was in the locker room a great deal. He played football, basketball, and baseball and occasionally worked in track. When he tried out for freshman football, he was almost laughed at by his coach, because there was no uniform small enough to fit him. "That's all right," Romney said. He took the smallest uniform, tied the loose places with shoelaces, and came out for practice. He played three years as scrub tackle and one year as guard.

Basketball was his best sport, and when Romney was a sophomore he tried out for the "midget team." One of the requirements was that each player must weigh 110 pounds or less at the beginning of the year, and Romney was a little overweight this time. Clarence C. Neslen, a teammate, says that to this day he can remember how hard Romney worked to make the team: "For two or three days he'd get up on the track trying to make the weight. And he'd run around that track fifty or a hundred times and sweat. Then he would go down to the steam room and sweat. And he curtailed his eating. I think that on the day of the weighing in we practically had to lift him onto the scales, he was so weak."

Romney was able to rise in the hierarchy of basketball from the midget team as a sophomore to the varsity as a senior. Always the last man off the floor, he was the first man out of the shower. "Basketball was his best sport, although he was not an outstanding athlete" Peterson says.

In baseball he was an outfielder and was not on the first team. It was in track that he revealed his true character, when he tried to run the mile. "He was not exceptionally speedy or fast, but when he entered a race he was in it to stay. Even if the other fellow finished a half lap ahead of him, he would finish the race. He was just that kind of a kid," Peterson adds.

Vadal Peterson also had young Romney as a student in his hygiene class. He remembers Michigan's governor in this way: "He would come to school with his fingers bleeding in the morning after lathing with a lantern late into the night. Finances were his big problem, but he was always prepared, and I talked to other teachers who said the same thing." Clarence Neslen related that he was not an outstanding student, but was "better than average." Official transcripts from the Latter-Day Saints High School show that he carried a "B" average.

Besides work, school, study, and sports Romney was active in a number of school clubs. He was a member of Ciceronia, of which Neslen was president. Ciceronia was an all-male group that met once a week at 7:30 A.M. for one hour. There was no instructor, but the group did have an adviser. Its twenty or so members would give talks on current events, debate among themselves, and study parliamentary law. The club also sponsored dances. Romney took part in few of the debates. "I was very active in athletics and student-body activities and the result was that I was more or less excused from debates," he says.

Neslen was mindful of the fact that the club was "kind of a snooty bunch of extroverts," and maintains that this description included young Romney. There was a club song that went like this:

> We are the Ciceronias.
> We are the Ciceronias.
> We're the first, last,
> Everything between;
> Leaders in every little thing.
> And we can argue,
> Debating is our specialty;
> And we'll convince you
> We're a great fraternity.
> So it's C-I-C-E-R-O-N-I-A—
> Ciceronia, that's us!

The active young man was also a member of the Boosters Club, the Student Board of Control, and the Student Council. Occie Evans, a fellow council member, recalled that in meetings Romney would "listen attentively and say little until he could offer a solution."[13]

Probably the most important school office Romney held was that of president of the student body, and in that role, his wife says: "He gave quite a few introductions and speeches. And it was funny, he used to duck his head as he walked up to the rostrum. He was very shy. He would put his head down and get up there and usually have a joke that would make everyone laugh and then tell whatever he had to tell."

Young Romney was also involved in dramatics, although he started by way of the back door. He tried out for the senior play mainly because he felt sure that Lenore LaFount, his sweetheart and a good actress, would get a part. To his utter surprise he landed the lead role of Mr. Archibald in Edward Childs Carpenter's *Bab*.

He was insanely jealous and didn't even want Lenore to dance with another boy. There was one scene in the play where Lenore was to be kissed. During dress rehearsal Romney watched this scene and was overcome with jealousy. He stormed onto the stage, grabbed the unsuspecting fellow by the shoulder, and said, "Say, that's all right. But you don't have to be so . . . this is only a practice period. You don't need to make a real thing out of it." It must have been difficult for him to remain calm throughout the rehearsals and the performance, but *The "S" Book* (the school yearbook) reported that "George Romney, as Mr. Archibald, gave an excellent dramatization."[14]

Even as a youth he was convinced that he was usually in the right. David Kennedy, board chairman of the Continental Illinois National Bank and Trust Company in Chicago and an old friend of the Governor, relates that Anna Romney had become quite concerned with the bold positive assertions that her fourth son often made. One evening at dinner she reprimanded him, saying, "Did it ever occur to you that you might not always be right?" The boy nodded assent. But the next afternoon Romney was dissertating to his brothers again without qualification. Suddenly he caught the knowing look of his mother, and an awkward pause followed. His last sentence had begun, "In my opinion . . ." After reassessing the situation, he started again: "In my *humble, but nevertheless correct,* opinion . . ." Anna Romney had to laugh in spite of herself.

Romney seems to have developed his skill in reading during this period. Vadal Peterson "could not remember seeing him without a book in his hand," and sister Meryl remembers his liking for a biography of Theodore Roosevelt and his quoting the Bull Moose leader's advice, "The best road to success is to do your present job well." Romney himself says that from the time he was thirteen he spent much of his time reading: "I worked summers, and when I traveled on the streetcar I always had a book to read with me."

Romney graduated from high school on May 28, 1926. The 1925 *"S" Book* carried this caption under his picture: "Serious, high minded, of noble nature . . . a real fellow."[15] In the 1926 edition there was a commentary on Romney's leadership as student-body president: "President Romney . . . worked in a manner that has put the student body ahead in probably more lines than for quite some time,"[16] and his sweetheart Lenore wrote a long personal note. She advised him, "Don't let this be your banner year . . . you can do with the future what you will."[17]

Throughout junior and senior high school Romney had been making the expected advances within the church. He rose through the normal stages of deacon, teacher, priest, to elder. A deacon is usually twelve to fifteen years of age, and his major duties are to prepare the meeting house and to collect fast offerings. The Saints suggest that each family fast one Sunday of each month for two meals, and that they give the money they saved to the ward organization to take care of the needy. (A ward is a division of the church consisting of five to nine hundred people.)

When a boy is advanced to the rank of teacher, his duties are to make about six visitations a month with an older member of the church. At the age of seventeen or eighteen a boy is elevated to the rank of priest. At this level he has the authority to perform baptisms, is allowed to administer the sacraments, and is often asked to speak, on almost any subject. At about the age of twenty the rank of elder is bestowed. Now a young man may be chosen to preside over a Young Men's Mutual Improvement Association, administer a Sunday-school organization, or go on a mission.

Missions are very much a part of the Church of Jesus Christ of Latter-Day Saints. As well as spreading the word of God, they have been a major influence in the growth of the church membership, which is now over two million. Romney's grandfather, father, brothers Miles and Charles, and both of his sons, Scott and Mitt, have made two-year missionary sojourns. Young George decided that he would like to go on a British mission in the fall of 1925, but there were complications, mostly financial. (Missionaries must pay their own expenses.)

Upon graduating, George wanted very badly to go. "Dad," he said, "if I have five hundred dollars in the bank at the end of the summer, can I go?" The elder Romney gave his consent, and George embarked upon his goal in earnest. He would get up at dawn every morning, prepare his own breakfast and a lunch, and then take a streetcar to work. At the end of the summer, bursting with pride, he approached his father one evening and handed him seventy dollars. "What's that?" Gaskell Romney asked. "It's my tithe," the young man said. He had earned seven hundred dollars that summer.

Young Romney left for the British mission in mid-October, 1926. He spent eighteen months in Scotland and six more in England. Scotland proved to be a difficult assignment, because whiskey making is a national industry and the Mormon sect, opposing drinking, could hardly expect to overpower the population. But young Romney was sent there to preach, and preach he did. He and David Kennedy, who was a missionary in Liverpool at the time, became good friends. Kennedy recalls Romney as a "very active, energetic missionary," and describes a typical day's activity:

The missionaries were always in pairs. One was a junior companion and the other a senior companion. In the morning, they would have a class together on the Scriptures, discuss what they were going to do during the day, and then go out on their assignments. Sometimes it was to visit the sick or the poor. Other times it would be a street meeting. Or it might be "tracting" (distributing gospel literature from door to door).

Quite often a young missionary was in charge of a group of Saints and served as branch president. It would be his responsibility to see that Sunday school and the worship service were held properly as well as to serve as main speaker at the worship service. The missionaries also presided over funerals, preached funeral sermons, and dedicated graves. The rest of their time was spent answering correspondence. "The work," Kennedy says, "consisted largely of study and aiding people with their problems."

One of the problems of any young missionary is how to secure an audience. George was enterprising. In Edinburgh he scribbled on the sidewalk in chalk: "Come out and see what Mormons are really like."[18] In Glasgow he resorted to a task-force approach: instead of the usual traveling in pairs he would take seven or eight missionaries into a community at the same time. This drew attention from the public and from newspaper reporters, often resulting in pictures and free publicity. He would also get up early enough to walk to work with the Scottish coal miners and pass out his tracts. "There's where we ought to make our contacts" he told the other missionaries.

Capturing and holding a street audience was difficult. It was on soapboxes in Scotland and in London's Hyde Park that Romney gained experience in public speaking. The Detroit *News* labels Hyde Park "the world's greatest rough and tumble forum of free speech."[19] Romney was "about as effective at handling hecklers as anybody we had," according to Kennedy.

On one occasion his traveling companion was telling a crowd how Joseph Smith, although illiterate, had read and reread the Bible. Somebody in the audience said, "If he was an illiterate, how could he have read the Bible?" "He was stuck," Romney says. "He couldn't answer it, so I pointed out that it was not correct to say that he was illiterate and that my companion had meant to say that Smith had very little formal schooling; that he had been given some educational instruction and could read, but was not educated as we mean the word at the present time." Romney was in great demand to speak before organizations of all types.

Romney believes that his missionary experience was one of the most valuable of his life, and explains, "When I got into the mission field, I was like many young men and women who go out on such a mission. No longer able to rely upon the faith of my parents or others, I had to make my own search and through my own prayers satisfy myself as to whether or not the cause in which I was engaged was right and whether there was a Creator. I spent many hours and days in the public library in

Glasgow reading religious books and praying on the campus of the University of Glasgow to get that conviction and certainty that came as to the existence of a creator."[20] The Governor believes missions important for providing direction in the life of any youth because "you have to decide what you really think and you have to acquire the ability to explain your beliefs to others."[21]

Two years and two months had elapsed when the young man of twenty-one arrived in time to spend Christmas holidays in Washington, D.C., with the LaFounts. He had corresponded weekly with Lenore while away. On January 2 it was a penniless but happy young man, who boarded the train for Salt Lake City. His future was before him. He was now certain that Lenore LaFount was to be his wife.

Back home Romney resumed part-time work for his father and enrolled in the University of Utah. Entering in January, he took Spanish, Social Science, Zoology and History; and in March he reelected a second course in Social Science and History. This time he was an "A" student. He was quite popular and received bids from several fraternities. His brother Miles and high-school chum Gerry Smith were members of Sigma Chi, and Romney decided to join. He was well received by the brothers. He liked people and loved to dance, but "really didn't have time for fooling around in a fraternity" according to Smith. Before he could become initiated, he had gone east.

In June, Romney started working for his father on a fulltime basis and registered for an evening course in speedwriting. The LaFounts soon returned to Salt Lake City for the summer, and the Governor fondly reports that Lenore's presence didn't help his class attendance: "I had seen her only two weeks in two and a half years, so I was really more interested in courting her than going to those night classes in speedwriting. I got to only six classes all summer."[22]

He dated Lenore daily. One night they had been out late at a dance and awakened Mr. LaFount on their return. "For goodness' sake," Lenore's father said, "hurry and get to bed!" The couple had a tennis date at five-thirty in the morning, and George promised to wake Lenore by whistling under her window. Soon the sun was up, and George was there whistling away. Mr. LaFount staggered to the door and muttered, "George, are you still here?"[23]

By the end of August, Romney had made up his mind to attend George Washington University so that he could be near Lenore. He took the remaining minutes of his last day in Utah to visit his mother's grave. Placing a flower before the stone, he knelt and meditated; then he promised his mother that he would make something of himself—that he would be a success.

3

Michigan Before Romney

"Michigan" is derived from two Indian words meaning "large lake." The twenty-sixth state admitted to the Union, in 1837, it now ranks twenty-second in area and seventh in population. The state motto, "Si quaeris peninsulem amoenam circumspice" ("If you seek a pleasant peninsula, look about you") is literally inaccurate, because Michigan consists of two peninsulas. Together they constitute an area of 58,000 square miles. Its peninsulas are surrounded by four of the five Great Lakes. The lower peninsula is sometimes likened to a glove, while the upper peninsula seems to resemble a long shark with its tail fin extracted and thrust into its belly. The upper peninsula was acquired as a settlement in the bloodless "Toledo War," in which Michiganites gave up their rightful claim (under the Northwest Ordinance) to that part of Ohio now encompassing Toledo.

Most Michiganites don't care whether their state is nicknamed the Wolverine State or a Water Wonderland, but feelings may be aroused if a Michigan citizen is labeled a Michigander instead of a Michiganite (or Michiganian). The suffix "der" had an unpleasant origin. Back in 1848, when Michigan's General Lewis Cass was a presidential candidate, someone incorrectly pointed out that etymologically "Cass" meant "goose," and a rhymster penned this quatrain:

> Oh, then look here; oh, then look where?
> In Michigan right yander;
> Do you not see old Lewis Cass,
> He looks just like a gander![1]

Cass became known to his opponents as a Michigander, and the term later was expanded to include all the General's supporters from Michigan.

The bottom portion of the lower peninsula is responsible for Michigan's reputation as an industrial state—its industry being essentially the automobile. Outstate Michiganites (those inhabiting the upper portion of the lower peninsula and the upper peninsula) depend largely upon farming, tourist trade, and mining for their livelihood.

Jackson, Michigan, claims to be the birthplace of the Republican party, although the first Republican meeting of sorts was held at Ripon, Wisconsin, on February 28, 1854. At the Ripon meeting abolitionist Whigs, Free Soilers, and Democrats voted to form a new party in the event that the Kansas-Nebraska bill (legislation repealing the Missouri Compromise of 1820, which prohibited slavery north of the 36° 30′ line, and allowing the extension of slavery into Kansas) was passed. Michigan, however, can claim the first formal Republican convention complete with platform and a full slate of candidates. The meeting that took place on July 6, 1854, was such a large gathering that the crowd overflowed Jackson's largest hall and was forced outside "under the oaks" (like the famous 1926 Scopes evolution trial). The convention adopted two major resolutions:

1. That . . . in view of the imminent danger that Kansas and Nebraska will be grasped by Slavery, and a thousand miles of slave soil will be thus interposed between the free States of the Atlantic and those of the Pacific, we will act cordially and faithfully in unison to avert and repeal this gigantic wrong and shame.
2. That in view of the necessity of battling for the first principles of Republican government, and against the scheme of an aristocracy, the most revolting and oppressive with which the earth was ever cursed or man debased, we will cooperate and be known as "Republicans" until the contest be terminated.[2]

Michigan was a Republican fortress from the birth of the party until the candidacy of Franklin D. Roosevelt, during the great depression. The very first November ballot for the state Republican party witnessed election of Republican Kinsley S. Bingham as governor, and the Republican sweep carried a majority of state legislators into office along with three of the four United

States representatives. During the thirty-four biennial elections between 1853 and 1932 the Republicans never lost the electoral vote for president, and lost the office of governor only twice (1890–92 and 1912–16). Three elections in the early 1900's found the Democrats without a single member in the state legislature!

The depression in the early 1930's affected most aspects of the American being, and it profoundly affected the politics of the state of Michigan; the year 1932 witnessed the collapse of Republican supremacy. In fact, the depression stamped "Complete Reversal" upon the usual November election. Not only was FDR the first Democratic presidential candidate to carry Michigan, but Secretary of State Frank D. Fitzgerald was the lone Republican survivor.

For the next decade the state looked like a two-party battleground. In 1934, the Republicans made such a mighty comeback that only the Democratic state treasurer and auditor general were evidence of the drastic 1932 changeover. The Democrats rode the Roosevelt coattails once again, in 1936, and the landslide was enough to carry in the entire state ballot. But the off-year election in 1938 found the Republicans repeating their 1934 performance. In 1940, although Roosevelt failed for the first time to carry Michigan, the Democrats were successful in electing the governor, lieutenant governor, and state treasurer.

In 1942, Michigan returned to Republicanism in an election that foreshadowed state politics for the next six years. Roosevelt carried Michigan narrowly, in 1944, but not one Democrat on the state ballot came within 100,000 votes of winning an office. Two years later Democratic disintegration was so complete that the number of Democrats in the U.S. Congress had dwindled to three. The Republican victory was so emphatic that the Democratic stronghold, Wayne County, fell to the GOP. The Democratic defeat of that year can only be described as crushing, yet it may be that the nadir paved the way for a new type of leadership in the Democratic party that was to play an important role in state politics for the next dozen years.

During the 1940's the Democratic organization in Michigan

declined in strength. Young, liberal-minded members of the party began a reform movement in 1947, when the Michigan Democratic Club was formed. At that time two labor groups (the Political Action Committee of the CIO and the League for Political Education of the AFL) were pushing for more liberal social legislation. With their support, G. Mennen Williams—a relatively unknown lawyer—became the Democratic governor in 1948; and Democrats were also elected lieutenant governor and attorney general.

In 1950, Williams was the only Democratic victor. The count was so close that on the morning after the election, newspapers proclaimed that the entire Republican ticket had been elected. Williams demanded a recount that reversed premature speculation by a 1,154 plurality. He was also the sole survivor of the 1952 Eisenhower sweep of the state, by a much larger recount margin.

Williams did not acquire political coattails until his fourth gubernatorial campaign. The 1954 election was truly a party victory, as were those of 1956 and 1958. But the 1958 voting brought about a curious reversal of roles. Williams had been a lone winner in the early fifties and successful at pulling in other Democratic nominees in 1954 and 1956. He had built a reputation as the strong man of his party. In 1958, however, his powerhouse was short-circuited. The Republican gubernatorial nominee, Paul D. Bagwell, made an exceptionally strong bid, while Williams trailed the entire Democratic ticket.[3] (Williams had reached the peak of his popularity in 1954, and his plurality had since then been decreasing. According to Michigan Secretary of State James M. Hare, that was one reason Williams did not choose to run for a seventh term in 1960. Instead he passed the baton to his lieutenant governor, John Swainson.) In 1960 the Democrats made it four straight in state-office sweeps, while John F. Kennedy pulled Michigan into the Democratic presidential column for the first time since 1944. (Richard Nixon was later to remark, "If George Romney had run for governor of Michigan in 1960, I would have been president!")

Hugh A. Bone, author of the political classic *American Politics and the Party System*, and historian George H. Mayer, in his *The Republican Party, 1854–1864*, agree in that "only rarely can winning issues be manufactured by party theoreticians or precinct workers; most always they are generated by the larger forces of history."[4] These larger issues generated by the forces of history were vital factors in the Michigan campaign of 1962, and an exploration of Michigan in the 1940's and 1950's is therefore essential to a comprehension of George Romney's political rise.

Michigan's sociological history during this period may largely be discussed in terms of population growth and the governmental and institutional attempts to cope with that growth. From 1940 to 1950 the population increased by more than a million, and from 1950 to 1960 it increased another 23 per cent, from six and a half million to nearly eight million.

The population had increased during the early forties because of the labor vacuum created when nearly 600,000 young men left for military duty. Almost anyone could get a job in a defense plant. People from the South migrated North in record numbers, and a large percentage were Negroes. In 1940 there were 216,000 Negroes in Michigan. By 1950 there were 450,000; by 1960 the number had swelled to 750,000.

Not only did the population grow rapidly, but the state experienced some important changes within its population composition and groupings. The various nationalities that came into the state often located in areas that became practically isolated. The Dutch settled in Holland; the Germans in Frankenmuth and Westphalia; the Polish in Hamtramck; the Finnish in the upper peninsula; and the Italians in Detroit. Detroit also had many Syrians, Greeks, and Arabs. The 1960 U.S. Census lists for Michigan 159,000 English, 59,000 German, 58,000 Polish, 37,000 Italian, 20,000 Dutch, 16,000 French, 14,000 Hungarian, 12,000 Jewish, and all other groups less than 10,000, making a grand total of 539,000 foreign-born.[5]

The war boom also caused a vast shifting of the population

groupings. The northern counties lost people to the manufacturing areas and particularly to the region around Wayne County. By mid-century Wayne County accounted for 38 per cent of the state population, and the four counties of Wayne, Oakland, Genesee, and Saginaw could boast over 50 per cent. The state had gone from 39 per cent urban in 1900 to 64 per cent in 1950.

Michigan experienced some unfavorable publicity during 1950-60, but the population growth and realignment continued. By 1960 more than 73 per cent of the state's nearly 8,000,000 population could be classed as urban, although the figure is somewhat deceiving. Many of the large cities actually lost people during this decade. There was a phenomenal growth in the areas on the fringe of the core city—suburbia. Warren grew from a township of 727 in 1950 to a city of more than 89,000 in 1960. Such population growth and realignment placed great demand upon state government for expansion of present services and for new services, presenting a serious challenge to the state's economy.

From 1940 to 1953 Michigan was one of the most industrious states in the nation. It had turned its talents to war production in 1940, then at the conclusion of the war focused attention on automobile production. The shortage of automobiles in the United States during the war meant that a vast market was available; and before the market had diminished, Michigan became involved in defense production for the Korean War, in the early fifties. Business thrived so well that in 1953 Michigan could almost be accused of having overemployment. (While a figure of 38.5 per cent is often considered to be the goal of full employment, Michigan had an employment force of nearly 42 per cent.)

But beginning in 1954 the state, in three short years, suffered a loss of about 130,000 jobs, whereas the nation as a whole had made a net gain of nearly 2,500,000. The recession of 1958 was especially severe in Michigan, where the unemployed numbered more than 400,000 and equaled nearly 16 per cent of the labor force. As late as 1962 the figure was estimated at nearly 300,000.

Several factors appear to have contributed to Michigan's economic problem. First, there was defense spending. During the Korean War and World War II, Michigan was a conspicuous producer of military equipment, but after the wars there was a significant shift away from wheeled vehicles, such as jeeps and trucks, to aircraft, electronic equipment, and missiles. Michigan had not planned ahead, with the result that neither the knowledge nor the facilities to absorb the change were available. Michigan lost 150,000 defense jobs in six short years.

The second and third factors concerned the automobile. Automation had made it possible for 100,000 fewer workers to produce more cars in 1960 than were produced in 1950, and the automobile industry was in the process of decentralization. Although the major automobile production was orginally in Michigan, it had slowly been moving to other parts of the country. In 1930 Michigan accounted for over 60 per cent of all automobile employment, but in 1962 the figure had dropped to 40 per cent.[6] Norman Barcus, research director of the Michigan Employment Security Commission, estimates that this decentralization process was responsible for the loss of 100,000 automotive jobs in the three years from 1954 to 1957 alone.[7]

Add to these three economic woes the national recession of 1957–58, a booming populace demanding increased state expenditures, a governor dedicated to social legislation (Williams was responsible for a state budget increase averaging $50,000,000 annually during his twelve years in office), support from state funds for the large number of unemployed, a state legislature unwilling to add new tax sources, a state reputation for having a poor climate for industry, and it becomes clear that Michigan was headed toward economic disaster.

Until the depression Michigan—like most other states—could not to be classed as a big spender. In the early 1900's expenditures were limited to education, such institutions as hospitals and prisons, and running the three branches of state government. In 1910 total appropriations amounted to less than $5,000,000. The major sources of revenue were taxes on land, buildings, and personal property, a liquor tax adopted in 1879, and an 1899 inheritance tax. The pre-depression years witnessed the addition of a weight tax on automobiles (1915), a tax on boxing and wrestling (1919), a corporations franchise and a building and loan association assessment (1921), an aircraft registration tax (1923), a gasoline duty (1925), and a gas and oil severance levy (1929).

Money problems continued to arise anew. Legislators realized that real-estate and personal-property taxes were an inadequate source of income. In 1932 a constitutional amendment had limited these two important tax sources to 1.5 per cent of assessed valuation, an amount far beneath Michigan's financial needs. When, as a result of the depression, tax delinquency was commonplace throughout the state, the Democratic-controlled legislature of 1933 responded by relinquishing these tax claims to local governments, replacing them with a 3 per cent sales tax.

More money became available, but the population increase and new demand for better schools, relief of the unemployed, care for the mentally ill, and other such state services continued. The tax on beer and wine was reimposed as prohibition ended. Michigan enacted a use tax and began to collect for unemployment compensation in 1937. In 1947 cigarette, diesel-fuel, and watercraft duties were placed on the books. A business-activities tax was imposed in 1953. (This tax paid no attention whatsoever to business profits and did not give a tax break to newly formed enterprises. It was largely responsible for Michigan's reputation as a poor place to do business.)[8]

Even with all these new sources of income over half of the total revenue came from the sales tax enacted in 1933. The heavy reliance on the sales tax meant that Michigan would have a great deal of money in good times but very little in bad. The late fifties were bad times!

The state of Michigan keeps its monies under two separate titles: the General and the Earmarked funds. The General Fund includes that money which the legislature is free to disperse as it may please, while the Earmarked Fund is bound by constitutional amendment or statute to be spent in specified ways. The amount of money placed in the earmarked category was another stride toward Michigan's financial crumble in the late 1950's.

The earmarking problem dates from 1939, when a constitutional amendment was passed providing that all monies acquired through gasoline and weight taxes be used only for improving state highways. Seven years later, in 1946, a second constitutional amendment (referred to as the Sales Tax Diversion Amendment) took a huge bite out of the General Fund. It returned 60 per cent of the total sales tax collected in any given year to local school districts and returned another one-sixth to local governments.

The war years had been good years, and Michigan continued to place its income in earmarked funds. The state legislature provided for $50,000,000 to be taken from the General Fund and placed in a Veterans Trust Fund. It also diverted 40 per cent of the monies collected through the 1947 cigarette tax into the earmarked category. And to make matters worse, in 1954 the percentage of the sales tax going to school districts was raised from 60 to 67 per cent, with municipalities still claiming their one-sixth.[9]

Having so much of the state income tied up in earmarked funds became a serious problem in the late fifties. Since the money in most instances was taken from the General Fund by constitutional amendment, it had to be returned to the General Fund by constitutional amendment. In the late fifties the state actually controlled only about a third of the budget, for General Fund expenditures. All the rest of the funds were earmarked.

The seemingly obvious solution to any financial need would be to release the earmarked funds by constitutional amendment, but this simple solution could not be realized, because from the time G. Mennen Williams became governor in 1949 through 1960, there was a severe political clash afoot.

During the Williams era (1949–62) the Michigan Democratic party built an extremely strong organization. Democrats were able to control the governor's office and many state-wide posts.

But the Republicans dominated both houses of the legislature. The Liberal Williams found himself a victim of the 1908 constitution allowing Conservative control.

The constitution stated that the legislature was to be reapportioned every ten years starting in 1913, but the outstate majority of lawmakers simply did not take action. Token efforts were made in 1913, when Wayne County was granted one additional seat in the Senate, and in 1925, with Wayne County gaining seven representatives. In 1943 the House reapportioned itself again, making it possible for Wayne County to have twenty-seven seats (it was entitled to at least ten more), but the Senate stood inert. Finally, in 1952, the numbers of representatives and senators were increased by constitutional amendment from 100 to 110 and from 32 to 34, respectively. This helped only a little.

In 1955, Gordon Baker, in *Rural versus Urban Political Power,* placed the forty-eight states in five categories on the basis of urban underrepresentation.[10] Surprisingly enough, Michigan—under represented as it was—was not to be found under the "severe" classification! (In 1955, according to the U.S. Supreme Court one-man-one-vote principle, there were eight states less fairly represented.) Michigan, however, was not well off. In 1960, 42 per cent of the population elected 64 per cent of the senators, while Wayne County contained 34 per cent of the people and elected only 20 per cent of the senators.[11] Not only were Democrats disfranchised, but also the more liberal urban Republicans. The result was, as Richard L. Milliman, Romney's press secretary from 1962 through 1964, points out, "the main voice for Republicanism in the State became the conservative majority leadership in the Legislature."[12] During the entire Williams era the Senate was a conservative bulwark, and only during the 1959–60 sessions could the Democratic governor claim at least a 55–55 split in the House.

Williams was an ardent New Dealer. He pushed what Conservative Republicans called "the welfare state" forward on all fronts. In his six terms as governor of Michigan spending rose from $500,000,000 to more than $1,100,000,000. During these twelve years Williams saw to it that Michigan more than tripled its yearly expenditures on education and highways and more than doubled its support for the mentally ill, and he became much more concerned with public welfare. Consequently he gained quite a national reputation. In 1958, *U.S. News & World Report* carried an article titled "Michigan Again and Then to Washington?" and articles on Williams appeared in *Time,* the *Nation,* the *Saturday Evening Post,* and the *Reporter.* Before the payless payday occurred, there was every indication that Williams would be the Democratic vice-presidential nominee in 1960. (Williams announced that he would not be a candidate for a seventh consecutive term early in the year and voiced support for Senator Kennedy three months later. He regarded Kennedy's choice of Lyndon Baines Johnson as a personal affront. Kennedy could not be blamed, however. He knew that the religious issue would make the election a close one and that he needed to add strength to the ticket. It wasn't so much what Williams had done to Michigan but what the American people thought he had done that mattered.)

According to former governor John B. Swainson, what ensued during the last Williams administration was "almost a personal vendetta against G. Mennen Williams, because the very same men who voted for expenditures would speak out against appropriations." Even two-time Republican gubernatorial nominee Paul D. Bagwell believes that "the Republicans of the Williams era practiced a form of hypocrisy!" Any doubt that this was "Let's Get Williams" year for Senate Republicans is erased by a telegram mailed to the twenty-two Republican senators during the 1959 legislative session by a Michigan Manufacturers' Association lobbyist. It read: "You have him [Williams] over the barrel for the first time in ten years. Keep him there 'till he screams 'Uncle.' God bless each of you."[13]

The 1959 legislative session killed any hope Williams had of becoming the Democratic vice-presidential nominee, but the political conflict had greater ramifications than the reputation of one man. Michigan throughout the Williams era was at the crossroads. The state was testing two diverse philosophies of government, and the strain upon its finances could be seen as early as 1957—although the overt manifestations were delayed until 1959. Would

Michigan push forward with humanitarian, liberal, and social legislation, or would it swing back toward the conservative expenditures
of the early twentieth century? Williams and Company was dedicated to the former position, while Conservatives in the Senate
(twenty-two Republican versus twelve Democrat) were even more
stringently, perhaps even pigheadedly, clinging to the latter. Each
time Williams proposed new expenditures the request would be
whittled down before being passed. When it came to locating new
tax sources, it was a different story, however. The ultraconservative
senators stalled such requests and tried to tide over by adopting a
patchwork of low-yield taxes. For a few years the Republican
"Neanderthals" pleaded that expenditures were too great and that
the state was really in no great financial squeeze, but as the financial picture worsened they shifted their argument from lack of
need to the means by which more money could be raised. Governor
Williams sought enactment of a corporation profit tax and a personal income tax. The former was repeatedly voted down by the
Republicans on the ground that it would drive industry away from
Michigan, and the latter did not have popular support. (Twice
Michiganites had overwhelmingly rejected such a proposal in the
1920's, and newspaper polls cautioned that the voters' opinion of
an income tax had not changed in the least.) The Republicans
wanted to increase taxes on gasoline, liquor, cigarettes, and beer—
the so-called nuisance taxes. They also supported a 1 per cent increase in the sales tax.

It was on this disgruntled basis that the liberal Democratic
governor and the conservative Republican Senate existed until the
pressure became unbearable in 1959. As the legislative session
opened, Williams, the Senate, and the majority of Michigan's population knew that something had to be done. The national recession
of 1958 had caused overestimation of revenues by some $43,000,-
000, and recession hit the city of Detroit with such force that
the state treasury was forced to take over the public welfare
program in that area. (The state usually paid 30 per cent of
the general relief cost and the town or city the other 70 per cent.)
The General Fund plunged into the red. On February 4, 1959,
Williams warned that if nothing was done to correct the situa-

tion, Michigan would be left with a staggering year-end deficit of $110,000,000.[14]

Michigans infamous "payless payday" was April 29, 1959, although for some months prior to that date newspapers and periodicals had been announcing the coming attraction. On February 13, *U.S. News & World Report* had noted that Michigan was "living off the cuff"; on March 2, *Newsweek* headlined, "Michigan: How to go Broke"; and on March 23, *Time* put "Financial Disaster" in bold type. So the arrival of the payless payday was not entirely responsible for giving Michigan its unfavorable publicity: it had already earned a reputation for being a problem state. The payless payday drew more publicity because it was an overt symptom of inward sickness. Within the next six months articles dealing with the payless payday appeared in *Business Week*, the *Reporter*, the *Saturday Evening Post*, the *Nation, Time, Newsweek, U.S. News & World Report*, and untold newspaper columns. But the payday fiasco was the icing on the cake; the top of the iceberg. It did not come as a violent shock to those familiar with state finances, but it was not exactly expected either.

The General Fund had slipped into the red in 1957, and then plummeted at an incredibly rapid rate, yet larger and larger expenditures were requested by the Governor and approved by the legislature. (Even in the face of the payday crisis itself Williams was requesting an additional $50,000,000 in state spending for education, mental health, and pay boosts for government employees.) The 1908 constitution had set the state's debt limit at the ridiculously low figure of $250,000. Michigan was in a bind. It was necessary either to spend less or to raise money through new taxes. Clearly the actions of Williams and the legislature barred the first alternative, and their conflicting philosophies on taxation disrupted the second.

It should be noted that Michigan is now—and was at the time of the payless payday—one of the nation's richest states. The financial mess that engulfed its government in the late 1950's was due not to a shortage of financial assets but to a shortage of immediate cash in the General Fund to meet governmental obligations. On the

date of the overt payday manifestation Michigan's General Fund
debt totaled $117,000,000, but there were various earmarked funds
containing more than $170,000,000![15] So the state had money.
It was the conflict between the Governor and the legislature that
caused Michigan to waver on the brink of disaster for two years.

All through 1958 and up until March, 1959, Michigan drifted
from one financial crisis to another. The previous year had witnessed liquidation of the state's $19,000,000 liquor inventories and
reconfiscation of $10,000,000 in special funds set aside for veteran
bonuses; still money continued to go out faster than it came in.

One of the special funds that were not constitutionally earmarked was the $50,000,000 Veterans Trust Fund, which is in-
vested in U.S. government bonds and yields approximately $1,200,-
000 a year to be used in assisting Michigan veterans. But every
time Williams drew this possibility to the attention of the Republican senators, they ignored it. Williams continued to plead for
a corporation profit tax and a personal income tax. The Republicans held their ground, asking for an increase in the sales tax
from 3 to 4 per cent. In February, 1959, Williams appealed to the
large business interests to pay their taxes in advance (moving due
dates from July to April). His call was answered, and nearly
$36,000,000 rolled into state coffers, but again the measure pro-
vided only a temporary reprieve. April 29, 1959, found the
treasury unable to meet the payroll for 325 employees (including
all 114 legislators). Williams warned that unless immediate action
was taken, the same fate awaited 28,000 other Michigan employees.

The statement proved to be an idle threat. The payless payday
ended with no other direct casualties. It lasted only five days and
consisted of a delay in pay to only the 325 employees. But the rest
of the iceberg—what was the extent of that?

According to Paul D. Bagwell, the GOP gubernatorial candidate in 1958 and 1960, Michigan's financial woes "involved many
millions of dollars, and included the payroll of state employees,
funds due to the state universities and colleges which they in turn
used to meet their payrolls, and all the creditors of the state of
Michigan—the people who sell goods and services to the State."
Democratic State Chairman Neil Staebler paints a similar picture:

We had been building up these many years with insufficient tax receipts to match appropriations. The Legislature kept refusing to get new taxes, and consequently we were "in the red." "In the red" means that the General Fund would have had that much of a deficit if all of its obligations were met. The obligations consisted of payments to various State funds—retirement for example—and other statutory obligations of the State, plus bills due vendors. Michigan had tried to hold a 30-day policy on payment to vendors. That slipped to 60 and then to 90 days. So the deficit was reflected in these obligations to State funds and vendors.

One little-known fact concerning the April 29 event is that it was planned to be a political smasheroo. It was intended to shock the Senate Republicans into giving in, before they would see Michigan subjected to payless paydays and national disrepute. Williams had pushed for new taxes on income, he had requested a corporation profits tax, he had asked to borrow the Veterans Trust Fund. All his suggested actions were stymied. And so he resolved to press his point by a national dramatization of Michigan's plight. Neil Staebler, close Williams adviser at the time, presents us with this succinct account of that decision:

> Many legislators were pooh-poohing the idea that there was a crisis, and, early in 1959, the idea was proposed that there be a kind of dramatic demonstration. So the decision was made—and carried out—to let the treasury be empty on the day the Legislature got paid. This was accomplished by using the funds coming in and paying on past obligations. So, come payday, the General Fund really did not have funds available to meet the legislative payroll.

John B. Swainson, lieutenant governor at the time and next governor of the state, in 1960, explains how the plan operated:

> . . . The basic condition of a state can be dramatized on any given day. At this particular time it became a situation of whether or not you robbed Peter to pay Paul. You could do a number of things: deny funds for conservation, welfare or any number of enterprises. And I'm sure that at the time it was hoped that by demonstrating the need with state employees, maybe this would encourage the legislature to appropriate sufficient funds. Of course it didn't work out that way. We had a cliff hanger for about seven days. The desired result did not materialize.

A result that did materialize was additional publicity giving

Michigan a worse reputation than it already had accumulated. Previous warnings that Michigan was about to go bankrupt seemingly came true, although the state was not broke. Another negative result is pointed out by Republican Paul Bagwell:

Now the consequences of that [1959 crisis] are tremendous. And we're still paying for it. The average citizen doesn't realize that at the same period of time—and shortly thereafter— we were floating millions of dollars in bond issues on the bond market—and because of the reputation the state got from failing to meet its payroll at that time our bond rates went up from ¼ per cent to ½ per cent. Over the lifetime of those bonds, at one time, I figured it was costing the people of this state an additional 16 to 20 million to build their roads, schools and other things they were financing on the bond market.

Yet by another set of criteria Williams was successful. He certainly succeeded in focusing national attention on Michigan that put pressure on the legislature. Responding to the immediate crisis the Republicans passed a series of bills in late August that raised the business-activities taxes and the intangibles tax. The legislature also adopted a 1 per cent use tax, although Attorney General Adams warned that the use tax was really a veiled increase in the sales tax, which was constitutionally limited to the 3 per cent level then being assessed. Within sixty days Adams was supported by a 5–3 Supreme Court decision.

The legislature was called back for a special session in December of 1959, and it resorted to a patchwork approach once more. A package of nuisance taxes (levies on telephone bills, liquor, beer, and cigarettes) and an increase in the business-activities tax by some $9,000,000 were the result. In 1960 the legislature finally authorized borrowing the Veterans Trust Fund, and in November, 1960, Michiganites approved an amendment raising the sales-tax limit from 3 to 4 per cent. The resulting $110,000,000 revenue was collected as of February 1, 1961. The nuisance taxes expired on July 1, 1961, but were reimposed when the General Fund ran a deficit of $85,000,000 on July 1, 1962.

In the early sixties what Michigan had been hoping, waiting, and praying for back in the late 1950's finally began to materialize. Unfortunately for the Democratic governor, John Swainson, it took too long to gain sufficient momentum to be visible to the naked public eye in terms of a General Fund surplus. The awaited event was a sharp upturn in business—in fact the beginning of an unprecedented boom—which meant that a 4 per cent sales tax would rake millions more into the state cashbox.

The Political Prelude

ALTHOUGH George Romney did not arrive in Detroit with large crowds cheering, his Michigan debut did not go unnoticed. The front page of the Detroit *Free Press* carried this small item on September 29, 1939:

> Selection of George W. Romney as manager of the Detroit office of the Automobile Manufacturers Association was announced Thursday after a meeting of the board of directors of the organization.
> Romney has been representative of the aluminum industry at Washington for several years. With Mrs. Romney and their two children, he will take up his headquarters in Detroit, when the new offices of the association are opened in the New Center Building.

At the age of thirty-one Romney had been stepping in high company. The Automobile Manufacturers Association board of directors included Paul G. Hoffman (Studebaker), B. E. Mutchinson (Chrysler), W. S. Knudsen (General Motors), A. E. Barit (Hudson), E. C. Fink (Mack), and C. W. Nash (Nash). The position as manager of the Detroit office had taken Romney from Washington, D.C., where he had spent the past nine years.

Romney had gone to Washington in the fall of 1929, because he heard jobs were plentiful there. He enrolled in night classes at George Washington University and set out to find a job. Barely twenty-one and a Mormon Republican from Utah, he landed a position as stenographer with Senator David Walsh, a Catholic Democrat from Massachusetts. Walsh liked him and soon changed his duties from taking dictation to tariff study.[1]

For the wages of $120 a month Romney became an expert on the Hawley-Smoot tariff bill, a major issue of the day. It became his lot to analyze each section of the bill and to summarize all the arguments that were received from any source. His work therefore involved some interviewing in the Senator's office and gathering of information from foreign embassies, the Library of Congress, and the Tariff Commission. He often sat next to Walsh on the Senate floor during debates to provide pinpoint tariff information.

Senator Walsh was serving on the Senate Finance Committee, and Romney got to meet Wisconsin's Bob LaFollette, Texas' Tom Connally, and Kentucky's Alben W. Barkley at close range. He listened to Nebraska's George Norris, Pennsylvania's David Reed, Indiana's Jim Watson. He worked with two men who served as secretary of the Senate: Leslie Biffle and Felton Johnson. Two of the most important people with whom Romney came into contact were not involved in politics, however; they were executives of the Aluminum Company of America (Alcoa). Alcoa was also interested in tariffs, and J. E. S. Thorpe and Safford K. Colby had requested some specific information from Senator Walsh's office. They considered Romney's great detail beyond the call of duty and offered to pay him an extra dollar or two for his services. Romney would not hear of it, and the executives were impressed. They offered him a position as an apprentice trainee. The initial salary was to be $125 a month, with double that at the end of his apprenticeship, when he would receive a spot in the company's Washington office.

It was a hard decision for a young man of twenty-two. He liked his job, and he liked Senator Walsh equally well. He wanted to attend the Harvard School of Business Administration. But he could double his present salary by September—opportunity was knocking! After three quarters of a year as a senatorial assistant he joined Alcoa, in June, 1930. Years later he was to reflect upon his months with Senator Walsh:

> It was a wonderful experience. I had practically all of American industry spread out before my eyes, and I had to judge for the Senator the worth of the opinions expressed. I had a clear view of the workings and thinking of all segments of American business.[2]

Romney left Washington and moved to Kensington, Pennsyl-

vania, where he spent the next three months learning the manufacture, processing, and uses of aluminum. He was highly regarded
by the management, and his request for a sales assignment at Los
Angeles was granted in mid-September. Romney proved successful
as a salesman and was given two weeks off for a honeymoon in
early July. He married Lenore LaFount—a high-school classmate
two years his junior—on July 2, 1931, just six days before he turned
twenty-four. The couple set up housekeeping in Santa Monica in
a one-room apartment. Two months later Romney was called to
Washington, and his salary doubled. The Romneys rented a two-
room apartment at the Kennedy-Warren, where they remained for
the next two years.

Romney became a lobbyist for Alcoa, as well as a representative for the Aluminum Wares Association. It was all part of his job,
but modern observers would have labeled Romney a social climber.
He constantly entertained people of importance for the aluminum company, went to parties at the White House, and joined the
National Press Club. He was out five or six nights a week. He became a member of the Burning Tree Country Club in Bethesda,
Maryland, making important contacts on the golf course. Gerry
Smith, a high-school classmate of Romney who was in Washington
at the time, chuckles when he recalls that Romney first learned to
play golf on the country courses with him until he got good enough
to play at the private clubs. "Then," says Gerry, "he didn't play
with me any more!" Smith also recalls a remark Romney made to
him after an industrial-league basketball game for which they both
played: "You know, Gerry, you've got to be willing to bet every
cent on yourself." "Apparently Romney really believed it," says
Smith, "because he was living in an apartment that was way over
his head."

All indications are that Romney was a successful lobbyist. Officially he was to "keep abreast of all the legislation concerning
aluminum." On one occasion, when he clearly exceeded this definition, he was rebuked by Senator Otis Glenn of Illinois: "Young
man, I did not come to Washington to run errands for the business
interests of my State."[3]

Romney was a devoted employee of Alcoa. In 1934 he went

so far as to appear at a Beaux-Arts ball clad as a knight. Mrs. Romney had made his costume by dipping washrags in aluminum paint. But as time passed he grew dissatisfied. Alcoa had been under attack for being a monopoly since 1924. The Federal Trade Commission ruled in 1930 that it was not a monopoly, but small companies that bought aluminum continued to press for Department of Justice action. Romney had to give Alcoa's retort. He relied primarily on the company's low yearly earnings of 6 per cent and the fact that aluminum had to compete with other metals, such as copper. One factor that placed Alcoa in a bad light was that Andrew Mellon, Secretary of the Treasury under Harding, Coolidge, and Hoover, was a stockholder. This led Senator James Couzens of Michigan to charge Mellon with conflict of interest. Mellon was removed with the election of Roosevelt, but the monopoly charge grew in force. Romney found the charge distasteful, but the incident most directly related to Romney's decision to leave Washington had been the appointment of Edward B. Wilbur to the newly created office of Washington manager. Romney felt that he should have gotten the position. He took this as being indicative of Alcoa advancement policy: "As near as I could figure it, I would have been ninety by the time I rose to the top."[4] Consequently, when the Automobile Manufacturers Association offered him a position as manager of its Detroit office, in 1939, he jumped at the chance.

Romney had come to Michigan through the efforts of Pyke Johnson, the Washington representative and vice-president of the Automobile Manufacturers Association. The two men had met through the Monday Club—a group of trade-association men that lunched weekly at the Press Club or the Washington Club. Johnson was a former sports editor of the *Rocky Mountain News* and had known the Romney family through several all-conference selections he had made in the past. The men became fast friends, and Johnson picked Romney as a member of the newly formed National Recovery Administration Trade Association Advisory Committee.

In 1939 Johnson was made executive vice-president and general manager of AMA. Johnson wanted to stay in Washington, but the board of directors voted to move activities to Detroit. Johnson asked Romney to come to Detroit. As a job applicant Romney went, was passed by the board, and was formally voted Detroit office manager on September 28, 1939—although he did not set up shop until January. At thirty-two Romney had a fine job indeed at a salary of $12,000 a year.

The Romneys arrived in Detroit a family of four. Two daughters had been born to them: Margo Lynn (June 6, 1935) and Jane LaFount (March 18, 1938). They rented a house in Grosse Pointe for a short time and bought a large three-story home in Detroit. The last two members of the Romney family, George Scott (June 7, 1941) and Willard Mitt (March 12, 1947), were born there.

As Detroit manager of AMA, Romney became engrossed in a study that determined his future thinking about the role of the automobile in America. The study dealt with automobile use and revealed that the average American was using his car more for short, essential trips—such as going to the corner store, to church, or to work—than for long journeys. Romney read "basic transportation" into this utilization of the automobile, and that was one reason he became so optimistic about the economy car when he became president of American Motors some fifteen years later.

At the same time the study was being undertaken, Romney started procedures to remove the ceiling on the dues of the organization, which he felt were unfair. AMA had a budget of about $1,000,000, and members contributed in proportion to cars produced, but there was a ceiling of $40,000,000 for any one automobile line. This proved to be a handicap both to the smaller automobile companies and to AMA revenues.

In a few months the restructuring of the budget was successfully completed, and Romney became involved with the Automotive Committee for Air Defense, formed at the request of President Roosevelt. General Arnold had advised the President that medium- and heavy-range bombers were to be the critical elements in the war, and the Automotive Committee handled the liaison dealing with the subassembly of airplant parts in four short months.

After Pearl Harbor, December 7, 1941, Romney's role in defense work became vital indeed. He served as managing director for the newly formed Automotive Council for War Production. Until then automobile manufacturers had subordinated new model changes to the production of airplane subassemblies; now there was to be total conversion to war production, and the Automotive Council became all that was visible of AMA only two months later. After serving as spokesman for the newly formed council and explaining the goals and purposes of the committee at regional conferences of automotive concerns in Detroit, Chicago, Cleveland, and New York, Romney supervised a census of tools and equipment, backed a drive that turned up tons of scrap metal, organized committees that allowed defense contractors to explain methods of production to newer producers, and established a manpower division dealing with problems of the workers. In short, he worked up a system that enabled companies to share their production methodologies for the good of the nation.

In June, 1943, a race riot broke out on the bridge between Detroit and its famous recreational area in the Detroit River, Belle Isle. The riot involved the death of thirty-four, injury to more than seven hundred, and the jailing of over one thousand persons. In direct response Romney teamed with Victor Reuther (brother of UAW President Walter Reuther) in organizing the Detroit Victory Council. The council was later to serve as one of Romney's prime examples of "what a free people could do while working together" (voluntary cooperation). The council arranged for sitters to care for children so that more mothers could work, organized automobile pools, investigated housing shortages, and rerouted bus transportation to make commuting for war-production purposes more feasible.

The Automotive Council for War Production became defunct on October 1, 1945, but not before it had been responsible for the production of more than 3,000,000 wheeled units, four-fifths of all tanks, three-quarters of all aircraft engines, more than half the Diesel engines, and one-third of the machine guns produced.[5] So the council had been wonderfully successful in terms of materials produced; but it went an important step further under Romney's foresight. Near the end of the war he persuaded government officials to expedite cumbersome contract-termination procedures that threatened to handcuff automobile production for months. Romney's efforts enabled automakers to go fairly smoothly from wartime to peacetime production, thus averting heavy unemployment.[6]

The transition was not completely free of discord. By the end of the war the scars had not entirely healed from the race riot of 1943. The Detroit Victory Council had labored to ease racial and war tensions but had met with only limited success. Then, too, there were numerous strikes in the supplier industry, and it was extremely difficult to get steel. There was a lot of labor unrest. Romney analyzed the problem in these words:

> Today the big common problem is to set a pattern for the country, to work out our peace problems . . . We have to do four things: Shift the national spotlight away from troubles and differences to achieve and accomplish; get every nose pointed in the direction of common interest; create a desire to work together; and help get going through example, so that others will want to do the same.[7]

His solution was a celebration marking fifty years of automobile production in the United States. It was also the one hundred and fiftieth year since the American flag was raised in Detroit, and so plans were made for the Automotive-Civic Golden Jubilee. Romney headed up the automotive portion, and the Detroit Common Council appropriated $100,000 for the celebration. The Golden Jubilee was celebrated throughout the United States by more than four hundred communities. In Detroit the ten-day celebration started May 31 and cost nearly $400,000. Activities included huge parades, awards to those who had contributed to civic and automotive progress, and hundreds of speeches. Tom Mahoney credits the jubilee with creating the groundwork for social reforms undertaken almost immediately afterward.[8]

The jubilee made the person of George Romney widely known in industrial circles. At the end of the war he had urged the Automobile Manufacturers Association to continue the cooperative cohesiveness that had been exhibited within the War Production Board. His efforts were not rewarded, and once again he began to look to greener pastures.

Romney was now a man with highly impressive credentials crisscrossing his Walsh, Alcoa, AMA, War Production Board, and Golden Jubilee experiences. He had also been appointed by President Harry S. Truman as an employer delegate to the Metal Trades Industry Conferences of the International Labor Office in 1946 and 1947. As a result of these qualifications he was offered the vice-presidency of Packard and almost simultaneously a post as executive assistant to the president of Nash-Kelvinator. The Packard offer included elevation to president within a two-year time span and a salary of $50,000, but Romney did not feel that two years of preparation before becoming the top official of a company was sufficient. He took a full month to decide, because he felt "the decision would probably determine my last employment and vocational opportunity."[9]

On April 1, 1948, Romney usurped Assistant Public Relations Manager John Conde's office at the Nash-Kelvinator Schaffer and Plymouth home office.

It is hard to determine why Romney thought the Nash-Kelvinator offer at all attractive. He did not have the total confidence of President Mason and did not gain it immediately. For over a year he had no real power over slipshod practices and lax procedures within the company, and the company was not in a sound financial position. Nevertheless, Romney dug in with enthusiasm. He started by learning the business from the bottom up. He took the Milwaukee training course for service men, worked at the side of hourly employees, talked to each and every foreman; and he studied books and reports on automobile engineering, designing, and styling. When he felt he had a firm grasp of the operating procedures, he moved to the policy and administrative phase. The latter segment of his on-the-job training proved to be the wedge he needed to break into top administration.

Romney had been talking with the little people in the appliance and automobile divisions, and he decided that there were several problems within the organization that could stand attention. He did not like the way Mason tried to make every person with authority report directly to the boss. It was a time-consuming procedure, and Romney must have been as taken aback by it as he was with Michigan's hydra-headed 141-department administration when he became governor. He observed that there was no clear-cut labor-relations policy, and it was evident that lax labor standards allowed during the war would have to be changed on a large scale. He drew these observations to Mason's attention with a formal written statement ten months after becoming his assistant, suggesting procedures for improving communication channels. This focus on improved communications was pushed forward with more vigor as Romney's power increased.

Mason gave Romney his first important assignment almost by accident. Romney had been appointed employer delegate to the Metal Trades Committee meeting in Geneva, Switzerland. Between planes in New York City he spoke briefly with Mason, who was just returning from an automobile show in Paris. Mason had been impressed by the designing work of Italy's Pinin Farina and asked Romney to "get that man to design cars for us."

Romney succeeded, and that made him look inches taller to George Mason. The mutual respect between the two men grew as Romney began to take a keen interest in Mason's dream of a small, lightweight automobile. Mason had been possessed with the small-car idea since the depression. He was so delighted by Romney's optimism that he appointed him to head up the presentation of the new N.X.I. (Nash Experimental International) in January of 1950. Romney worked hard on the project, which proved unsuccessful because the N.X.I. could not be produced as cheaply as Mason had hoped.

But 1950 was Romney's year. Still working on the small-car idea, he associated himself with the Metropolitan and the Rambler. He didn't know it, but the Rambler was to be his vehicle to fame and fortune as he had not imagined.

Romney preferred the name Diplomat because it sounded well when teamed with the company's Ambassador model, which was larger. Top executives preferred Rambler. In 1950, company sales set a record, but Rambler sales were less than 16,000. Twelve months later the number of new Ramblers on the road rose to more than 50,000, and Romney was rewarded for his efforts with the title of vice-president.

Romney now pushed for tighter organization and greater communication on all levels. He was appointed chairman of a policy-determination committee that had no direct power, simply the power of suggestion. Somewhat later he formed a committee on employee information. One outgrowth of his committee work was a series of town-hall meetings open to all salaried employees. These monthly discussions concerned departmental functions, and provided an opportunity for employees to get to know one another. The meetings were complete with bell-ringing town crier. The response was favorable, and Romney hired a former AMA associate to fill the newly created post of director of communications in 1952.

In the meantime Romney and one of the other vice-presidents developed an ideological clash. R. A. De Vlieg, in charge of manufacturing, felt that most management-labor communications should take place through union representatives. Lax labor standards and apparent lack of effectiveness in presently channeled communications caused Romney to disagree. When the Kelvinator division of Plymouth Road slipped into the red at the end of 1952, De Vlieg recommended that the plant be closed, since it was "obviously inefficient." Romney took issue with De Vlieg, reasoning that if the slipshod work practices were stopped and improvements made in mechanization, the division could be made profitable once again. He wanted to take his case directly to the workers. In January of 1953 the conflict ceased. Romney was named executive vice-president—second only to Mason.

Romney resolved to follow the dictates of his conscience and appeal directly to the workers for a fair day's work. Speaking over a microphone and on company time, he told them bluntly that productivity would have to be raised or the plant would be closed. Union leader Matt Smith struck the plant in protest. Romney wrote to the workers at home. So did Smith. During the next six months workers were on strike almost a third of the time, but Romney finally emerged victorious.

In early 1954, Nash-Kelvinator merged with Hudson, and

American Motors resulted on May 1. All mergers present problems for executives concerned with overlapping of costs and effort, but American Motors was shaken severely while in its infancy. On October 3, 1954, George Mason was stricken with pneumonia and five days later he died. It was Romney who delivered his funeral eulogy and Romney who assumed his titles of chairman, president, and general manager on October 12.[10]

When he became president, American Motors was not in a sound condition. Romney found himself "with an outmoded plant, a perilous shortage of cash, cars that weren't selling, and the overhead of two auto companies."[11] The company was losing millions of dollars each year.

Romney hired a new sales manager in the person of American Motors ex-president, Roy Abernathy, established an eleven-man policy committee to advise on major decisions, and engaged in advertising policies that made enemies in the automobile industry. He cleaned up slipshod labor practices, satisfied dealers with a Volume Investment Fund and launched a company-wide economy drive. He encouraged executives to take a cut in pay, setting the example himself. He stopped the manufacture of Hudson and Nash and emphasized the importance of employer-employee relationships.

At the same time he became the apostle for the "compact" car—a term he coined. In the dry years—the years American Motors was in the red, 1954–57—Romney was constantly crusading before creditors as well as employees and the general public. Wherever he spoke, he commanded respect by his abounding optimism and sincerity. One of AMC's creditors was the Continental Illinois National Bank and Trust Company, and David M. Kennedy, chairman of the board, remembers an occasion when Romney had been pleading his cause. After the meeting ended, Kennedy approached Romney and asked, "George, could you possibly be wrong?" Romney replied, "Oh, I'm convinced!" When Kennedy pointed out that executives of Ford, Chrysler, and Chevrolet saw no future for the compact car, Romney said simply, "They're wrong!" Kennedy concluded with a chuckle, "He persuaded me and our senior money lender. That's how sure he was."

Romney was forced to deal also with a creditor of a different sort. Louis Wolfson had a reputation for being a stock raider, and in July, 1956, he owned 200,000 shares of American Motors. Romney persuaded Wolfson that there was a bright future ahead and even talked him out of his desire to have a personally selected young man on the board of directors. Wolfson bought another 240,000 shares and wanted AMC to trade stock and finance his acquisition of some other companies. Again Romney refused. By that time it was obvious that American Motors was going to make it. The last quarter of 1957 proved to be profitable, and both the Rambler and Romney were off and running. Romney celebrated by moving into a $150,000 home in Bloomfield Hills.

In his capacity as compact-car apostle it was not uncommon for him to travel seventy thousand miles in a year. He had made the decision that his company could become profitable only through the economy-sized car, and that was that. He felt sure that logic was on his side—represented by the car-use study made back in 1939 and just plain common sense. He resolved to make employees recognize that AMC made quality products with the slogan "Build each car as if it were your own." He inspired a sense of identity with the company by trying to keep all workers informed. He organized an Employee Preview as an annual company affair; held in Milwaukee Stadium, it drew as many as forty thousand employees and their families to his annual "state of the company" address.

At the same time there seemed to be a ground swell of support for the compact car from other sources. In March, 1957, Lowell Harris, in the *American Economic Review,* pointed out that eight hundred square miles of space would be created if every automobile were twelve inches shorter. New York Traffic Commissioner Wiley stated that any increase in automobile size would be "sheer madness," and he was backed by Mayor Wagner. Los Angeles Mayor Norris Poulson pointed out that large automobiles were the number one cause of air pollution. In 1958, *Consumer Reports,* an unbiased nonprofit organization, listed the Rambler as the "only current U.S. contribution to economical motoring." Even cartoonists got into the act, using such full-page ads as the fisherman who got hooked (he found he had a "whale" of a gas bill), the dragon slayer who stabbed the large car monster in the gas tank, and the father who had to rob his children's piggy bank to pay for gasoline. Around this time, too, "Beep, Beep," a song describing how a Rambler outruns a Cadillac, was fourth on the hit-tune list. Many businessmen adopted a Rambler for sales travel, and some companies employed them by the fleet. To top it off, a Rambler won the 1959 Mobilgas Economy Run.[12]

The strategy that worked for American Motors in 1957–58 was nothing that hadn't been used before. It simply had the advantage of timing and cumulativeness. Fortunately for Romney, the make-or-break year for American Motors coincided with the 1958 national recession. The American people suddenly became economy-minded. Americans took an abrupt interest in ways to save their pennies, and Romney not only gave them a means but provided sociologically defensible reasons for choosing a Rambler. By utilization of the term "compact" instead of "small," a Rambler customer was "frugal," not "cheap." Romney had been pushing for three years now, and the economic condition of the country made his listeners much more susceptible. Suddenly people could see that "Romney was right. All of that extra metal was a waste of money." Reading the economic signs perfectly, Romney announced in his third annual Employee Product Preview speech at the Milwaukee Arena on September 14, 1957: "The future is here. *This is the year!*"

Romney really needed a symbol. And when the Detroit *News* published an editorial concluding that "bigger bodies and bigger engines must stop or the private automobile will go the way of the dinosaur," Romney took full advantage of it. He had his chief speech writer, Howard Hallas, develop a talk using the *News* article as its central theme. Mrs. Romney wasn't sure (she advises the Governor on many of the speeches, more so than his speech assistants), but the speech proved highly successful. The dinosaur image caught the fancy of the American public. Romney used the theme again and again. Soon he had concocted a prehistoric menagerie with which he would parody the modern-day Big Three automobiles. His collection included Brontosaurus, Triceratops,

Demetrodon, Pterodactyl, and Stegosaurus, which last he described as "perhaps having the highest development of the dinosaur in terms of useless non-functional decorative treatment." He stressed that "the principal factor in their extinction was the fact that they kept getting bigger and bigger and finally got so big they were unable to live."[13] The dinosaur thus became the Romney trademark during his compact-car crusade. He belittled large cars by calling them "gas-guzzling dinosaurs" and pointed out how ridiculous it was for cars weighing two tons to run a 118-pound housewife three blocks to pick up a package of bobby pins.

American Motors became a profit-making corporation in 1958. It remained that way for three years after Romney left to seek public office.

By 1956 Romney was a well-known executive. He was chairman, president, and general manager of American Motors as well as newly appointed president of AMA. But there was a civic side of Romney too. He played the leading role in meeting a Detroit public-school financial crisis, was responsible for the formulation of Citizens for Michigan in reaction to the Michigan financial crisis, and became a delegate to the state Constitutional Convention.

Romney became engaged in his first civic-duty work while his company was in dire financial straits. He had inherited a $70,000,000 debt upon becoming president of American Motors in 1954, and the company proceeded to lose another $7,000,000 in 1955. When Romney was asked by William Merrifield, president of the Detroit Board of Education to serve as chairman of a Citizens Advisory Committee on education in late December, 1956, American Motors was in the process of reporting an additional fiscal-year loss of nearly $20,000,000.[14]

Merrifield explained that the school-age population in Detroit had exploded with such force that a five-year building program had been exhausted in thirty-six months, and that millions of dollars in new taxes would have to be raised. Someone was needed to head up an independent study of the financial needs of the Detroit schools. Romney accepted.

The 270-member Citizens Advisory Committee really consisted of nine different committees: a forty-member city-wide committee and eight regional groups. Operating from its headquarters at Chadsey High School, the first meeting was held on February 28, 1957. Romney, as leader, began the study believing that economy in spending might be all that was needed but trying to be open-minded. Speaking before an audience of Detroit principals and supervisors in November of 1956 he had stated that the committee would be "fact-finding, before fault-finding." He spent every other Thursday night presiding over meetings and pored over hundreds of reports. Finally he became convinced that mere economy would not be enough; it would take more money. Supported by fact, he started a crusade that earned him the title of "spokesman for a better Detroit." Before civic groups of all types he spread the word that more money was needed and education was the "foundation of democracy."

In April, 1957, Detroiters had voted down a proposal that would have given $33,000,000 to the city for building classrooms during the next twenty-four months, and a review of the data on Michigan's economic health (traced in Chapter Three) will show that 1959 was not an ideal time to try to get more money from the citizens. Nevertheless, on April 6, 1959, only days before the payless-payday crisis, Detroiters approved a $90,000,000 school-support package: $60,000,000 in bonds and $30,000,000 by way of raising property taxes from $4.50 to $7.50 per $1,000 valuation. The committee also presented 182 proposals to the Detroit Board of Education, which the Detroit *Free Press* labeled as "bombshells that will reverberate for some time."[15] Besides appearing on the cover of *Time*, Romney received an honorary Doctor of Laws degree from Wayne State University and the Detroit teachers' annual civic award for his time, effort, and financial contributions.

The success of the Detroit school committee made George Romney consider such an approach for Michigan's financial needs. The possibility crossed his mind for the first time a good six months before the April 29 cash crisis, because he knew that Michigan's financial problems went deep.

With Romney playing the dual role of host and instigator, dinner for seven was served at Detroit's Sheraton Cadillac Hotel on April 28, 1959. The group reportedly met to pool their frustrations over Michigan's financial plight. Six week later, in mid–June, a second meeting was held at the Student Union Building on the Michigan State University campus in East Lansing. This time, membership having expanded to fifteen, Citizens for Michigan was born.

Although it had been patterned on the Detroit School Needs Committee, it was a new idea on a statewide basis. Romney knew that to make his organization successful he would have to inform all citizens as to its goals and worth; so in early June he embarked on his third major crusade, through the vehicle of a Detroit press conference. For his Citizens for Michigan he was requesting an original membership of about a hundred interested persons who would serve as "citizens only" and would therefore place the needs of the state above group and personal objectives. Financing would be solely on an individual basis, with no member being allowed to donate more than one hundred dollars. (This was aimed at keeping the group completely independent.) Romney carefully spelled out the fact that no new party was forming and that the committee existed merely to study and advise the officials of Michigan on methods of solving the state's financial problems. More than two hundred Michiganites responded at a Lansing meeting one week later.

In September, Romney was formally designated chairman of Citizens for Michigan. He proceeded with plans to expand membership by planning a series of regional and local meetings throughout the state. Eventually three areas were pinpointed for close scrutiny: the extent and financing of government services, an examination of the state's present constitutional structure, and the problem of Michigan's economic growth.

Although CFM gained wide support from the public and the press, not everyone found the "third force" approach to his liking. August Scholle, president of the Michigan AFL-CIO, was neither a friend of George Romney nor a backer of his citizen-group idea. Scholle, who met Romney during the early 1940 War Production

Board discussions on manpower, has never cared much for Romney. In a February 8, 1960 letter that is now famous he advised Walter Reuther that Romney was "a cog in the Republican party machinery" and warned that "our participation in the Romney Citizens for Michigan Committee might conceivably boomerang on us when on some future occasion Mr. Romney may declare the Republican party the only party free from domination by an economic pressure group." Scholle could not have hit the nail more squarely on the head. Except for the question of Romney's motivation—which is examined throughout the remaining chapters of this book—that is precisely what happened.

In late January, Romney appeared before a meeting of CFM and expressed his belief that the citizen effort would need considerably more than the present two thousand members if it was to be successful. He had spoken to state Republicans a few days earlier and was reported to be considering running for U.S. senator on the Republican ticket. The announcement was to occur at the January 30 meeting, but when his motives for establishing CFM were connected to the seeking of national office by a former president of the League of Women Voters, Romney backed out. He felt that CFM would crumble and fall apart if he went through with his originally planned decision. He was probably right.

Walter Reuther reasoned that Romney was likely to push ahead with CFM whether labor joined the effort or not, that a boycott of CFM would leave labor open to charges of not assisting in a solution to Michigan's financial woes, that labor might just as well try to influence the group from within. The result was that labor sent Leonard Woodcock, Jack Conway, and Judah Drob as representatives.[16] One of the most significant finds of CFM was that the state constitution was badly in need of revision.

State constitutions in the United States have an interesting history of their own. Massachusetts held the first state constitutional convention in 1779, and more than half the states have constitutions that were adopted during the nineteenth century. Massachusetts, New Hampshire, and Vermont have not revised their constitutions since the day they were written in the eighteenth century.

Michigan has been somewhat more active in the area of constitution making than most states, having held revision meetings in 1850 and 1908. In addition there had been attempts to revise its 1908 constitution ever since 1926.

Michigan has had four referendums on the question of constitutional revision: Revision was voted down in 1926 and 1942 but gained support in 1948 (850,000 to 800,000) and 1958 (820,000 to 610,000). Due to a 1908 constitutional stipulation, however, a majority of those voting on the issue was not sufficient. Article XVII required a majority of those voting in the *election,* and since many people chose not to vote on the constitutional issue, the revision session could not be held. (More than 2,000,000 people voted in 1948, and in 1958 the number casting ballots was 2,300,-000.) It was clear that Article XVII would have to be changed.

Romney's Citizens for Michigan Committee on Structure of Government gave its formal report in April, 1960, and on May 21, CFM gave complete endorsement to a constitutional-amendment effort that had been suggested by the Michigan Junior Chamber of Commerce and the Michigan League of Women Voters. The proposal became known as the Gateway amendment.

The Gateway amendment was an initiative petition and as such required signatures of citizens equal in number to 10 per cent of those voting in the last gubernatorial election—about 330,000 providing a safe margin for error. The Jaycees and the Women's League started to gather these signatures in January, but by mid-April had only 15,000. As of May 21, 1960, when the CFM group announced its support of the amendment, only 85,000 signatures had been collected. The CFM announcement gave the effort a boost, and on Romney's birthday, July 8, 332,000 signatures were filed with the secretary of state.

Reaction to the Gateway amendment did not respect party lines. Among Democrats, Governor Williams and Secretary of State Hare favored the amendment, while Lieutenant Governor Swainson and AFL-CIO President Scholle opposed it. Two-time GOP gubernatorial nominee Paul Bagwell endorsed the amendment enthusiastically, but the conservative and rural elements of the party said no. In addition to the three organizations mentioned the Gateway amendment was supported by the Bagwell Boosters, Detroit Bar Association, Michigan Congress of Parents and Teachers, Michigan Education Association, Michigan Municipal League, Oakland County Citizens League, United Church Women of Michigan, Wayne-Oakland-Macomb Counties Building Trades Council, American Association of University Women, Dearborn Chamber of Commerce, and Lansing Building Trades Council. Opposition to the amendment came from local government officials who saw a constitutional convention as a threat to their status: the Michigan Manufacturers Association, Michigan Retailers Association, Michigan Sheriffs Association, Michigan Township Association, Michigan Justices of the Peace Association, County Road Association of Michigan, Michigan Asphalt Paving Association, Michigan Bankers Association, Michigan Construction Equipment Association, Michigan Farm Bureau, Michigan Real Estate Association, Michigan Good Roads Federation, Michigan Savings and Loan League, Michigan State Grange, and Portland Cement Association.[17]

On November 8, 1960, the Gateway amendment was approved by a margin of 350,000 votes. Only about two-thirds of those casting a ballot chose to voice an opinion. Passage of the amendment brought new support from organizations that had opposed the suggested change in Article XVII for the Con-Con question itself, which would be decided on April 3, 1961. Most important of the new supporters were AFL-CIO, UAW, and the entire Democratic party; and there were several of Con-Con's previous foes who had ceased hostilities. With the public largely apathetic toward the question, Con-Con was approved by a narrow 23,421 votes, with only one third of the state's three and a half million registered voters participating. Delegates to the convention were chosen by the respective parties in a July 25 primary, and on September 12, 1961, their number was cut to the final 144 delegates. The first session opened on October 3.

The 144-member body was predominantly Republican (99–45), although each party had divisions within its ranks. It was decided that the convention would have one president and three vice-presidents. George Romney had been elected by a 3–1 landslide in Oakland County and more or less expected to head the Con-Con body. But a deadlock between Republican factions at a party caucus a week before the convention began caused both Romney and conservative-bloc leader Edward Hutchinson to be bypassed. When Hutchinson led the first dozen ballots, Romney lost his temper and alienated many of his fellow delegates. Finally, on the seventeenth ballot the title of president was awarded Stephen S. Nisbet, a retired vice-president of Gerber Products. Romney and Hutchinson became vice-presidents, and Tom Downs, an attorney for AFL-CIO, became the only Democratic member of Con-Con's top four leaders.

Michigan's constitutional convention lasted seven and a half months. Roughly speaking, the constitution-making procedure entailed three phases. Phase one lasted about three weeks and concerned operating procedures: organization, staffing, and rule formation. Phase two, the committee phase, involved provisions and hours of committee hearings. The last phase consisted of full body debate on committee work and adoption of provisions to be submitted to the Michigan electorate.

The 144-member body began on a bipartisan note. But strangely enough this was shattered as the convention progressed by the person most desiring a bipartisan convention: George Romney. Romney had been mentioned as a gubernatorial candidate as far back as December 4, 1958, when Allan B. Clink formed a citizens' committee to draft George Romney for governor. But as the months passed Romney made no bones about his position and asserted, "If drafted, I will not accept; if nominated, I will not run."

It was Romney, however, who shook the convention on December 3, 1961, when he announced that he was giving consideration to seeking the Republican gubernatorial nomination. Romney's announcement received considerable publicity in the Detroit newspapers, and on January 18, Detroit Mayor Jerome Cavanagh accused the press of "plotting to thrust George Romney on the public as a political personality!"

Just one week earlier Romney had debated August Scholle, president of Michigan AFL-CIO, on the subject of legislative apportionment and had gained himself a wide following by convincing doubters that "a corporation president accustomed to the quiet of a board room could handle himself against an experienced labor leader schooled in the give and take of union halls."[18]

On the same day that Romney debated Scholle he became involved in a dispute concerning former president Harry S. Truman. Formal invitations had been extended to both Truman and Eisenhower to speak before the Con-Con assembly, with the understanding that one would not be allowed to speak unless the other accepted. Eisenhower had spoken a month earlier, and now Truman notified the body that he was not coming and indeed had never accepted the invitation! This action tended to make the heavily balanced Republican body seem narrow-minded in seeking outside advice to construct a new constitution. Romney felt that the Democratic reversal was an attempt to embarrass him, since he had initiated correspondence with both distinguished guests.

Toward the end of the month Democratic State Chairman Joe Collins accused the Republican-convention delegates of being more concerned with George Romney as a candidate for governor than with a better constitution. In early February a mass of press releases informed the public that Romney had begun a twenty-four-hour fast to help him decide whether he would run for governor or not. August Scholle accused Romney of being a "big clown": "This business of trying to put on an act of having a pipeline to God in order to become Governor of Michigan is about the greatest anti-climax to a phony stunt I've ever seen."[19]

Naturally Scholle's comments set off a clash between the two men. After announcing he would be a candidate for governor, Romney told Scholle that the same pipeline was open to everybody. Scholle struck back with a biblical quotation: "And when thou prayest, thou shalt not be as hypocrites are: for they love to pray in the synagogues and in the corners of the streets, that they may be seen of men." (Matt. 6:5). He added insult to injury by accusing Romney of "running hard since last October" and using Con-Con to advance his personal goals.

On February 16, Rev. Joseph C. Walen got into the battle

and scolded Scholle for scorning any man's religious practices. Finally the matter of the Mormon fast was brought to a halt with a real surprise. Democratic Governor John Swainson announced that he had been raised in the Mormon faith!

The religious issue being dead for the moment, the Democrats released a series of attacks on Romney. Lieutenant Governor T. John Lesinski wrote Romney a letter asking him to testify before the Senate Taxation Committee and explain a tax program that he would endorse. The move was calculated to show that Romney could not convince Republican legislators to vote for an income tax any more than could Swainson.

Neil Staebler, a candidate for United States Representative, accused Romney of using the Republican party to get himself elected but shunning the Republican label. These attacks were followed quickly by requests that Romney plead before the Michigan legislature for strong civil-rights legislation and a minimum-wage law. The idea seemed to be to press Romney to show some of his leadership abilities—or better yet, his lack of such abilities.

A significant development took place in the constitutional convention at this time. A large majority of the delegates were Republicans. But the fact is that there were really three parties represented, because the Republicans were split into two groups: the "moderate" or "liberal wing" headed by Romney, and the "old guard," "farm delegates," or "veto bloc" under the direction of D. Hale Brake. So it was necessary for the Republicans to give and take among themselves to make use of their majority.

On March 16, Romney announced an accommodation agreement between the Republican factions designed to settle all major issues remaining in the convention. To obtain support for some measures that he wanted, Romney had to give concessions. Four major concessions were his goal of a house apportioned on a straight population basis; his desire for the governor to appoint all six members of the State Administrative Board; his wish that the fifteen-mill property tax limitation be erased; and his plans for more flexibility in earmarked funds.[20]

The Democrats immediately accused Romney of selling out his principles of good government. They maintained that he had

been "traded out of his pants." D. Hale Brake solved the problem by giving Romney a pair of large green pants for St. Patrick's
Day, and Romney retorted that he always bought suits with two
pairs of trousers!

In attempting to justify his actions in the face of severe
criticism by the Democrats for the next several days—and throughout the coming campaign—Romney made a number of public statements. Probably his two most potent were these:

> No one finds it harder to compromise their objectives more than
> I do. But we were faced with total defeat or 80 per cent victory.
> I think it best to take the 80 per cent victory.

> Idealists want 100 per cent achievement. But pure idealism doesn't
> build from where we are to where we want to go—the constitution
> is a one-shot deal. There's no subsequent session where you can try
> again.[21]

The convention recessed on May 11 until the sine die meeting on August 1, and as might be expected, the constitution became a political football. It was treated as "Mr. Romney's constitution" or at the very least "a Republican document." Romney
had announced on February 10, 1962, that he would seek the
governorship but vowed that he would not be an active candidate
until Con-Con adjournment. He kept his promise.

5

Get Michigan on the Move:
The 1962 Campaign

THERE is great similarity between the Kennedy "get this country moving again" campaign of 1960 and that presented by Romney to the people of Michigan in 1962. Michigan had suffered economic problems that hit their climax in 1959, and Democratic State Chairman Neil Staebler accurately predicted that in two to four years there would be a backlash against those in office. Staebler, of course, meant the Republican Neanderthals, but the backlash extended into the office of governor.

From the very start it was obvious that the economy of the state would be the major issue in the gubernatorial election. Governor Swainson would be forced to defend his record and prove that Michigan was moving ahead at a satisfactory rate and that he had rendered positive actions within his two-year term. Romney, on the other hand, would be pushing the Kennedy arguments of 1960: "Michigan is not functioning at full capacity . . . let's get Michigan on the move."

In his State of the State address to the Seventy-first Legislature on January 11, 1962, Governor Swainson outlined what his administration had accomplished in his first year of office. Unfortunately he had little concrete achievement in his favor. "Michigan," he said, "is moving ahead. There are signs everywhere that our economy is on the way up." He pointed out that defense industries entered 1962 with an increase of $40,000,000 in back orders over the 1961 fiscal year. He pointed to the reduction in the army of the unemployed from a high of 422,500 in March, 1961, to 205,000 in November. He painted vivid pictures of expanding industry, noting that sixty-one new operations had been launched within the state in 1961 (the most in five years). He cited twenty-six industries that had moved in from neighboring states and indicated that nine plants previously closed down had gone back into production. He ended his presentation by saying, "Michigan is marching forward again. We are growing. We are regaining our economic might. Our prospects are bright. They can be even brighter if we but have the alertness and aggressiveness to press forward."

Michigan voters were confronted by Romney's contention that this was not enough. The state's money problems had not been solved: unemployment was high. "Michigan," said Romney, "needs leadership."

The unsuccessful GOP candidate of 1958 and 1960 paved the way for a Romney victory in 1962. Paul D. Bagwell, when an undergraduate at the University of Akron, had worked part-time for Ohio County Chairman Ray Bliss. He studied two years in the graduate school of Wisconsin, and taught at Michigan State University in 1928, when Michigan was on the old caucus system. Bagwell served as state chairman of Citizens for Eisenhower in 1952 and 1956, was nominated for auditor general in 1956, and led the Republican ticket that year, while GOP gubernatorial candidate Albert E. Cobo went down to defeat. It was Bagwell who set many valuable precedents for Romney's campaign.

Two of the most important precedents were in advertising and labor. The lesson in advertising was what to avoid. Bagwell supporters had relied on a cheap kinescope process for television spots for their candidate. Bagwell says, "My television spots did more to wreck my campaign than to help it." His daughter joked that she thought her father was applying for the job of master of ceremonies for "Shock Theater," a late TV series thriller narrated by a ghoulish-looking graduate student at Wayne State University. His image was so bad that it became a good way to draw a response from an audience, Bagwell says. "During the last week of the 1960 campaign I could appear before any audience in the city of Detroit and open by saying, 'I'm here for the purpose of destroying the image that's been created for me by my commercial TV spots'—and I couldn't say anything funnier!" Most of the Bagwell commercials were ten and twenty-second segments. He had no telethons and a few fifteen or thirty-minute exposures, other than the debates with Williams and Swainson. Romney learned a valuable lesson.

Romney was also able to observe Bagwell's attempt at cracking the labor-Democratic alliance. In 1960 Bagwell brought Ken Fabel, one of California's top UAW-CIO organizers, back to Michigan. Fabel devoted full time to the Bagwell campaign and developed Bagwell Booster clubs within Buick, Chevrolet, and A C Spark Plug plants. These clubs circulated petitions demanding equal time for their candidate on company bulletin boards and in the union halls. In addition the candidate did much of his own labor-vote seeking. "I worked the factory gates in 1958," Bagwell reflects, "and those men had never seen a Republican there! I couldn't get Republican volunteers to man the gates with me, so I got high-school kids to stand out and pick the literature up. It looked very bad. Sometimes they would throw it on the ground and spit on it."

It was Bagwell, too, who crashed the major Labor Day Rally in Detroit for the first time. There is a picture in a Detroit newspaper of his 1908 Oldsmobile sitting in front of Walter Reuther at Detroit's Cadillac Square (Bagwell had bought the 1908 automobile from the duPont family to underline that the state constitution adopted in 1909 was as outdated as the vehicle). All these efforts met with limited success. Whereas a labor worker could not be found sporting a Bagwell button in 1958, Bagwell carried the heavy labor counties of Genesee and Muskegon in 1960—the first time for a Republican since 1946.

Another service rendered Romney by Bagwell was isolation of the issues. Most of the major issues of 1958 and 1960 were still present in 1962. Bagwell had concerned himself with the need for a new constitution, reorganization of the administrative branch of government, the flight of jobs and industry out of the state, and the financial irresponsibility of the Democratic administration in its long years of domination.

Finally it was the liberal-imaged Bagwell who first attempted the task of shoring up Republican support. This was not easy, because of the conservative posture of the party. Many of the GOP Old Guard did not want Bagwell to lead their ticket and did not contribute to his campaign fund. Bagwell states, not entirely in jest, "I spent more time fighting Republicans in 1958 and 1960 than Democrats!"

All these factors united to make it a formidable race for the office of governor of Michigan in 1960. It was a close race indeed, with Bagwell picking up 49.5 per cent of the vote but losing to Democrat John B. Swainson by a 41,612 plurality.

The Constitutional Convention recessed on May 11, 1962, and though Romney had done no active campaigning up until that time, he nevertheless was a man in motion. He asked Arthur "Mighty Mite" Elliott, Jr., to serve as his campaign manager only three days after announcing his decision to become a gubernatorial candidate, in February. Elliott was a fellow delegate to the Constitutional Convention and a Romney admirer. He began work right away with two aims: to develop a campaign structure of personnel and to introduce George Romney to party leadership throughout the state. The second goal was of prime importance, because the outstate Republicans were not at all sure that Romney was a good choice. They resented Romney for one or more of five reasons.

First, they were not sure that Romney was a Republican. His role in Citizens for Michigan had established a nonpolitical image in their minds. Furthermore, Romney had made statements in the past that tended to confuse them. Shutting the door on any speculation that he might run for senator or governor in 1960, Romney had said, "I am not currently a Republican. I was, but I'm not now." He explained his position by saying that he felt he could make a more valuable contribution on a nonpartisan basis: "I consider the public service I can make through

CFM more important than being a candidate for public office." Romney did stress that the statement applied only to 1960. Other quotations such as "I'm not a member of any political party" were made in a CFM environmental setting, when none of the members were expected to act in a partisan sense. Democrats to this day are still saying Romney "flip-flops" on being Republican or not being Republican as his whim dictates. There is no truth to the charge. When Romney's dream of independent action burst, he labeled himself an Oakland County Republican to separate himself from the conservative image the party had gained within the state. This description puzzled hard-core members of the party even further.

Second, outstate Republicans were not happy with his economic views. In 1958, shortly after American Motors had become a profit-making corporation, Romney surprised everyone in testifying before Senator Estes Kefauver's antitrust subcommittee when he advocated the breakup of General Motors and Ford into smaller companies. Romney went so far as to propose antitrust laws that would force divestiture when any company engaged in a single industry exceeded 35 per cent of the market. This was the first time any executive in the automobile industry had made such a suggestion, and it just about gagged Old Guard Republicans within Michigan who thrived upon big business—the automobile industry—for their power base.

Third, Romney had gone on record while working with CFM as favoring a state income tax. The Old Guard wanted no part of an income-tax package. They had been fighting Williams and Swainson on that issue and thought it would be awkward at best to have a candidate or governor from their own party supporting such a thing.

Fourth, many conservative Republicans were boiling over a statement Romney had made in the national television program "Meet the Press," in early January of 1962. Romney painted a gray picture of Michigan's political history rather than the customary black and white, conservative versus liberal, portrait. He said that labor was presently controlled by the Democratic party—which was all well and good. Then he said that big business had dominated the Republican party within the state. In short, Romney said of the past, "A plague on both your houses." Barry Goldwater, six weeks later, visited Michigan and praised Romney for being a "dedicated man of flawless integrity," while adding that "the myth that business dominates the Republican party in Michigan should be exposed for the fraud it is!" It was no fraud.

Last, they resented the George Romney they had seen at Con-Con. True, he had agreed to the March package deal with D. Hale Brake. But here was a man who had been in favor of a House apportioned on straight population (which would cut down the number of conservatives elected to office); backed the idea of appointing the six-member State Administration Board (which would give the governor far too much power); wanted to increase the property-tax limitation; and wanted less earmarking of state revenues. In addition Romney had gone on record in mid-January as being dissatisfied with the Republican image within the state; if he were the GOP candidate for governor, he "would begin the task of remolding the Republican party to fit his concepts of a dynamic and pressure-free citizen-run organization."

From the very beginning Romney was aware of the rumblings within party ranks and fully realized that he needed to wage a preliminary battle to quiet GOP sniping before challenging Swainson. Without underestimating his task Romney began a chore that could be described as how to win Conservatives and influence Republicans.

In early February Romney returned from Washington, where he had received only lukewarm support from Michigan congressmen, and dined with twenty-two GOP state senators in Lansing. After he had discussed the possibility of running for governor for nearly three hours with the infamous veto bloc, Senator Charles R. Fienstra of Grand Rapids commented, "He's got a good head, but it's not been cultivated in the area of government!" From mid-April until mid-May Romney attended a series of get-acquainted sessions with party leaders in each Congressional District. On July 8, 1962, he celebrated his fifty-fifth birthday by throwing a party at his Bloomfield Hills home. It was more than a party—it was a county chairmen's luncheon, at which Montgomery Shepard, a northwestern Michigan conservative leader who had once threatened to oppose Romney in the August 7 primary, issued a statement that he was 100 per cent behind Romney. This, in spite of the fact that he wore a "No Income Tax" pin on his shirt! Romney did not gain full support of his party until the August 7 primary.

On February 13, Romney resigned from American Motors. He was elected to the newly created post of vice-chairman, continued as a director, and was granted leave of absence to pursue the GOP gubernatorial nomination. At that time Romney was AMC's largest stockholder, with 104,200 shares. He retained his holdings during the election.

In April, Romney's staff completed a poll that had been conducted for two reasons: to locate the issues and to see how the people of the state viewed the candidate and the party. The poll revealed that Romney's image was one of strength at that early stage and that Swainson was less popular. When viewing the parties, the opposite was true. This led Elliott and others on the Romney campaign staff to conclude that it would be detrimental to Romney to emphasize the party label.

Largely on the basis of that poll, Romney asked John Dempsey (new director of television Channel 2 in Detroit)—who had always been a Democrat—to be state chairman of a group that became known as the Romney Volunteers. Dempsey was successful in establishing 146 chapters scattered throughout all eighty-three of Michigan's counties. The volunteers numbered eighty thousand by election time and were financed by the Romney for Governor committee. The volunteers did several things: they located Romney supporters and got their names on a list, canvassed Democratic areas, set up headquarters, passed out materials, and organized rallies. The group was mostly responsible for the "Name Only" bumper stickers in 1962 and 1964. After all, many of the members were Democrats for Romney!

The first real issue outside Con-Con activities also evolved in April. The executive and legislative branches of the state government had made several attempts at obtaining fiscal reform via an income tax during the early months of 1962. Swainson had on January 26 proposed a tax package, designed to produce $71,000,000 additional annual revenue, the Senate Taxation Committee had proposed its program aimed at raising $59,000,000 (omitting an income tax), and the House Taxation Committee had also offered a tentative solution. None of these plans was acceptable to all, and a compromise program was adopted in the Senate on April 25. No sooner had the bill passed than a motion was made to reconsider. Five days later the bill was defeated.

It was evident that no new income tax would be accepted and that some form of fund-raising would be necessary. Relenting toward what he felt to be the lesser of two evils, John Swainson allowed the nuisance taxes to be reimposed (and in some cases outrageously raised). The new tax measures that went into effect on July 1, 1962, without his signature allowed for an increase of 1 mill in the corporate franchise tax, an increase of 2 cents per pack in the cigarette tax, a second 4 per cent tax on liquor, a 4 per cent use tax on communication services, and a 428 per cent increase in the beer tax. The last measure formed the first anti-Swainson interest group of the 1962 campaign.

Swainson had campaigned on the platform that he would allow the nuisance taxes to expire. It was a promise he meant to keep, and technically he did. They expired in June 1961; but they were reimposed one year later. If they had not been allowed to lapse for that one year, Michigan's financial picture would not have been so dismal in June, 1962. Those taxes raised over $50,000,000 in their 1960–61 levy and would have cut the $85,585,815 General Fund deficit by more than half. The brewing industry was upset. Not only had Swainson not kept his promise to cut out the $1.25 per barrel tax, he had allowed the tax to be raised to the ridiculous figure of $6.61 a barrel.

The second major economic mistake by Governor Swainson was the veto of the Bowman bill. Early in 1962 the Detroit city council and the state government were in search of additional funds. They decided to impose a 1 per cent income tax on all payrolls, including those of non-residents who worked within Detroit. Roseville Senator John T. Bowman introduced a bill that passed the legislature disallowing the tax on non-residents. Swainson vetoed the bill; hence suburban areas were up in arms. It was common to hear Democrats in these areas declaring, "Swainson will never get my vote again!" or, "I won't vote Republican; I'll just stay at home!"

A third anti-Swainson group was formed by Michigan dairy workers. Michigan has been plagued by a milk-pricing problem for years. Leading chain groceries used milk as a loss leader. Swainson promised to do something about this problem and did. The McClean bill was passed in 1961, but the wording was bad and actually fixed the price of milk. Swainson vetoed the new legislation and as a result lost friends. In October of 1961 a small sign draped in black was placed on the Dairy Workers Union Building in Detroit. It read: "In memory of John B. Swainson who broke his promise."

In addition to these economic actions Swainson made some campaigning errors that would haunt him. He did not appear at all the functions his predecessor G. Mennen Williams had attended, such as the Upper Peninsula Fair at Escanaba. Of course, as acting governor he had had a number of duties to perform, and his artificial limbs limited his movements; nonetheless, he was expected at a score of events from which he was absent.

Another personal campaign error that might be singled out occurred in August. Invited to address the National Convention of Jewish War Veterans in Detroit, Swainson spoke not as governor of Michigan but as candidate Swainson, lashing out at the "Republican Neanderthal men of the state legislature." It would have been a dandy of a speech at a Democratic rally, but this audience did not expect a partisan harangue. Jewish War Veterans National Commander Theodore Brooks remarked, "We didn't expect the Governor would deliver a partisan speech, but since it was, I think the other candidate should have equal time." Consequently Romney was invited, spoke on a nonpartisan basis, and received a standing ovation from the two hundred delegates at the convention. Swainson had thus made it possible for Romney to make political hay. In fact, the incumbent Governor made enough campaign miscalculations to justify a criticism offered by an enterprising Detroit newspaper reporter: "It's getting to be a question whether George Romney if elected shouldn't find some appointment around Lansing for John Swainson. The political custom is to reward those who have been helpful during the campaign. . . ."[1] In all fairness to Swainson, he had been taken in. Romney had broken an eight-year tradition by making a strong political speech at the Ionia Free Fair only two weeks earlier. The occasion had been a joint appearance of the candidates, however, and this gave an illusion of fair play that the incident spoken of above did not carry.

Oddly enough, it was Governor Swainson who started campaigning first. On May 11 he announced for reelection at the Democratic party's Jefferson-Jackson Day Dinner in Detroit, saying that he would wage war on the "disdainful Republican record of obstruction and reaction." He linked the Republican party to all that was bad in the state and pledged that he would fight adoption of the new state constitution.

Romney opened his campaign a week later. On May 17, he attended the Holland Tulip Festival opening. For the first time since 1948, no Democratic leader was present for the street-scrubbing ceremonies. The 50,000 people got a glimpse of George, Lenore, and young Mitt Romney dressed in Dutch costumes and wooden shoes, pushing brooms with the other street scrubbers along a one-mile parade route. The crowd roared when Mitt drenched his father with water several times. After having been seen by this large number of Michiganites and holding a press conference before the parade, Romney still insisted that the campaign had not yet started. Commenting on appearing ahead of his Democratic opponent, Romney stated, "It always pays to be on the job early!"

The Romney campaign opened officially at its Detroit Industrial Building headquarters the next day. At that press conference Romney revealed a plan showing remarkable political adroitness. It was not altogether new, largely a matter of semantics. When questioned on taxes, Romney casually announced that he did *not* favor an income tax! That statement was bound to raise a few eyebrows, since it was widely known that he had subscribed to the

CFM call for a flat-rate income tax when he headed that group, and he had again voiced public support for the plan when Swainson asked him to help on fiscal reform in February. Romney said that the major issue of the election was jobs and that he was for "fiscal reform." To be sure, he was in great demand for the next few weeks to explain what he meant by his term; and he clarified his position by saying that an income tax was only one side of the Michigan tax problem. As he saw it an income tax in and of itself would "not solve anything other than the state's deficit." What he had in mind was administrative and fiscal reform that would spur economic growth and create jobs. Speaking before the Detroit Press Club on May 25, Romney explained his emphasis on complete fiscal reform rather than on the income tax:

"While I do not believe the state's job, fiscal, and tax problems can be solved without the enactment of an income tax, it is not clear that we need higher taxes. The fundamental tax need is to shift the burden away from the low-income families, property owners and industry—particularly new business—while providing help to local government. . . . What makes total administrative and fiscal reform absolutely essential is that it is one indispensable element in stimulating economic growth or jobs."

It was not until September 13 that Romney finally announced a fifteen-point program which, he said, would "assure Michigan of the economic growth needed to regain the nation's confidence." Main portions of the plan called for eliminating unnecessary spending, reducing the state deficit quickly so as to establish a sound financial base, streamlining state governmental organization, consolidating promotional efforts of the state, utilizing the talents of retired citizens, eliminating the business-activity tax, taking full advantage of federal programs, strengthening the tourism program from its $650,000,000 to more than $1,000,000,000, and conducting a "dynamic personal selling campaign to let the nation and the world know that Michigan is rolling again."

Now the campaign was in full swing. Neither of the candidates had had primary opposition, and each represented a different political philosophy. Swainson was much more the political animal who reacted to each situation with politics in mind. He believed that all accomplishments were made from within the parties and saw nothing so drastically wrong with the state that enough money would not cure it. He saw the Democratic party as the party of the workingman and the Republican party as the party of big business. Romney, on the other hand, felt that the ultimate power of politics rested with the people—not necessarily the parties. Parties to him existed because they were necessary instruments. He believed that the state had lost much of its power by lack of initiative and had thus encouraged federal encroachment. He believed that an independent administration under the Republican label could take the lead among the states in local and state problem solving. These viewpoints allowed the coming campaign to be viewed as a race between a man and a machine.

Swainson was G. Mennen Williams' personal choice as his heir. Swainson had successfully conducted the 1960 campaign and was now trying to get himself reelected. He was a veteran of World War II who had lost both legs below the knee when as a nineteen-year-old army private he walked on a land mine during French combat in 1944. He had a boyish, sincere campaign manner and a solid Wayne County Democratic labor organization behind him. He was finishing his first term as governor of a great industrial state at the age of only thirty-seven; but he had some drawbacks.

John S. Knight describes Swainson as a "so-so Governor with no clearly defined ideas for the solution of Michigan's problems other than to follow the dictates of Scholle and Reuther."[2] *Newsweek* referred to "John Swainson's placid regime."[3] Other words used to describe the young Governor were "ineffective," "lackluster," "colorless," and "one who had hardly inspired." Veteran capitol reporter Bob Popa gives a more accurate picture of the Democratic Governor: "He had the unfortunate reputation of being sort of a bland, colorless candidate. He was pretty colorful, but he didn't come across that way to the voters. He was a man who couldn't project warmth. He spoke in a stilted fashion . . . a sort of Victorian syntax." On a person-to-person basis John Swainson is often described as "a hell of a nice guy," "wonderful to work for," and "a man deserving of loyalty." Without doubt, he is a man of high integrity who was hurt by his inability to project a dynamic image and the "time for a change" backlash that Neil Staebler had predicted in 1959!

In contrast, Romney was a bright young star on the Michigan scene. He had headed a successful drive for Detroit school needs, had been a leader in CFM and a prominent force in pushing for a constitutional convention, and had made headlines constantly during the convention; and—most important of all—he had the reputation of being a financial wizard. But Romney, too, had drawbacks. He was of a minority religion, he was not clearly a member of the Republican party, and he was something of a political novice.

This last point is underscored by a battle within his own party that Romney himself touched off in May—a flareup that sputtered throughout the campaign. On May 18, the day he officially opened his campaign, Romney publicly urged that Fourteenth District Republican leader Richard Durant relinquish his position because he was an acknowledged member of the extremist John Birch Society. Two months later Durant had not acted and in a private meeting on July 28 Romney demanded his resignation. Still making no headway, Romney foolishly put his prestige on the line addressing a breakfast meeting of candidates for precinct delegates in the Fourteenth District the following morning. He did not mince words when he scolded, "If delegates from this district reelect this man, then you will have repudiated me!"

Tension mounted until Durant made it public that he had given up his membership in the arch-conservative society, and Romney reacted with what he felt to be a suitable acknowledgement: "Assuming this is a complete severance from Birchism, it eliminates, in his case, conflict between the Republican party and that organization." Swainson, seeing that Durant had only resigned from the organization—not repudiated its principles or aims —charged Romney with another sellout.

Romney was clearly feeling his way on the issue and wished that his verbal pronouncement would put an end to the matter. How wrong he was! Only three days later, a ward leader in

Detroit wrote Romney a letter revealing that Durant had given her Birch literature only twenty-four hours after making his renunciation public. Durant evidently had not severed his connections with the society, and Romney was in a predicament. He could not afford to further alienate the Old Guard Republicans, and he no doubt felt that he had gone as far as he could. On September 1 he made a feeble attempt to turn the tables on the Democrats who had been accusing him of compromising with Birchers. Trying to spread the extremist issue to both parties, he mentioned Communist infiltration as a problem in the Democratic party at a press conference:

REPORTER: Do you consider this [Communist infiltration] currently as being a problem in the Democratic party?

ROMNEY: Yes, I do.

REPORTER: Do you think it is a problem in the state Democratic party?

ROMNEY: I don't know. I simply say that it has been a sufficient problem on both sides.[4]

Although not directly accusing the state Democratic party of harboring Communists, Romney clearly implied it. The Democrats, assembled for their state convention in Grand Rapids, were more than ruffled. The group passed an official resolution calling Romney a "political slanderer," and the party state chairman, Joe Collins, sent a telegram of protest to the National Fair Campaign Practices Committee. His strategy not working well, Romney announced a few days later that he would rely upon the Romney Volunteers in the Fourteenth District.

Judd Arnett had predicted the 1962 campaign in Michigan would be somewhat "off the beaten path,"[5] and those who knew Romney as a business executive warned that the campaign would be something to behold. That Romney was a workhorse and a bit unorthodox most political observers knew—but they didn't know quite what to expect. The GOP gubernatorial candidate offered a long list of Romneyisms revolving around moral principles, nonpartisanship, and unorthodox solutions to governmental problems.

The first Romneyism was made public on June 2, when

Romney announced that he would stick to a six-day work week because of his "personal conviction that Sunday should be devoted to church and family life." He vowed that his staff would leave the Sabbath open "without exception." Swainson probably wondered what kind of religious nut he was squared off with, and Gus Scholle groaned loud enough to be heard in Lansing.

Glenn Engle of the Detroit *News* describes Romneyism number two: an "unorthodox though systematic" campaign practice of using questionnaires.[6] In February, when he announced that he would become a candidate for governor, Romney added that he would ask for guidance from all citizens of the state, saying, "I am not afraid of the voice of the people. I welcome that voice and I want to hear it!" By June members of his campaign staff had started circulating questionnaires on state problems to make good their candidate's promise—or at least to make it look as if he meant what he said. The questionnaires were passed out in person, many of them by the candidate himself. The voters were asked about such matters as what tax they thought the legislature ought to levy if it was found necessary, the organization of state government, and other important issues. There were ten statements to be marked on a Likert-type scale of agree, undecided, disagree. One such statement was, "I believe our State government must be completely impartial and just in administering the laws and must not favor any 'special' people or groups." The voters were asked to spend four minutes and four cents "to improve the State of Michigan." About 150,000 of the questionnaires were distributed by August 5, and over 2,000 had been returned by that date. The statements were arranged so that Romney stated his views and then asked the voters whether they agreed with him or not. Most of the returns showed a high degree of agreement.[7] The device appealed to the independent voter in the state and was actually a method of persuasion. After all, if you agreed with what Romney stood for when you marked the questionnaire, didn't you more or less commit yourself to vote for him?

A third Romneyism was the introduction of the door-to-door campaign in Michigan by the candidate himself. Starting this face-to-face campaign the day after his fifty-fifth birthday, Romney invaded neighborhoods on a random basis, ringing doorbells and shaking hands over fences and at factory gates. The favorable reaction in most instances is characterized by George Walker of the Detroit *Free Press.*[8]

HOUSEWIFE A: I told my husband George Romney was coming up the sidewalk and he told me I must be crazy and that I'd better go back to bed!
HOUSEWIFE B: Surprised? I never heard of such a thing . . . a millionaire going around ringing doorbells!

While these remarks tend to indicate that Romney was already regarded by many as a celebrity, there were a few disbelievers. In Detroit a housewife took the questionnaire from the Republican candidate and threw it onto her front porch, saying, "Detroit will never be like it was. You can't stop manufacturers from moving out!" "Oh, yes I can," Romney replied. "Oh, I know you promise all kinds of things but once you get in office you won't do anything," she continued. Romney paused for only a moment and retorted, "I never started anything yet I didn't finish. I straightened out a financial mess at AMC and I can do it for the state." "It would take a miracle to straighten things out in Michigan," she said, starting to walk away. But Romney replied in a clear, deliberate, and confident voice, "I believe in miracles!"

Romneyism number four aroused the ire of Governor Swainson the most. Beginning September first, Romney appointed a two-man team to investigate the safety of a Berrien County bridge over the I-94 Freeway that crosses the entire southern part of the state. Swainson had promised earlier to make any state records available to the Republican candidate during the campaign. Romney took advantage of the offer, and when a few days later he appointed a second team of experts to review the records and procedures in the offices of the auditor general, treasurer, and controller, Swainson bristled at his "colossal gall" and labeled Romney's inquisition squads "a shabby political game."

Undoubtedly the most significant Romneyism was a continuation of the Bagwell desire to shatter the labor political curtain. Since the 1948 victory of G. Mennen Williams, labor's influence in the Democratic party had been common knowledge,[9] and Romney well knew that he would have to make substantial inroads in the labor area if he was to succeed. Actually it seems that labor made a series of miscalculations that enhanced Romney's possibilities. On August 30, Al Barbour, Wayne County AFL-CIO president, made a public statement to the effect that Romney was not welcome to attend the annual Labor Day Rally to be held at the Michigan State Fairgrounds.

Romney decided that he would attend the festivities anyway, and it proved to be a grueling day. There was to be a parade to the fairgrounds, and Romney decided to participate. He arrived at the parade's starting point at 8:30 A.M. and promptly got into an argument when he tried to shake hands with three men standing on a street corner. The parade got under way. Swainson rode in an open convertible behind a brass band. Romney walked ahead of the band and along the curbing so that he could shake hands with the people who lined the route. Upon arriving at the fairgrounds, Romney assumed a seat in the rear of the band-shell area. He listened to Swainson's speech and a photographer captured "lonesome George" as he sat there on the back of a bench with several empty rows between himself and the Democrat-labor celebration. Attending took courage in Romney. Several union members would not even shake his hand, and at one point the marching unit of the UAW Local 155 whipped past him singing, "Swainson is our leader, we will not be moved." But Romney was not discouraged. That evening he was an uninvited guest at the Muskegon Labor Council picnic.

Romney told reporters the next morning that he had "penetrated a political curtain." He felt that his appearances in Detroit and Muskegon had demonstrated that AFL-CIO was "not a monolithic voting bloc in this state despite the efforts of some leaders to make it appear that it is." The cold fact is that he had not penetrated any barrier. But he had started the labor osmosis. A few days later he was refused admittance to a Cadillac local. People became aware of the charge Romney was making, and labor leaders were forced to make statements denying that the union was dominating the political will of its members.

Romney's first big break was to come on the union-sponsored television show, "Telescope." Romney charged that Swainson had recently made several "distortions" on the program, and requested that he be permitted to correct them. Guy Nunn, the quick-witted, sharp-tongued UAW commentator, agreed, but before the show could be aired there was a public hassle over who would foot the bill. Nunn originally said he would gladly accept Romney's money, and Romney mailed a check for $1,040 to cover the cost of the program. Upon receiving the check, Nunn changed his position, saying that UAW programs were paid for in advance by the year and could not be sold or resold. Nunn wanted it understood that Romney could have his money back and that under no circumstances would the check "be considered payment for the program." In a letter to Nunn, Romney indicated that he felt it was neither moral nor right for UAW members to be arbitrarily taxed to pay the cost of broadcasting opinions they might not support. (The UAW constitution provides that ten cents a month of each member's dues be placed in the UAW Citizenship Fund, part of which was used to pay for "Telescope.") Nunn pointed out that upon special request the ten-cent fee could be spent in some other way. Finally UAW President Walter Reuther intervened and suggested that Romney donate the check in dispute to the American History Foundation. Romney complied.

The show itself was hardly less spectacular. It was taped on September 22 in the CKLW studio, Windsor, and shown the following evening over Channel 9. A large audience was watching.

Guy Nunn, who had a reputation for bringing out the worst in people, started the show with a long statement that led listeners to believe that the UAW had actively sought out Republican gubernatorial candidates for a program appearance over the previous twelve years—which was little short of a direct lie. Romney got in a few licks about the union-published paper *(AFL-CIO News)* presenting only one side of an issue, and nailed down five distortions he felt Swainson had made in the previous Sunday's show. Nunn then started firing questions of the "When did you stop beating your wife?" variety. But Romney was looking for that technique and refused to fall into the trap: "Mr. Nunn, would you let me answer one or two questions at a time? You're listing a lot of points there that I want to comment on before you go further, because you're already listed two distortions of fact." Nunn was intent on smearing Romney and constantly interrupted and changed the subject. Tempers flared, and several times the two men spoke over one another:

ROMNEY:	Now, again, let me stop right here.
NUNN:	May I continue, Mr. Romney, please?
ROMNEY:	No sir, no, sir . . .
NUNN:	May I continue?
ROMNEY:	No, sir, I insist that when you throw in as many misstatements as you've just thrown in in the process of asking me a question that I have the right . . .
NUNN:	May I . . .
ROMNEY:	No sir you have thrown in so many of them that I can't do it.
NUNN:	May I put it very simply like this?
ROMNEY:	No, sir, I want to correct what you've already thrown into this picture in the way of distortion.
NUNN:	Don't you want to answer the real question?
ROMNEY:	No, sir. Number one, you let me finish!

Judd Arnett commented that while Romney came out the right way through the telescope, Nunn came out with the lens reversed.[10] Roscoe Drummond reported: "I've never heard a faster-talking TV commentator [than Nunn], but he didn't outface and he didn't outtalk Romney, who backed him into the corner, cut him off in mid-innuendo and, for the most part calmly, sometimes sternly, made his case."[11] The result was that the labor-domination issue grew in the public mind.

After the Nunn show Romney received several invitations to speak before union groups. On September 27 he was invited to Teamsters Local 326, and by the middle of October he had been invited to UAW Local 155, Carpenters Local 983, UAW Local 1233, and a few others. But some of the invitations were traps, with no sincere wishes to hear his point of view. On three different occasions Romney debated labor leaders before union audiences where catcalls, jeers, and other forms of disrespect were the order of the day. E. S. Patterson intentionally called him "Mr. Romley" throughout their debate on October 16, and on October 19 the governor-to-be was forced to debate standing under a billboard-size poster that urged the election of his opponent.

Usually Romney remained unruffled, but at times his composure was slightly shaken. His comments to individual union members depended upon their manner when approaching him. If someone smiled and said, "I'm for Swainson," Romney might reply, "That's your privilege." But if the person spoke in a mocking tone or insisted that labor should vote Democratic for no reason at all, Romney might retort, "Why, you're stooges. You're perfect stooges." Once a labor man said sternly, "You can't brainwash me!" Romney hesitated only a moment, looked the man in the eye, and replied, "You've already been brainwashed." When, finally, Warren Creekmore, president of UAW Local 280 announced that he would support George Romney for governor, it was clear to all that the political curtain was beginning to crack.

Hugh A. Bone believes that the arguments that develop in any campaign grow out of two sources: the nature of the candidate, and the imagination of his managers or the political and economic environment of the moment.[12] The issues of the Michigan gubernatorial campaign of 1962 fall nicely into Bone's classifications. A number of minor charges went back and forth between Swainson and Romney that lend themselves to the first category, but the more serious and prevailing issues were indeed the ones dealing with the political and economic environment in Michigan as the campaign began.

Some of the minor issues raised by Romney were that the Democratic party was taking Negro votes for granted; that Swainson was inconsistent in that he first stated progress had been impeded by the Republican-controlled legislature and later in the campaign started pointing to all the "great achievements" chalked up by his administration; and that there was some sort of "federally organized rescue mission" being carried on, since many prominent Democrats were visiting the state to help Swainson get reelected.

The Democrats seemed to level more minor charges at Romney. They accused him of conducting a campaign against August Scholle, campaigning without the Republican label, having presidential ambitions, opposing medicare for the aged, and donating money to extremist groups (it was reported that Romney had donated a hundred dollars to Americans for Constitutional Action in 1960).

But all the verbal hocus-pocus failed to hide the real bread-and-butter issues of the campaign. There were in essence three: the people of Michigan wanted leadership, jobs, and an end to the state's financial problems.

On the question of leadership Romney was clearly on the offensive. He began as early as May by saying that Swainson was led by labor, and he generally expanded upon this point, noting that Swainson "had concerned himself with special-interest groups" and had "accomplished absolutely nothing." Using particulars, he criticized Swainson for referring to Republican legislators as Neanderthals. "He's been throwing mud and calling people names —people whose cooperation he must have if he is elected. This is simply additional evidence of the fact that we're in for more stagnation and stalemate for another two years in this state if he's elected."

When Swainson charged that Romney should have done more to promote fiscal reform in the legislature, Romney retorted, "John Swainson, I'd like to say this to you as directly as I can. What you are saying is that you thought I, as a private citizen, should step over and do your job as governor. This is one of the biggest admissions of failure on your part you could possibly cite. It simply means that you couldn't do your job!"

Romney even went so far as to set a set of criteria, saying that the person in the governor's office—

1. Should be free from control of narrow interests.
2. Should treat all citizens equally.
3. Should have the capacity to work with others.

4. Should be able to unify conflicting elements in the state.
5. Should care about individual citizens.
6. Should use state funds frugally.

During the campaign he condemned Swainson on all six counts, and the only thing the governor could do to counteract the indictments was to remind voters that Romney had refused to lend his leadership when it was requested that he plead for a state income tax before the legislative tax committee; to deny that labor influenced his decisions; and to point to what he considered to be the accomplishments of his administration. (Swainson spoke about the state's excellent highway system, increased assistance for public programs such as schools and the mentally retarded, and a seven-year nadir for unemployment.)

There is not much doubt that Romney won hands down on the leadership issue. On the eve of the election Al Sander of the Associated Press characterized Romney's typical campaign personality: "He presented the image of a man who could do great things, a man who had done great things, a man who picked American Motors up by its bootstraps and could do the same thing for the state of Michigan."

The exact employment problem in 1962 is a hard thing to determine because of conflicting reports. Swainson placed the figure at 4.9 per cent, but Norman Barcus of the Michigan Employment Security Commission felt it was nearer 6 per cent,[13] and Harold C. Taylor of the Upjohn Institute for Employment Research noted that there was an employment gap between the number of jobs available and the number of jobs needed for full employment of about 300,000.[14] Regardless of the figures we accept, it can be taken that Michigan's unemployment problem was still acute.

Throughout the campaign Romney was charged by the Democrats with being a "Wisconsin industrialist," because, when serving as president of American Motors, he had moved Hudson manufacturing from Michigan to Kenosha, Wisconsin, and combined it with Nash and Rambler production. Sarcastically, they repeatedly asked him how he would bring more jobs to Michigan by moving all the plants to Wisconsin. Romney pointed out that the success of American Motors in Wisconsin allowed the company to buy four times the number of automobile parts in Michigan that it had previously needed. He contended that the demand for parts caused a greater job increase in Michigan than the unemployment caused by Hudson's leaving. He also contended that UAW President Reuther agreed with the move in 1953.

The employment issue reached its climax in the first of three television debates between the two candidates. Swainson maintained that ninety-five out of every hundred persons in Michigan's working force were employed. Romney charged that these figures were misleading, because 126,000 people had either moved out of the state or dropped out of the working force because they could not find employment. Romney felt that the true figure of unemployment was in the vicinity of 9.2 percent. Neither man was being mendacious—MESC data released after the debate supported both candidates.

While Swainson had been unable to get fiscal reform and had angered dairy workers, the beer industry, and suburban Detroiters by his economic acts concerning issue three, Romney was playing down the term "income tax" and emphasizing the term "fiscal reform." He spoke as if Michigan's problems could be solved solely by cutting down the operating costs of government. And in the final analysis voters on the issue were faced with the knowledge depicted by Detroit *Free Press* political writer Tom Shawver: "Over and over voters who did not know much else about the Republican candidate made the obvious comparison between the state government's nagging money troubles and those that once plagued American Motors."[15]

Election eve found Romney at the Pick Fort Shelby Hotel in Detroit. Although he trailed in actual votes in the early hours, weathervane precincts isolated by Romney's polling expert, Walter DeVries, forecast a win. Romney did not say, "I've won" until Swainson conceded, at nearly 2 A.M. Then Michigan's new governor—the first Republican in fourteen years—emerged wearing a dark-blue suit and his well-known dinosaur tie and tie clasp. In the terrace room the crowd was going wild and upon Romney's entrance they sang "Stout Hearted Men" while balloons floated through the air. Richard Nixon, losing in California, called to wish him well.

Earlier in the evening George Romney had hugged his wife Lenore and said, "Glad to see ya." He hesitated for a moment, and a broad smile wrinkled his rugged features. "Glad to see ya," he reflected—"that's all I've been saying for months." And for Romney the phrase would long continue as an active part of his vocabulary. He defeated John B. Swainson by 80,573 votes.

Keep Michigan on the Move:
The 1964 Campaign

THE 1964 campaign was destined to be conducted on a different basis than that of 1962, for three major reasons: Romney was now an incumbent governor with a record; 1964 was the year of a presidential race (one of the zaniest of all time); and the state of Michigan had undergone what must have seemed a miracle to its citizens. In many respects the 1964 campaign was the antithesis of the one just twenty-four months earlier. Whereas the key question in 1962 had been, Who is responsible for the Michigan mess? it was now, Who is responsible for the progress?

Michigan's newly elected forty-first governor started out like a ball of fire. Only two days after his victory he invited the State Administrative Board (of which he was the only Republican member) to a get-acquainted breakfast. On Friday morning he met with all eighty-one GOP lawmakers on the Michigan State University campus, and added the sixty-three Democratic lawmakers for good measure at a later luncheon meeting. Romney, reliving his lobbyist days for Alcoa, was attempting to give every lawmaker individual attention. And he didn't forget to thank those who had helped him in his campaign. Most of his newly appointed twenty-six-man staff was composed of loyal campaign workers, and telegrams were sent to all GOP county and district chairmen over Romney's signature. (Even Richard Durant in the 14th district received one, but this was a mistake made through Western Union!)

Immediately after the election Romney began grinding out the 1963–64 state budget. He asked the budget division to cut 10 per cent from all departmental recommendations, and he followed by appointing a special task force of financial experts to find ways of performing state services more efficiently. Next he put forth a hold-the-line budget of $547,000,000 (only $35,000,000 more than the 1962–63 state expenditure). Romney dubbed his budget "prudent, because it lives within its income, and progressive because it provides for the future." Breaking from tradition, he delivered his message in person.

Republicans, such as House Majority Leader Robert E. Waldron and Speaker Allison Green, seemed to think that Romney's position of "no new programs we cannot afford" and a balanced budget made sense, but Democratic leaders voiced opposition, including House Minority Leader Joseph J. Kowalski, Representative Michael J. O'Brien, and Senator Charles S. Blondy. The opposition consensus was that Romney's budget was not nearly as progressive as was needed. And the Democrats were not incorrect in their view. Educational needs were surely slighted (Wayne State University had requested five million more and received under one million). But Romney did not pretend to act as if he were meeting the state's educational needs. He fully recognized that his was only a stop-gap school budget and promised that he would make up for it next year. His goal was to wipe out Michigan's poor reputation by putting the state back on a strong fiscal base. This, he reasoned, could be accomplished only through a balanced budget—and, indeed, by repaying the state deficit. It was simply a fact that had to be faced.

Next Romney took firm hold of his party. In mid-February the Republican State Convention in Grand Rapids adopted a platform that could easily have been written by Romney himself. Such Romney goals as restoring confidence in Michigan, increasing citizen participation in party affairs, balancing the budget, and supporting the new constitution were plainly stated. In addition Romney's campaign manager, Art Elliott, Jr., was named state Republican chairman. Chalk up two for Romney.

But the biggest boon to Michigan's new dynamo occurred on

April 1. It was ironic that on April Fools' Day, 1963, while Wayne State University's *Daily Collegian* carried a front page of Romney's face under a Kennedy-type hair style, Michigan voters ratified the new constitution by the razor-thin plurality of .6 per cent. The vote was all-important, for not only had Romney toiled in the drafting and become a political candidate on the strength of the document, he had literally stumped the state in its support. His political prestige was on the line. Chalk up three for Romney.

Only four weeks later Romney's leadership emblem got a new coat of varnish. The legislative session ended on April 27 with Romney getting almost everything he had sought. Romney himself reported that of the sixty-five things he requested, the legislature had given him more than 80 per cent. And there is no reason to shun this self-appraisal as biased. Anthony Ripley of the Detroit *News* confirms that: "Governor Romney emerged from the first legislative session under his administration today with most of his program enacted."[1]

What precisely had Romney been able to achieve? In the first place he succeeded in holding the budget figure almost exactly at the $547,000,000 he had requested in January. Second, he failed on only two major pieces of legislation: a minimum-wage bill and strong legislation against housing discrimination. In the way of new legislation Romney could boast: a bill requiring voters to register every two years, establishment of a Construction Safety Commission, authorization of funds to be spent on expansion projects at universities and institutions, provision for federal aid to dependent children of the unemployed (later nullified by the NDEA department), revised jobless-pay eligibility, several bills in the area of economic development, a special fund of $750,000 to finance studies for job creation by state universities, two additional judges added to the Wayne County Circuit Court, and the future establishment of regional mental-health centers. Not at all bad for a four-month session!

By the June 7 formal adjournment Romney's record had not changed significantly. Of the 288 bills passed, only three had been vetoed. Romney was in such high spirits that he broke precedent again and personally thanked both houses for their efforts formally. That was not the full thrust of his appreciation. An elaborate party at East Lansing's Walnut Hills Country Club went beyond precedent-breaking; it was precedent-shattering! Chalk up four for Romney.

But the entire year was not to be charted by Romney's rising star. During the first power-packed meeting he had announced that he planned a special session on fiscal reform "sometime after Labor Day." Most political observers felt that this would be the real test of Romney's leadership—and they proved to be correct.

The special session began on September 11, but Romney had been working for tax reform from the moment the regular session ended that June. On June 10 he revealed eight possible plans for tax revision, stressing that they were for discussion only. For the rest of that week he met with representatives from thirty or so statewide interest groups to discover what they felt a tax reform program should include.[2] During the week of June 17–24 he traveled to sixteen cities across the state talking to nearly two thousand citizens, group leaders, and local officials. July and August were spent meeting with legislators and sounding them out. After all this groundwork Romney and his staff proposed a twelve-point program on September 12. The plan imposed a state income tax of 2 per cent personal, 3½ per cent corporate, and 5½ per cent on financial institutions, while exempting food and drugs from the sales tax, repealing the business-activities tax, improving the corporation-franchise fee, reducing school-property taxes by one fifth, allowing for a senior citizen homestead tax deferral, and stipulating equitable property-tax assessment. In addition the plan allowed for local options and assured support for existing earmarked funds that might be affected by the change.[3]

While most Republicans praised the package, some hesitated to endorse it, and some openly opposed it. Some leading Democrats, such as former Governor Swainson, Lieutenant Governor Lesinski, Congressman-at-Large Staebler, and Secretary of State Hare, seemed to think it was "well-balanced." Two of the most disgruntled Democratic leaders were Gus Scholle (who saw nothing in the package to benefit labor) and Detroit Mayor Jerome Cavanagh (who envisioned a $10,000,000 tax loss because the 1 per cent city income tax was to be trimmed to ½ per cent on suburbanites who drew their paychecks within the city).

On September 13, after listening to Romney's plan and the introduction of twenty-three bills that mirrored his tax package, the legislature recessed. The rest of September and early October saw the House and Senate taxation committees hold a number of public hearings across the state to sample public reaction to the tax reform. Meanwhile Romney was still vigorously talking up his program. On September 23 he met with representatives of the groups he had spoken with in June, explaining how his program met with their earlier suggestions. By the first of October he had begun a tour of more than twenty Michigan cities that covered more than three thousand miles and brought him face to face with some eight thousand citizens.

When the legislature reconvened in October, Romney asked House and Senate leaders for suggestions that might improve the program or increase chances of its passage. Both Democratic leaders (Blondy and Kowalski) felt that there was not much use discussing the tax package until Romney could promise Republican support; so Romney went to work on his majority-party lawmakers. (Democrats were later to charge that Romney had bypassed them and concerned himself only with Republicans in seeking support for tax reform.)

Originally Romney presented twelve points in his tax-reform package. However, this soon proved to be an unrealistic goal. Complaints were filed immediately; Romney listened, but refused to modify his plan until well into October.

As more and more support was sought Romney went from one extreme to the other. First, he deleted a section dealing with property-tax relief for senior citizens (who objected violently to a property-tax deferral with the state getting first rights to their estates after death). Next, he tossed out a portion dealing with the beer tax (Democrats cried "special interest" when it was discovered that Malcome Lovell, a Romney staff member, was a former vice-president and present stockholder of a brewery that would benefit from the legislation). By the end of the eight-week session Romney had made so many concessions that *Business Week* accused him of being willing "to make changes for anyone."[4]

Romney did not make these changes willingly but because the Republicans were divided on tax revision. The very idea of a personal income tax—no matter what the amount—was still poison to the twelve Old Guard Republicans who remained in the Senate. The twenty-three Republican Senators were split into blocs of twelve conservatives versus eleven moderates on the basis of the 1962 election. Joining with the Democratic legislators in the Senate, the Old Guard element all but killed Romney's tax package by sending it back to committee on November 6. All eleven negative votes were from moderate Republicans.

The final dirge was played on November 14, when the House voted 47–44 against the tie-in amendment that would have assured consideration of the entire tax package. In the final tabulation 37 Republicans and 7 Democrats voted for it, 16 Republicans and 31 Democrats voted against it, and 5 Republicans and 12 Democrats were absent.

In round two, the first special session of 1963, George Romney had been a failure. When asked how the tax defeat affected his national image, it was a tired George Romney who replied, "I couldn't care less. The citizens of Michigan are the losers."

Romney had been hurt and disappointed, but there was a new constitution to be implemented. He called the legislature together again, for its shortest session of the three (December 4–20). There were disagreements over some of the suggested bills. At one point Romney threatened still a fourth session between Christmas and New Year. The pattern of the third session was a mixture of the first two in terms of success, but Romney signed all sixty-nine bills pertaining to the new constitution.

Looking back at his first full year in office, Romney noted that it might have cost him a cool million dollars in terms of salary, bonus, and American Motors stock options as compared with a governor's $27,500 salary and his extra expenses. All in all, though, Romney felt that being governor of Michigan had been "a priceless experience."

There was only one legislative session in 1964, and it lasted from early January until the end of May. Bill Burke of the Lansing *State Journal* summarized the session: "Romney steered most of his 1964 legislative program through."[5] Some of the legislation dealt with setting up a new state Court of Appeals, overhauling welfare laws, requalification for ADC-U benefits, establishing a uniform statewide city income tax, creating a state scholarship program for Michigan high-school graduates, exempting tools, dies, jigs, and fixtures used in automobile production from taxes, and accelerating the state capitol-development project. And Romney's budget of $624,000,000 was closely adhered to.

Every four years national attention is focused on the important task of picking a leader who will bear the most prestigious title in the world: The President of the United States. It transcends any individual state or local political race in terms of coverage by the news media. Yet it probably is state and local leaders who will have the most direct influence on the lives of the people. Perhaps the men running for governor, senator, or mayor should be selected when their individual merits may be judged in detachment from the great presidential siege. None can escape; the Romney effort of 1964, therefore, did not take place in a political vacuum.

Shortly after his victory in November, 1962, George Romney was touted as a dark-horse candidate for the presidency. Surely he disavowed any such desire by pledging to the people of Michigan that he would not seek greener pastures at the national level in 1964. But a man who inspires cannot always control the zeal of his disciples. Second, success itself causes attention to be focused upon such a person. And in Romney's case there was a third factor: a feeling of personal patriotism that simply meant he had a duty to serve if his country needed him. All these factors when combined with his geographical movements outside Michigan contributed on three occasions to make it look as if Michigan's governor had presidential ambitions.

Acquisition of the new constitution and success with the first legislative session first caused national attention to be focused on Romney in early 1963. And Romney himself added fuel to the fire by a short vacation that began on the heels of his first legislative session on April 29. The vacation was spent with the J. Willard Marriotts, close friends of Romney's for more than thirty years. Alice Marriott was the stepdaughter of Utah Republican Senator Reed Smoot and the GOP national committeewoman from the District of Columbia since 1960. Willard Marriott had been a member of the American Motors board of directors since 1959, was president of the Morman stake in Washington, was owner of a chain of motels, and was president and chairman of the board of Hot Shoppes, Inc., a large East Coast restaurant chain.

Romney attended a congressional dinner in Washington on Tuesday and addressed the U.S. Chamber of Commerce on Wednesday. On Thursday, May 2, some three hundred businessmen attended a Marriott party in Romney's honor. To the New York *Times* this was evidence that Romney was being launched as a candidate. Romney was in Washington again on May 9 for a testimonial dinner, and again on May 22 when he appeared before the National Press Club. Success couldn't be suppressed. The May Gallup poll showed Romney to be the choice of 18 per cent of the Republican voters!

But in his Press Club address Romney mentioned the word "Michigan" seventy times and began his talk simply with "I came here today to sell Michigan." Although the event itself would have it that Romney was seeking national publicity, the content of the speech was indeed indicative of Michigan's official business.

Romney told the story of a newly crowned king who wanted to be the very best ruler that his country ever had; so he traveled far and wide to learn how. The king finally realized that the way to be the best ruler would be to pay attention to what happened in his own kingdom. Romney phrased the message to a schoolroom lyric:

The best kings are those,
In this and all other lands,
Who tackle the problems under their nose,
With the tools that are under their hands.

He may have been signaling that he was withdrawing from presidential speculation. Taking his own advice after that May 22 appearance, he sternly adhered to matters within the state. The first Romney boomlet, as Novak labeled it, had ended.[6]

With the defeat of his fiscal-reform package Romney was rapidly eased out of presidential speculation. But on November 22, John F. Kennedy was assassinated, and the rest of the year was spent in mourning for the late President. While the people wondered what effect his death would have on the country, the parties wondered what effect his death would have on the coming election, and the would-be-candidates wondered if and how their political fortunes had been changed.

By late December, 1963, Romney had carved out what his personal role was to be in the 1964 election. He announced that he would stay in public life "on a full-time basis" and indicated that he would accept a number of outstate speaking engagements in order to "exert such influence as I can on national affairs." He thus made it clear that he was going to pursue an adequate Republican national platform. (Shortly before the 1960 election Romney had accused both Nixon and Kennedy of evading three basic issues: excessive concentration of union and corporate power, utilization of United States agricultural techniques to alleviate world hunger, and the drift of power to the government in Washington. He wanted to be sure that these topics and a few others would not escape discussion in 1964.)

Of course, all this set off new speculation that Romney was a candidate. It began when Romney made his second appearance before the National Press Club, on January 7. Instead of selling Michigan, Romney now concerned himself with "the Republican opportunity in 1964." He listed seven specific problems that he felt were facing the nation, and enumerated six procedures the party would be able to utilize in seizing the election-year opportunity.

Not only was the speech worthy of a candidate, but in the question-and-answer period Romney dropped a bombshell. Asked how he would respond to a draft-Romney movement, he replied:

> I realize that I am being discussed by others as a candidate. Many people have talked with me and urged me to become one. This is inevitable in the current situation considering my present position as governor of the great industrial state of Michigan. I have no way of knowing whether such a demand will develop; it would be presumptuous to assume it will develop. However, if it should, like any concerned American, *I would of course have a duty to accept.* . . .

Immediately afterward the Governor attended an open house at District of Columbia Republican headquarters, chatted with Cliff Folger (a top GOP fund raiser), and capped the day off with another reception at the Marriotts' (this one included Republican state chairmen from all over the country).

That was all the press needed. Romney was again in the race, according to the headlines. The announcement left Republicans at home badly shaken, for they felt it would hurt him with the 1964 legislative session about to begin in Michigan. Immediately upon his return Romney met with and convinced them that the chance of a draft was remote. For any opportunistic interpreter, Romney had found a way to release himself from his pledge not to become a candidate: he would acquiesce to a draft. Were the two different? Was Romney cutting too fine a line? The truth is that Romney was ensuring that public attention would be paid to his remarks concerning the Republican platform. It was a clever publicity stunt—typically Romney. And then, too, there was always the outside chance that the party really would need a candidate if Rockefeller and Goldwater committed "primary" suicide!

On January 11, Romney was given modified favorite-son status by the Republican State Central Committee, and by February 9 he was off on his fourth visit to Washington in almost as many weeks. Appearing on "Meet the Press," Romney criticized the Johnson administration, disagreed with Barry Goldwater, and on the question of his own draft status responded, "I haven't felt any real breezes yet!" With that effort his second boomlet collapsed, and Romney again withdrew to attend to matters at home.

There was to be one more Romney boomlet—a rather ephemeral affair at the June Governors Conference in Cleveland, when Romney took strong issue with Barry Goldwater, front runner for the GOP presidential nomination. The relationship between these two political leaders was to play a prominent role in the 1964 Michigan election, and it deserves careful examination.

The Romney-Goldwater relationship was doomed from the beginning on both the personal and the ideological levels. In their minor associations while Romney was president of American Motors they had met and found nothing to personally admire in each other. Furthermore, Romney seemed radical to Goldwater in making his request for the breakup of General Motors and Ford back in 1958, and he puzzled the Senator with his jabbering about citizen participation (Goldwater was a strong party man). The relationship was bound to worsen when the two were forced into examining each other's "unorthodox" views. Romney felt that Goldwater was shallow, and Goldwater felt that Romney was an opportunist. Both seemed to have reason for their beliefs.

Back in May of 1963 when Romney vacationed with the Marriotts he had telephoned Goldwater for an appointment. Goldwater consented; and he was surprised when a host of reporters showed up for the meeting. The Senator felt that Romney was taking advantage of the situation to gain publicity.[7] From that moment on Goldwater was a bit suspicious of Romney's motives. On the other side of the coin, Romney felt that Goldwater's discussion of the issues was superficial and that some crucial issues were not even dealt with. He disagreed with many of the Senator's positions and solutions.

The crucial relationship between the two men for the political year of 1964 began when Goldwater made a political appearance at Grand Rapids on January 6. The occasion was a hundred-dollar-a-plate fund-raising dinner, and the fact that it was Goldwater's first official appearance as an avowed presidential candidate was a fluke. The dinner had originally been scheduled for November

23 but was postponed after the President's assassination. On the surface things went well. Romney supped with Goldwater, and the two men made polite chatter. But the next day Romney's speech at the National Press Club in Washington seemed to Goldwater to be a knife in the back. Romney said that "a party representing one or a few narrow interests cannot indefinitely survive in this country," and there was little doubt that he had the Goldwater philosophy in mind.

Nothing had been said about differences in philosophy at the previous night's dinner. In fact, the only private conversation between the two men had taken place in Goldwater's hotel suite during the twenty-minute break between the press conference and the dinner. So Goldwater again had reason to question Romney's motivation. He resolved that Romney wouldn't get another chance to make him look the fool. From that point on the "private talk over positions" that Romney repeatedly asked for in public had no chance of realization.

Then came the third and last Romney boomlet: Cleveland. The National Governors Conference beginning on Saturday evening, June 6, and lasting until June 10 has been recorded by both Theodore H. White and Robert D. Novak,[8] but the two accounts differ in many important respects. The participants themselves cannot agree on exactly what happened. The likeliest interpretation seems to be as follows:

On the evening of June 6, Romney arrived in Cleveland after playing negotiator for a strike at Hillsdale, Michigan, which had seen him call out the National Guard in the interest of public safety. He had presided over an all-night bargaining ordeal in his office and had been instrumental in securing a settlement in the ninety-nine-day-old Essex Wire Corporation strike, between the company management and the International Union of Electrical Workers. It was a tired Michigan chief executive who arrived in Cleveland. But Romney, a man of boundless energy, caught his second wind crisply when informed of what had happened that day. Early that morning William Scranton had received a telephone call from General Eisenhower. He drove to Gettysburg, spent more than an hour with the General, and emerged as an all-but-avowed candidate. Romney was informed by responsible Pennsylvania Republicans that the official announcement was to come over Sunday's "Face the Nation" national telecast.

Romney had hoped the Governors Conference would concern itself with federal-state relationships, but he sized the situation up quickly. If this was going to be a successful last-ditch moderate stand against Goldwater, Scranton would need all the help he could get. Somebody would have to lend a helping hand. Somebody would have to take the lead. Somebody would have to prepare the way for Scranton's announcement. Right then and there Romney decided he would be the man.

By the next morning Romney had drafted a strong anti-Goldwater statement, and he went before a breakfast meeting of all the Republican governors (except Scranton, due to arrive at any moment) to discuss their reaction to it. Most of them thought it unwise, but Romney—still expecting Scranton to announce his candidacy—held a press conference immediately after the meeting. And to the amazement of all, he read the entire statement. It contained the strongest anti-Goldwater tone used up until that time:

> The Republican presidential candidate currently enjoying a preponderant support from elected Republican National Convention delegates has voiced public views that do not square with the principles for which the Republican party stands on the basis of its past record and heritage . . . consequently, I have decided that *unless I can have* an early opportunity for adequate private discussion with Senator Goldwater about his indicated views. . . . And if his views deviate as indicated from the heritage of our party, *I will do everything within my power to keep him from becoming the party's presidential candidate. . . .*

The rallying cry thus sounded, Romney withdrew to his suite to observe Scranton's expected announcement over "Face the Nation." The announcement never came. Scranton's intended statement was in his pocket, but a phone call from Eisenhower and the lack of cohesion among the Republican governors decided him not to read it. Romney left immediately after the show for Michigan, disappointment apparent on his face.

Oddly enough, it was the man who had just failed the leadership test, Scranton, who now picked up the baton for the liberal, or moderate, wing of the party. Holding a rapid series of conferences, he felt that he had started a gubernatorial draft-Romney movement before nightfall. The movement apparently had the triumviral support of himself, New York's Nelson Rockefeller, and Ohio's James Rhodes. Late that night Romney was informed. He said he would think it over.

Michigan's governor arrived on the Cleveland scene again Monday night after General Eisenhower held a unity session in the suite of conference chairman John Anderson, Jr., of Kansas. Romney talked privately with Eisenhower for twenty minutes but did not change his stance on the Goldwater candidacy: "Nothing he said caused me to change my position," Romney told reporters.

The next morning Romney breakfasted with Nixon to present his dilemma: Several governors now wanted him to make a run for it. He had made a commitment to the people of Michigan that he would not become a candidate, yet he had said he would be available for a sincere draft. Was this, in Nixon's opinion, a draft? Nixon was not sure.

After attending another breakfast, Romney met with Scranton, Rockefeller, and Rhodes in his suite. No sooner was the four-way conference over than Nixon made up his mind. To escape reporters, Nixon grabbed Romney's arm, and the two stepped into the men's room. There Nixon told Romney that it was indeed a "draft" and that he should take command while there was still time to head off the Goldwater forces.

By late afternoon Romney had reached his final conclusion. He decided that there was no sincere draft movement, because the governors were far from united. Of the sixteen Republican governors, he could rely on only two: Rockefeller and Scranton. Such support could not be called a draft in any man's language. Then, too, he had had an opportunity to speak with his press secretary, Richard Milliman, who was sternly against it, and other Republican leaders from the state, whose reaction was also negative. Once having made the decision, Romney wasted no time. "I will not be a candidate. I am available for a draft, but I'm not a candidate and I'm not going to become one," he declared. Romney was, however, going to spend the next five weeks before the convention traveling in the hope of strengthening the party platform! (This proved to be unnecessary, for on June 12, Scranton finally declared candidacy.) For three days, Sunday through Tuesday, Romney's third and final boomlet had sputtered. From a personal point of view it was the closest Romney had come to being a presidential contender. As principles and duty dictated, he had weighed the evidence and decided against it. For the presidential year of 1964, George Romney was through.

The path leading to the Cow Palace in San Francisco had been a long one and ever narrowing. Nelson Rockefeller became the first avowed candidate about three weeks before the Kennedy assassination, and Barry Goldwater made his announcement on January 3. Both had been losers in the March New Hampshire primary, falling victim to a large write-in vote for Henry Cabot Lodge. Rockefeller scored a surprise victory in the mid-May Oregon primary, but Goldwater scored an upset victory in California's June 2 primary. With the 86-vote California delegation safely in his pocket, Goldwater had all but clinched the nomination. He needed only 655 of the total delegation, and supporters now claimed he had far in excess of that number.

There would have been no opposition to Goldwater's nomination after the California primary had not William Scranton made his decision on June 12 to seek his party's highest honor. Even then there was no real opposition; but it did add a new dimension to the picture. Scranton had been aroused by Goldwater's vote against the newly passed civil-rights bill (as well as by the willy-nilly self-image he had created in Cleveland). There is also a good probability that he had been stirred by Romney's proposal to campaign on the issues—although the Scranton-Romney interpretations of such a campaign were built on entirely different conceptions.

The convention saw Goldwater's supporters humble the so-called Eastern Establishment of liberal-moderate persuasion. There is no point in reporting the activities of a convention that has been adequately covered. Important for our purposes is the role that George Romney played in that chaos.

Although he had observed one back in 1936, Michigan's governor was appearing at his first national convention. As the leader of the seventh largest bloc of delegates he would be expected to play a major role in the proceedings even under normal circumstances. But circumstances were not normal. Romney had been drawing further and further away from the party's almost sure nominee, and he had been pushing for a platform that he could support since long before the Cleveland fiasco. On that account he appeared before the platform committee to present five weaknesses that he felt the party document exhibited: a poor civil-rights plank, a weak stand on extremism, no specific disapproval of right-to-work laws, no measure ensuring judicial review of decisions made by federal administrators, and failure to recognize population as the key factor in apportionment plans for state legislatures.[9]

Not making much headway with the committee, Romney resolved to carry two of his objections to the convention floor. There were platform changes scheduled to be introduced by the Scranton forces in the areas of extremist groups and civil rights, but Romney did not see eye to eye with the Scranton statements, which specifically named the John Birch Society as an extremist group and also declared the new civil-rights bill constitutional. Then, too, there was the realistic fact that a proposal from the weak "other side" (Scranton) would almost surely be defeated by the 2–1 conservative majority.

First came the Scranton extremist proposal. It was supported by a bitter Nelson Rockefeller, who was anything but vague in showing his disgust for some of the "kooks" backing Goldwater. He taunted his audience and drew so many boos and catcalls that it took him twelve minutes to deliver a five-minute speech. At one point when the boos had subsided, Rockefeller served up this comment: "This is still a free country, ladies and gentlemen. . . . Some of you don't like to hear it [hate and fear tactics of extremist groups], but it's true." It was a classic example of what not to say to a hostile group. The amendment failed.

Now George Romney made his way to the speaker's platform. He began:

> I am not here to aid any candidate, and I am not here to detract from any candidate. . . . I am not here to criticize this platform. I'm here to improve it. I make this urgent plea for your open minds and hearts for the purpose of giving the candidate to be selected by this convention a better opportunity to win this fall. . . .

Romney compared extremists of the modern day with those in existence during the Know-Nothing era and read several Lincoln quotations on the subject. It was a good speech, with none of the provocative Rockefeller elements. It drew neither catcalls nor more than scattered applause. It was defeated, not so much on merit as for the gratification and show of power by the Goldwater delegates.

Later Romney spoke in favor of amending the civil-rights section of the platform. This too was voted down. Conservatives had yearned to be in control of a convention for years, and they weren't letting go one iota. There was to be no compromise on any part of the customary trinity power that would serve to unify the party: platform, vice-presidential choice, or national party chairman. All were to be hand-picked from the Goldwater right wing.

Goldwater was nominated on the first ballot, receiving 883 of the total 1,308 roll-call vote. Then Romney did something that startled many in the Republican mainstream—he moved that the vote be made unanimous! Was Romney going to endorse Goldwater? The answer was to come in short order. Romney was being a good sport, but that was to be his sole effort toward party unity. His future course was set. Romney would "accept, but not endorse" his party's standard bearer—whatever that curious division might mean.

There is one other part of the ecology surrounding the Michigan campaign of 1964 that needs to be set forth: the Michigan economy. It was destined to be one of the two major issues of the campaign. Whether prosperity was to be attributed to Romney's record was certainly a matter for contention, but on the improved economic condition of the state there could be no debate. Gene Roberts of the Lansing *State Journal* took advantage of the then faddish coloring books spoofing political personalities to say: "This is 1964, and you can color Michigan green, like money."[10] It was no overstatement. Not only had the $85,000,000 General Fund deficit been eliminated but there was a surplus of $57,000,000 in state coffers when the fiscal year ended on June 30.

And that was not all. New factories were being built at about double the rate of the previous year, according to Bernard Conboy, director of Michigan's Department of Economic Expansion. Fourteen new industries had moved into the state, five once-defunct businesses had reopened, and Michiganites themselves had launched seventy new operations. Unemployment hovered near the 5 per cent level, below the national average for the first time since 1957. And the best was still to come. Industrial expansion within the state for the first few months of 1964 made the previous year's total seem as though Donald Duck's miserly Uncle Scrooge was holding the purse strings. As the campaign progressed it appeared as though Huey, Dewey and Louie were loose in his money bin!

Upon this scenic stage Michigan's gubernatorial election took place, with Democratic Congressman-at-Large Neil Staebler and George Romney heading up the cast of characters. Staebler announced candidacy in early January, and although he was by no means the unanimous choice of his party, he was destined to have no primary opposition. (The Democrats had started their intra-party wars back in 1960, when Staebler and Williams supported Kennedy for the Democratic nomination. They had done so with the expectation that Williams would be the party's vice-presidential candidate. Understandably the resultant hostilities between the new President and the state Democratic party created mild irritations during the 1964 campaign; but the second intra-party issue was much more serious. Early in 1963, Joe Collins, Staebler's hand-picked state chairman, was ousted by a Swainson-labor coup, and Zolton Ferency took his position. The change caused a deep and bitter split between Swainson and Staebler forces.)

Neil Staebler was no new name in Michigan politics. An Ann Arbor real-estate builder, he had served as party chairman throughout most of the Williams era. When Williams departed in 1960, Staebler became a national committeeman. In 1962 he consented to be a candidate for the lame-duck congressman-at-large seat—an offer that most prominent Democrats declined because the office would be abolished when new district lines were drawn (Michigan had been granted an additional representative in Congress due to its population boom). Staebler proved to be the top Democratic vote getter in 1962.

If Neil Staebler was no new name, he was a new face, having had only limited exposure during his 1962 election. He had vowed that it would be his "first and last campaign," but his belief that he could dethrone the Rambler king and his desire to regain control of the state party united to change that pronouncement. He would have been better off if the vow had been kept.

If Neil Staebler had problems, so did Romney, and believe it or not, two of them were party problems that did not involve Goldwater—at least not directly. As early as the Staebler announcement in January, Republican senators were suggesting that the expected General Fund surplus be returned to the taxpayers. Romney succeeded at squelching that parasitic thought in the bud. The Senate Old Guard got under Romney's skin from time to time, but in April they made his blood boil. Acting without his knowledge or approval, they united with Democrats to form a coalition and rammed through a congressional reapportionment plan. Since the Republicans got nothing in return, Romney reasoned it was a poor bargain. During the Republican State Convention that May, Romney repudiated the Republican deviates as "political quislings."

The Conservative—Liberal rift within the party was demonstrated secondly by the gubernatorial candidacy of George Higgins, a sixty-three-year-old auto dealer and former state senator who challenged Romney in the Republican primary. Higgins was a persistent if mild thorn in Romney's side, from the time he entered the race on April 23 until the September 1 primary. He badgered Romney by accusing him of "being a supreme egotist," "not being a member of the Republican party," and "having utter disdain for the national standard bearer." Romney ignored the pain. When asked about his feelings toward Higgins, Romney would say, "Who?" He did not spend a cent in the primary struggle that saw him defeat Higgins by an 8–1 margin. Higgins was more a symbol of conservative dissatisfaction than a political threat.

Last, the intraparty strife was frayed by Romney's cool reception of Goldwater at the top of the ticket. Party leaders felt that Romney was making a big mistake in divorcing himself from the party. But Romney had set his course, and he would not swerve from it, despite constant pressure.

From the time Romney had left San Francisco he made his firm stand a matter of personal honor. He would campaign on state issues alone. Maybe Scranton would debate party principles and gloss over differences after the campaign—but Romney wouldn't. True, it was a matter of political expediency as well as principle, but those who say that Romney was shifting with the political winds simply don't know him.

Exactly how stiff Romney's stand was took time for the public to discover. Two real tests came in rapid succession. On September 26, Goldwater paid a campaign visit to Michigan and in Niles spoke with Romney on the same platform. The GOP presidential candidate took the opportunity to latch onto Romney's coattails by endorsing the popular Michigan governor without reservation: "I think he has done a good job, and I want to urge you to reelect Governor George Romney on November 3," he told the crowd. Romney did not reciprocate.

Later that same night Romney was to introduce the Senator at a rally in Detroit's huge Cobo Hall. By 8 P.M. more than twelve thousand screaming Goldwater supporters were ready and waiting. Decorum dictates that the presidential candidate be introduced as the next President of the United States, but Romney had a carefully worded statement prepared. He praised Goldwater as hard-working and dedicated but ended his brief remarks on an impersonal note: "Ladies and gentlemen, I am privileged to introduce our Republican *candidate for the presidency* of the United States, Senator Barry M. Goldwater." There was a slight pause as a hush gripped the throng. They were undecided whether to boo Romney for his detached introduction or to cheer their man. In one section the huge arena applause started, and in an instant the hall rang with applause and chants of "We want Barry! We want Barry!" Their idol was there.

Other than the Goldwater visit, Romney held constant with his "I will accept, but not endorse" comment. Asked if he would vote for Goldwater, he would snap back tauntingly, "I wouldn't vote for anybody else." Repeatedly on handshaking tours the question arose, and Romney answered. Yet each time the questioner seemed to expect more. Speaking before a group of Wayne State University students in October, Romney did go further. The sampling was heavily conservative, and the Goldwater query came. Looking as if he had been asked once too often, Romney answered as if he meant to settle the issue once and for all. "Look. I've said time and time again that I accept the decision of my party . . . that I accept but do not endorse the Senator. That's my position. . . . And if this means the political end of George Romney . . . then so be it!"

Although Staebler announced on January 4 that he would be a candidate for governor, and Romney made a similar announcement on May 16, the campaign did not get into full swing until after the September primary. The late start can be explained by a combination of three factors. First, Romney had a primary opponent, and that made it difficult for Staebler to attack Romney specifically. Second, much public interest was centered on the national party conventions to be held in July and August. Third, Michigan had had some problems with reapportionment[11] that forced postponement of the usual August primary date. When the primary ended on September 1, the official campaign was on.

It was evident from the very beginning that Neil Staebler would have a hard time projecting his image to the public. For one thing the Detroit *Free Press* and the Detroit *News* were on strike throughout the campaign (although the dearth was partially compensated for by an emergency *Daily Press* and by the *AFL-CIO News,* which is as profoundly Democratic as print will allow). Second, Staebler had some unfortunate personal mannerisms and characteristics. He wore outmoded clothes. He resembled an aging Adolf Hitler with long, stringy gray hair and a black mustache. He had a weak and gravelly voice and talked too much like the scholar he was. Last, there was the lack of real issues on which to attack his Republican opponent.

As a matter of fact, both candidates seemed to raise more minor questions than had been the case in 1962. Staebler accused Romney of being bull-headed, taking an election-year-only approach to mental health, double-crossing senior citizens, taking no action on air pollution, inadequately handling youth problems, having presidential ambitions, being anti-labor, and making phony education claims. Romney charged Staebler with being away from the state too long to know what was going on, promising so much that he would have to raise taxes to produce, striving for a welfare state, being obligated to labor, riding presidential coattails, and manufacturing his own opinion polls. (Toward the end of the campaign Staebler seemed to mention a new poll almost daily and Romney humorously referred to him as "Shave a point a day Staebler.")

There were several more clashes of intermediate importance: Ford-Canton legislation, the minimum-wage law, the Massachusetts ballot, ADC-U requalification, and the National Guard scandal.

In 1959 the State Supreme Court had rendered the decision that workers at Michigan plants of the Ford Motor Company were entitled to unemployment compensation when they were idled by a union strike at a Ford plant in Canton, Ohio. Since 1947, legislation had favored employers, stating that those laid off because of a strike elsewhere in a company were denied benefits. The 1959 ruling greatly favored unions, inasmuch as the employers, by contributing to the unemployment compensation fund, were in effect financing strikes against themselves.

Romney felt that the law was unjust and that the publicity

resulting from the decision was harmful to Michigan's economic growth. In 1961 and 1962 the Republicans had attempted to change the Ford-Canton ruling, but Democratic Governor Swainson vetoed both attempts as "unsatisfactory to labor." Romney had also felt that the two Republican legislation attempts were unfair but believed that his administration had established a proposition that would "treat employees and employers fairly." On May 21, 1963, he signed his compromise legislation into law. Throughout the campaign he had the dual task of persuading union members that he had not acted against their interests and that he had not shifted ground since his pronouncement that he would have vetoed the 1961 and 1962 legislation as Swainson had done. Staebler took advantage of Romney's actions with the charge "unemployment compensation laws have been undermined."

During his first year as governor Romney had unsuccessfully tried to get a minimum-wage law enacted. In 1964 he secured a bill that set a wage floor of $1.00 an hour and provided for an upward scale of $1.15 at the end of one year and $1.25 at the end of two years. The Democrats had sought a minimum-wage law for years but had constantly been defeated by Republicans. Romney finally persuaded enough Republicans to get action. Since his party had long been on record for supporting such legislation, about the only thing Staebler could do was to pronounce the law inadequate: "The minimum-wage bill covers only a small percentage of those workers who need it," he would say. Romney, on the other hand, announced that the law would "reach 200,000 workers immediately."

The Massachusetts ballot, named after the state in which it was first used, lists the candidates initially by office rather than by party. Michigan had used the party type for years, but the new plan was adopted by the legislature on May 19. The sometimes solid Republican majority wanted to render a Democratic slogan obsolete: "Make it emphatic—vote straight Democratic." The new ballot would make it impossible for the Michigan voter to pull one lever and vote for an entire party slate. The act was premised on the belief that more Democrats vote a straight party ticket than do Republicans. Romney signed the bill into law on May 29, and the Democrats announced that they would start a petition drive that same day to force a November referendum. Their drive was successful.

Since the Massachusetts Ballot Bill had passed the state legislature on straight party lines, the Democrats naturally expected it to be a prominent campaign issue. They condemned the new ballot by charging that it would "cause inestimable delay, confuse people—and, indeed, end the voter's free choice." The first two charges were plausible, but the third was ridiculous. Romney decided early in his campaign that the Massachusetts ballot was an optional item. He had enough of a burden already—why add an untested position to his headaches? He labeled the plan desirable but did not furnish strong support. Staebler and the Democrats spent much of their campaign time and money trying to make the ballot plan a partisan issue but met with little success.

John Swainson had attempted to qualify Michigan for Federal Aid to Dependent Children of the Unemployed (ADC-U) in 1961 and 1962 but without success. He had had to deal with Republican majorities whose conservative bent would not allow such federal intrusion. Romney was successful in getting such a bill in 1963. The law was aimed at qualifying ten thousand jobless Michiganites for federal payments, which would switch them from local welfare payrolls at a saving of nearly $9,000,000 a year. The Health, Education, and Welfare Department questioned the law as discriminatory. Romney maintained that the law met federal standards for qualification, and he resented the federal government's implied power that it could define unemployment for a state. He refused to make the necessary changes, and the state was refused federal funds.

In 1964 a new ADC-U Bill was passed, and this time Michigan did qualify. But Staebler took advantage of what he called Romney's costly goof to point out that it had cost Michigan taxpayers more than $20,000,000 in needless property taxes. Romney could only retort that the federal government's NDEA had changed the ground rules after the law had been written (as appears to be the case) and underscore the fact that his Democratic predecessor had failed to qualify Michigan for the federal funds for two consecutive years.

Much work had to be done in order to make what happened in the National Guard an election issue. Nonetheless, the workers were found, and the week end before the election it was one of the hottest issues of the campaign. The fiasco began on October 9, 1964, when Romney dismissed the state adjutant general and two other top Guard officers on charges that they had been involved in a land, money, and liquor scandal. The irregularities dated back to the 1950's and included such things as selling 2,800 state-owned lots, recording the sales improperly, spending the proceeds illegally, claiming improper travel expenses, not observing federal pay schedules, and diverting armory maintenance funds. Romney acted on a report that had been filed by his Democratic auditor general, Billie Farnum, on the advice of the State Military Board, and—so he thought—on the advice of his Democratic attorney general, Frank Kelley.

The dismissed officers cried "terrible miscarriage of justice," and the scandal took on political implications when it was discovered that Lieutenant Colonel W. Merritt Peterson, husband of the Republican candidate for the U. S. Senate, had been among the innocent purchasers of the illegally sold land.

Things seemed to quiet down as a number of investigations were undertaken; then, four days before the election the issue was taken out of the closet. On October 31, Attorney General Frank Kelley advised Romney that he had acted illegally in removing the three officers. Kelley contended that the officers could be removed only by a court-martial. Romney, who was campaigning in a Detroit suburb, was not given the courtesy of advance notice, and he was shocked and angry. He felt that he had "acted on advice from members of Kelley's staff" who were present when the decision was announced. He stopped his press-car driver and called an immediate curb-side conference. Visibly shaken, his voice quavering, he discussed the situation for almost half an hour.

After giving the background Romney opened up for questions. He was asked why the Attorney General had issued the advice. Romney, convinced of the injustice of the release, answered:

Why does he issue it? As far as I can see he's issued it for political purposes. And this he's done before . . . I've told you all along that we've got an Attorney General who gives instant opinions for political purposes. And you can't run state affairs on that basis. You can't run anything on that basis . . . and I'm getting fed up with this situation where these people sit in and take one position in conferences and then turn around and do other things in public.

The Governor fired off a six hundred-word telegram to Kelley asking him to "explain his failure" originally to advise legal action through court-martial. For the next two days letters were published that had been sent back and forth between Romney and Kelley, but the issue was very much up in the air when the election was held on Tuesday. Romney was correct; he had been taken for a ride.

There were only two major questions that the campaign rested upon: Romney's relationship to Barry Goldwater, and whom or what to credit for the state's economic boom.

Democratic strategists felt they stood a good chance of winning the governorship if Romney could be provoked into a Goldwater endorsement or if they could at least establish a close link between the two. Not recognizing the depth of the chasm between the two men, Democrats devoted a large portion of their campaign labor to development of a Romney-Goldwater connection (Staebler dwelt upon it in all three of his televised debates). That the pitch did not sell is evidenced by the large number of split-ticket voters: over 40 per cent of those votng for LBJ voted for George Romney.

As for state prosperity, there was never any question during the campaign of its existence. Romney gloated over it, and Staebler freely admitted that things were going well; he simply objected to Romney's taking credit. He maintained that "Michigan prosperity comes from national prosperity," while Romney rebutted, "If the argument is sound, then why did Michigan fail to keep pace with the nation in the 1950's?" It was, as the *State Journal* pointed out, "a cheerful debate."[12] It was a debate that Staebler lost.

The Detroit *News* four days before the campaign predicted that Johnson would win by a landslide and that Romney would win by 150,000. Many thought the poll optimistic. There were even those on Romney's staff who felt that the Johnson tidal wave might sweep their man under. State Republican Chairman Arthur Elliott would go as far as 200,000.

As the polls closed and the votes began to come in, Romney sat with a few close advisers in the presidential suite of Detroit's Statler Hilton. At 9 P.M. Walt DeVries announced, on the basis of his weathervane precinct analysis, that Romney would win by 100,000. By 10 P.M. he had raised the estimate to 200,000. Romney went to work on his victory statement, while his staff passed the word that Romney had done it—he had bucked Barry Goldwater and successfully retained his office!

It was a different George Romney who emerged that night—quite a change from two years earlier. He looked older, more mature, wiser. The dinosaur tie and clasp had been replaced by a gray tie sporting several elephants. He was proud of the victory, as he had every right to be. He had surpassed the fondest hopes of most of his admirers by trouncing Neil Staebler with a 400,000 plurality. And the victory was made even more impressive by the fact that the new Democratic President had swept Michigan by more than 1,000,000.

Romney, whether he liked it or not, was to be the subject of presidential speculation for the next four years.

The Action Team:
The 1966 Campaign

REAPPORTIONMENT and the Goldwater debacle of 1964 presented George Romney with a problem of the first magnitude: Democratic control of both houses of the legislature.[1] The state Senate had gone Democratic by a 23–15 margin, and the House was now to be run with a 73–37 edge for the donkey. Since both majorities were barely short of the number needed to override a governor's veto (25 and 74, respectively), many observers speculated that trouble was brewing for the GOP's new knight in shining armor. More than one political analyst drew an analogy between the Williams era in the late 1950's and the coming legislative session. After all, hadn't the Republican Neanderthals deliberately wrecked the presidential chances of Democrat G. Mennen Williams by wielding their majority power?

As the warning winds blew back and forth in capital gossip circles and the press columns Romney spoke in optimistic terms: "I expect to do all in my power to promote bipartisan support for major programs. After all, there was a greater degree of bipartisan action in the last twenty-two months than is generally appreciated. About seventy-four per cent of all major bills adopted had the support of a large bloc of Democrats in both houses," he noted. And Romney's optimism seemed to be echoed by the opposition. Democraic House Speaker Joseph J. Kowalski, when asked if Democrats would run their own show responded, "I don't know. The Governor has the prerogative to present a budget and the right to present messages to the legislature. We may have to have our own program, but where we agree with the governor, if the program

is right, then I imagine we'll support it. If he lives up to his prom-
ises, we will be glad to support him."[2]

And with these glittering generalities both parties went to work
on establishing priority programs for the 1965 legislative year.
Soon Senate Democratic leaders announced that the top two items
on the Democratic agenda for the legislative session would be
revision of the workmen's compensation law and property-tax
relief for senior citizens. Two weeks later, when Romney listed
eleven priority items, an Associated Press release noted that "Republican Governor George Romney and the Democratic legislators
already are agreed on what has to be done by the 1965 legislature."
Romney's eleven areas for action included finances, education,
traffic safety, youth, constitutional implementation, strengthening
of local government, conservation, agriculture, welfare, tax relief
for senior citizens, and revision of workmen's compensation
benefits.

The 1965 Michigan legislature sounded the opening gavel on
the second Wednesday of the new year, as the constitution required.
By April 28 a box score of progress after sixty-four working days
looked like this to capital reporter William Kulsea: "A few hits, no
runs and several errors." The hits were bills covering senior-citizen
property-tax relief and workmen's compensation. Kulsea noted the
status of Romney-Democratic cooperation at the time: "Democrats
and Republicans say the fight between Governor Romney and legislators for political advantage is a stand-off. Neither has been hurt
yet, and both are doing a good job."[3]

The lawmakers began a summer recess on June 26 and returned
for a one-day mop-up session on July 29, when they agreed to
return for another attempt at tax reform in September. The fall
session skirted the fiscal-reform issue, and on October 15 they
recessed again for a one-day session on December 9 and then until
the sine die meeting on December 30. There were no special
sessions involved, because Democrats wished to maintain a
political advantage: in special sessions the governor may dictate
what issues are to be considered. During this long, drawn-out session seven major areas of conflict developed between Romney and
the Democrats.

The first crisis revolved around something that both the Democratic leaders and the Governor were on the record as favoring: revision of the workmen's compensation law. Acting on the basis of three separate reports (by Weldon Yeager, director of the State Workmen's Compensation Department; a legislative study committee; and the Governor's Workmen's Compensation Study Commission), Romney proposed expanding benefits over a three-year period by some 50 per cent. Democratic lawmakers in the House, not thinking this was fast enough, passed their own version of the bill. When Romney threatened to veto it, Senate Democrats convinced their lower-house brothers that some sort of compromise would be necessary.

On May 8, Governor Romney, House Speaker Kowalski, and Senate Majority Leader Raymond D. Dzendzel issued a joint statement: "We have agreed today on a workmen's compensation bill which will make Michigan's act one of the best, if not the best, in the nation." The House bill had put the benefit level at $64–$93 on an immediate basis, whereas the new compromise bill provided for increased minimum and maximum weekly benefits for injured workers on a progressive scale. The present scale of $33-$57 would be eradicated on September 1, 1965. It would rise to $58–$91 at that time and be extended to $61–$92 and $64–$93 each September for the following two years. The new compromise bill was praised by the *Michigan AFL-CIO News* as "the first significant improvement in nine years."[4] The old compensation law had without doubt been in need of major improvements. Democratic priority number one had been taken care of.

The second area of clash dealt with appointments made by Romney. The necessary Senate appointment approval began to take on a partisan coloring on March 10, 1965, when Democrats seriously toyed with the idea of rejecting two Romney appointees: Ardale W. Ferguson, a Republican businessman from Benton Harbor, to the State Highway Commission, and Charles P. Davey, a Birmingham insurance man, to the chairmanship of the State Athletic Board of Control. Democrats had a precedent for such action dating back to 1962 (when the Republican-controlled Senate failed to confirm the appointment of August Scholle, president of the state AFL-CIO, to the Conservation Commission) but took no action because they feared that playing politics would give them a public black eye. By October such fears had dissipated, and the Democrats rejected two Romney appointees: Frederic Hilbert, a former state senator, as head of the Labor Department, and Wilfred G. Bassett, a seven-term state representative, to the Workmen's Compensation Appeal Board.

Disgruntlement number three concerned the second Democratic priority item: tax relief for senior citizens. On the opening day of the 1965 session Romney appointed a blue-ribbon commission to investigate methods of relieving heavy property-tax burdens to those over sixty-five. Democratic lawmakers in the House did not want to wait until April or May for the report to be made, and on March 19 passed a bill that would cost the state $20,000,000 to $40,000,000. Romney responded by saying that the state couldn't afford to relieve senior citizens "that much" and threatened to veto the legislation unless additional sources of income were proposed.

The Senate substituted virtually a new piece of legislation expected to cost $12,000,000 to $15,000,000. The new bill exempted persons sixty-five years and older from paying property tax on the first $2,500 of assessed valuation on their homes and stipulated certain limitations that the House bill had not included: a gross-income "means test" of not more than $5,000; a homestead of less than $20,000 cash value; Michigan residence of seven consecutive years; and disallowance of "renters' subsidy"—a discount for elders who rented. Romney was ruffled that the Democrats had drafted their legislation before reading his blue-ribbon report, but the legislation was signed on November 3, 1965.

Controversy number four centered on the 1963 constitutional requirement that Michigan reorganize its 130 state commissions and boards into not more than twenty departments. The constitution stipulated that this must be done within a three-year period; and since the legislature had not acted on the measure in 1964, time was running out. If it did not act in the 1965 session, the right to reorganize would fall to the Governor's office by executive decree. Democrats therefore wanted badly to achieve reorganization in 1965. In May a major area of contention developed between what Romney wanted and the recommendations of a

House committee headed by Democrat E. D. O'Brien. Romney wanted a "single executive" at the head of each new department, whereas O'Brien wanted a commission.

Once again Romney threatened veto, and a Democratic Senate-House conference committee drafted a new bill. Both sides made concessions, but Democrats seemed to yield the most. The compromise legislation called for nineteen major departments, seven headed by commissions. The twelve remaining "super departments" would follow Romney's request and be governed by single executives.[5] Since the constitution demanded four commissions, Romney had yielded only three new commissions while gaining state reorganization a year earlier than would have been possible had he been forced to veto the Democratic bill. He had also gained a propaganda tool to use in the 1966 campaign. Here was proof that he "had gotten along with Democrats"!

With a gracious nod in the direction of the payless-payday crisis—but certainly not approaching it in magnitude—the fifth area of dispute was the budget for the fiscal year 1966. Romney met with eleven legislative leaders as early as December 16 to sound out their thinking. He presented them with General Fund appropriation requests totaling nearly $996,000,000. (Budget requests are always much more than department heads expect to receive.) After the meeting Romney commented that "there was no effort to determine any final fiscal points by any of the participants. We discussed basic considerations in the 1965–1966 budget and in the course of this identified important decision areas." Democrats were quick to emphasize his poetic "only this and nothing more" summary.[6]

The next step was up to Michigan's governor. He formally presented his budget on February 2. It called for $788,000,000. "This figure," Romney said, "would assure a $72,000,000 treasury surplus on June 30, 1966." Within days State Superintendent of Public Instruction Dr. Lynn Bartlett denounced Romney's budget proposal in the field of public and elementary education as grossly inadequate. "It would appear that the Governor's program will do little to relieve local property tax of the growing burden it must carry in school support." He said that Romney's $31,000,000 increase fell some $60,000,000 short of the amount requested.

Democrats were concerned with the needs of education but were equally concerned with showing leadership separate from that exercised by the executive office. This need to assert themselves led them to a maneuver never before recorded in Michigan history: they killed all the Governor's budget bills! This coup de grâce fell on March 12. Why was it done? There are two versions. Democrats pointed out a constitutional limitation that forbade passage of any spending legislation until action had been taken on the governor's proposed budget. Since they wanted quick action on tax relief for senior citizens and workmen's compensation, they felt they must kill the bills to avoid later charges of unconstitutionality. "It was not a slap at the executive office," House Speaker Kowalski insisted. "This action will not affect the governor's budget recommendations. It is possible a majority of these bills will still be adopted. The action is merely one of procedure. It will clear the way for the legislature to proceed with its business in orderly fashion."[7]

Yet Romney would have it otherwise. As Republican legislators in the house wore black armbands (an idea instigated by Republican Marvin L. Esch), Romney asserted that "killing the budget bills might have serious implications for Michigan's hard-won fiscal integrity. It would return us to the old system by which Michigan dropped into a period of fiscal chaos. We would be going right back to one of the things that got us into trouble by sidestepping this orderly process required by the constitution." He also accused Democrats of trying to make the new constitution "look bad."

The final budget figure was slightly more than $820,000,000. This was $32,000,000 above the Governor's recommended spending offered in February but was halfway between where the Democrats and Romney wanted to go. Romney summed up the difference between his requested budget and the one he finally approved: "Except for the substantial increase in state school aid above my recommended increases, the budget total is extremely close to that which I recommended—in fact, less than 1 per cent above my request." As for the educational increase, the Governor realized that the schools needed more money. In early March he admitted that "education could use funds beyond those recommended" in the $788,500,000 request.[8] He was not against giving the schools more; but he wanted to safeguard the fiscal responsibility of the state.

The sixth area of disturbance concerned the Governor's veto privilege. In 1965, Romney erased a 1961 record set by John B. Swainson when he utilized that option on twenty-six pieces of legislation. The first veto of significance came on April 22, when Romney slapped down a four-year voter-registration bill passed by the Democratic majority. Romney had succeeded in getting a two-year registration plan during his first term of office and would not allow this "backward step." He felt that four years encouraged voter apathy. He also noted that under the four-year plan voters remained registered long after moving from the place of registration. Democrats favored the four-year plan as a boon to party voting. Three months later Romney was forced to veto the bill a second time.[9]

By July 24, Romney had signed 379 public acts, 2 local acts, allowed 2 bills to become law without his signature, and bagged 23 of his veto quota.

When the gavel sounded at the September meeting, Democrats had built up the momentum for an attempt at overriding two Romney vetoes. The first attempt came on a bill Romney had vetoed on July 10, concerning a $1,200,000 higher-education enrollment-contingency fund. The fund was to be used in the event that the state's seven smaller colleges and universities exceeded their estimated enrollments. Romney argued that such a fund would merely be an incentive for schools to build their enrollment. The second override attempt concerned a measure setting up new duties for the legislative auditor. Both gubernatorial decisions were upheld by a straight 21–13 partisan vote.

On October 28, 1965, Lieutenant Governor Milliken (acting on Romney's direction while he was on a European business tour) added the final three vetoes of the year, killing three multimillion-dollar bills: a $5,000,000 measure extending tax relief to senior citizens who rented quarters; a bill that would give $1,200,000 to state colleges and universities to compensate for unexpected enrollment increases; and a broadened base for the veterans' homestead exemption allowance that would cost the state an additional $3,000,000. This time Democrats were fit to be tied. They called the legislature back for an unexpected meeting on December 9 to attempt to overrule these executive decisions.

What happened at that one-day session can only be described as a smashing Romney victory. The Democrats had pulled out all the stops and planned what seemed brilliant strategy. What they needed, they reasoned, was for one of the three latest vetoes to fall; then the others would surely follow. Logic dictated that the attack be made in the House, where the Democrats needed only one Republican vote to buck the Governor. And that wasn't all. Careful consideration had established the veterans' homestead exemption as the most vulnerable area. By the ninth of December the word had gone out, and the House gallery was jammed with "cheering, jeering veterans."[10] Here was a large voting bloc witnessing the action of each House member. No wonder, then, that half a dozen Republicans were considering voting with the opposition.

But Romney went to the persuasion whip, and Republicans toed the line. He was elated—although he refrained from calling it a personal victory. Instead he passed out praise for the team victory, saying, "This was a great victory for the people of Michigan. The vote of Republican legislators was a public-interest vote. It was particularly strong in light of the extraordinary pressures they faced." With that effort the Democratic strategy collapsed, and the other Romney vetoes stood the test in the Senate.

Maelstrom number seven swirled around the old issue of tax reform. It was a somewhat bitter and experienced governor who faced the issue that in 1963 had made him taste the most severe political failure of his career. He was not about to make the same mistakes again. "When you go over the top," he said in November of 1964, "you learn who'll go over the top with you. Now I'm a second-term governor, and I know who'll go over the top with me."

In January he clarified his position even more. "I'm ready to go any time on tax reform. We've had plenty of studies and don't need any more. I'm prepared to sit down and work out a program whenever legislators are genuinely so inclined. If I put something out [a tax-reform program], it would be labeled a Romney Program and somebody wouldn't want to go along with it. I've made specific proposals. There isn't any doubt where I stand. But I'm not going to go through an exercise in futility. There are too many important things to do." With that statement he established his position for the 1965 tax-reform attempt. Romney if at all possible was going to make the legislators present a program.

On February 8, Romney's strategy yielded a dividend when Democratic Senator Basil Brown proposed a two-step fiscal-reform plan. Brown suggested adoption of the 1963 Romney plan as a starter, with a second step of changing the flat-rate income tax required in the constitution to a graduated tax. Romney's reaction was that Brown was "looking beyond the legislature for fiscal-reform support." Again Romney gained new wealth. Formal declarations favoring action on the tax question from the February 13 Democratic State Convention and the February 21 Republican State Convention followed rapidly.

Thus armed, Romney attacked the Democratic Senate Taxation Committee chairman, George Fitzgerald, for stalling: "It's been my experience that children, politicians, and lawyers can always find excuses for not doing things they don't want to do. Politicians seem to excel in this excuse-finding ability. I think it's about time for the members of the legislature to respond to my request that they indicate whether they agree with me that we need tax reform now." While Romney was demanding action from the legislature, Democratic State Chairman Zolton A. Ferency was sarcastically saying, "It's about time Romney made a proposal!"

In mid-March the Governor was picking up momentum. "There isn't any question that a treasury surplus of $105,000,000 will be wiped out within two years. We should not be lulled into complacency by our sizable surplus. The basic injustices of our existing tax structure remain with us, untouched and unresolved. We need tax reform now." Yet he announced that he would not accept a Democratic deal by yielding to a graduated income-tax plan.

Later when a Democratic House caucus gave reformists a green light to explore all avenues of fiscal reform, Romney proceeded with caution. He refused to comply when the caucus "respectfully invited" his specific proposals on reform. "I'd like bipartisan planning, not political hoopla," he said sternly. But explore the possibilities he must; and he broke political protocol by going to House Speaker Kowalski's office. What went on at that forty-minute meeting was described by Carl B. Rudow as "an Alphonse-Gaston impasse."[11] "We've got to know your program," Kowalski demanded. "Fiddlesticks and poppycock," Romney retorted. "You act like we don't know what we're doing," Kowalski volunteered. "We were for tax reform before you were on the scene," he said pointedly. "Then you'll be for my suggestion," Romney shot back.

At this time something that Romney had been ignoring finally began to exert its influence on his actions. He had said in 1963 after his tax-reform attempt, "I recognize that the ability to get action is affected by whether there is a surplus or a deficit in the General Fund." Unfortunately for the current tax-reform attempt, March sales-tax receipts were up by $3,000,000 from 1964, and each passing day showed that a huge surplus would be on hand that June. Romney therefore realized that there was little real chance for tax reform, and consequently he began to prepare for the probable, stressing fiscal integrity over fiscal reform. "I'd rather have both," he declared, "but if I have to make a choice, I'd rather protect the state's fiscal integrity." The thaw in Romney's icy push for tax reform was evident when he served up a patchwork do-it-yourself kit that contained twelve possible tax proposals and seven possible budgets for the next three years. He offered the plans for discussion and warned that Democrats had better produce a new source of money if spending proposals continued. The summer recess came without action being taken.

After Democratic leaders had agreed to discuss tax reform at the fall legislative meeting, Romney made one last effort—a two-day tax-reform conference at his Mackinac Island gubernatorial mansion. On August 12 he started a closed door session with eleven Democratic and nine Republican legislative leaders. He was in earnest at that meeting and at one point went so far as to say that he would accept a $1,000 per person exemption on a state income tax. (This was a position he had not accepted earlier; it was in reality a form of graduation that the constitution might allow and that he was already on record as opposing.) The conference possessed no lawmaking authority, but the score of lawmakers succeeded in narrowing six possible reform plans to two. These two plans were expected to be presented to the total legislative body in September, but they never got that far, because on September 22 a House Democratic caucus ruled otherwise. Speaker Kowalski summed it up: "We simply decided not to discuss the Romney tax package this fall."[12]

Romney had again been denied fiscal reform, but the 1963 and 1965 defeats were not at all similar in meaning. In 1963 Romney had gone out on the limb of leadership alone. When that was sawed off, his personal leadership image took it on the chin. This time he had assured himself of having ample company. The bipartisan approval of the twenty legislative leaders meant that the only real loser was the state of Michigan.

The second session of the Seventy-third Michigan Legislature was not so colorful, lengthy, or productive. Initiating action before the legislature officially opened, Democrats released a statement of goals to be sought in 1966 before Romney had a chance to make his directives known. A joint statement released by House Speaker Kowalski and Senate Majority Leader Dzendzel called for expanding state services within a balanced budget and without new taxes. The two Democratic leaders suggested legislation in four areas: consumer protection, constitutional reform, governmental reform, and public safety and law enforcement. If their goals were going to be as similar to Romney's program as last year, then why shouldn't Democrats go on record first and claim credit when new laws resulted?

When Romney delivered his State of the State message one week later, the similarities emerged. Democrats responded favorably to what Romney labeled total Michigan progress. "I'm quite pleased with the Governor's message because it indicates that the majority party and the Governor will be working this year toward accomplishing the same objectives," Dzendzel stated. Democratic Majority Floor Leader J. B. Traxler seemed to agree: "Frankly there doesn't seem to be any disagreement with the Governor's program." Romney's four broad areas of action included stimulating and encouraging greater personal, family, and private institutional effort; improving and strengthening the role of local government, broadening the scope and quality of existing state programs, and completely utilizing existing federal programs. He indicated that although tax reform was still needed, there was no dire necessity for it in 1966.[13] In spite of the cheery, agreeable attitude, the next few months were to resurrect three of the harassment games of the previous year.

Democrats were old pros when it came to game number one, Bury the Budget. When Romney requested $945,000,000 on January 28, they squashed his program in hours.[14] While Democrats insisted that the final budget would be "within 2 or 4 per cent either way" of the suggested budget, Romney told reporters that he didn't care which party label went on the final package, "just so Michigan had a good sound budget." Yet the educational need that had displayed itself in 1965 began to knock again at the legislative door, and once again Democratic solons felt the need to comply. Senate Democrats prepared bills that would cost $23,000,000 more for elementary and secondary schools, while House Democrats asked an additional $65,000,000 for that purpose. The requested amounts were at least $50,000,000 in excess of what was requested and put General Fund spending at more than one billion dollars. Revealing his gamesmanship, Romney played the flip side of a 1965 recording and again lectured the Democratic majority for authoring spending plans that could plunge Michigan into a "major financial crisis."

Fortunately for the Governor, two chance factors intervened to help dull Democratic desires: first, voters from all over the state deluged their representatives with warnings that if they eliminated the surplus, they had better not run again; and second, a twelve-day drop in automobile sales part way through the session made many lawmakers fear the possibility of a recession. These two ingredients when combined with Romney's constant warnings of a new payless payday were responsible for a budgetary pie of $972,000,000. It was a figure George Romney could accept.

The second game was Axe the Appointee. The Democratic Senate had failed to approve two Romney appointees in 1965, and they were out to double their pleasure in 1966. Democratic Senators practiced power politics in disapproving the appointments of Dearborn insurance executive Frank Padzieski and Detroit businessmen Frank D. Stella, Blaque C. Knirk, and Dale A. Feet. The first two appointees were for the Michigan Employment Security Commission; Knirk was for the Agriculture Commission; and Feet was Romney's choice for State Insurance Commissioner.

The third amusement was Vitiate the Veto. The 1966 version of the game was played with less gusto, however. On March 15, House and Senate concurrence sent a Veterans Tax Relief bill to the Governor that was virtually a carbon copy of the one vetoed in 1965. Romney said he would veto the bill again if it passed, and nine days later he did just that. He suggested the same alternative as last year, but the opposition decided to try another override on March 30. The attempt failed on a straight party-line vote, as it had on December 9, 1965. The fun and games died down on the veto issue until Romney declined to pass a bill eliminating the one-week waiting period for worker's unemployment compensation. Democrats tried again, without success, to buck the Governor on October 13—this time in the Senate.

For all practical purposes the second session of the Seventy-third Legislature came to a close on June 23.[15] By July 16, Romney had put his stamp of approval on 312 public acts and one local act and had vetoed only 14 bills. He was so pleased with his performance, he told an AFL-CIO political conference, that "to be perfectly frank, this legislature was easier to work with than the Seventy-second [where he had a Republican majority]." When Romney took his record with the Democratic legislature to the voters that fall, it was a record which he could well be proud of.

To Democrats it must have been apparent that evil omens foreshadowed the 1966 state elections for several months before the campaign began. As early as May 2, 1965, Detroit *News* political writer Glenn Engle noted that "Michigan Democrats, always boastful of a wealth of candidate talent for any office, are getting almost desperate for a 1966 challenger for Governor Romney." And Engle knew exactly what he was talking about. Three of the six biggest Democratic names in the state could be dropped from the lineup as injured or too old to play: John B. Swainson was now a nonpartisan circuit judge, Neil Staebler was securely back in his old position of national committeeman, and James M. Hare simply didn't have the zest or the desire to tangle with Romney. Secretary of State Frank J. Kelley and Detroit's young Mayor Jerome Cavanagh both looked like promising contenders, but neither warmed to the idea of a clash with the Republican white knight. Some party hopefuls told themselves that surely G. Mennen Williams, the Democratic haymaker of the fifties, would roar back on the scene. But the only person who seemed to get excited about taking on Romney was little-known Democratic State Chairman Zolton A. Ferency.

As summer turned to autumn, fall to winter, and winter to spring things did not improve. Four new names had been discussed seriously (at one point state spokesmen even tried to draft Secretary of Defense Robert S. McNamara!), while several political unknowns announced that they would oppose the Republican governor. The important names dropped were Representative John C. Mackie, a former state highway commissioner; Representative Billie S. Farnum, a former auditor general; Leonard Woodcock, vice-president of the United Automobile Workers Union; and state Senate Majority Leader Raymond D. Dzendzel—none of them an overpowering vote getter. As their turns came for consideration they took advantage of the public exposure offered by saying they were considering the race. Then, a few days later, they made acceptable-sounding excuses, said that Romney could be beaten, and bowed out of the competition.

It was plain that the Democrats had a serious problem when they approached the annual Jefferson-Jackson Day Dinner of March 26, 1966. Of the three big-name possibilities two had decided to enter the Senate primary, and the third had indicated he would make no gubernatorial move. On that basis party support began to crystallize around lame-duck State Chairman Zolton Ferency. Of the three thousand party faithful present at the fund-raising affair, about one in five sported a small red "Z" lapel patch. It was their way of saying, "It's about time we settled on a nominee!" The Zorro badges started a chain reaction among party leaders. Within days Frank Kelley, James M. Hare, Neil Staebler (who had searched the hinterland for an alternate), and House Speaker Kowalski had all gone on record as backing Ferency. Thus it was that the politically unknown party hatchet-man announced his office-seeking debut on April 19.

The crucial factor in the Ferency candidacy had nothing directly to do with the man himself. It was caused by the primary battle waged for the U. S. Senate seat between Detroit Mayor Jerome P. Cavanagh and Assistant Secretary of State for African Affairs G. Mennen Williams. Here were two men who (when both on the ticket) might have made a significant difference in the 1966 race. Although it is doubtful whether either could have defeated Romney, the combination might have prevented the Republican sweep that would ultimately occur. Strangely enough, Ferency encouraged the ensuing clash. In January he was quoted as saying that a primary-election fight between Cavanagh and Williams might strengthen the party's chances of holding both U.S. Senate seats. When asked to explain his reasoning, Ferency noted that "Williams hasn't run in this state for eight years, and Cavanagh has never campaigned outstate. They could both use the additional exposure."[16] Still, it was hoped that Williams would seek the Senate and that Cavanagh would make the supreme sacrifice and run against Romney.

Unfortunately for the Democratic party, Cavanagh had other ideas. On February 3, Williams announced that he had no intention of running for the governorship. Exactly one month later Cavanagh did the same. On March 7, Williams announced his senatorial candidacy, and two weeks later Jerry Cavanagh tossed his hat into the ring.

For the next six weeks the youthful and articulate Detroit mayor (he is thirty-eight), Roman Catholic lawyer of Irish descent, and father of eight, waged all-out war on the wealthy Princeton-educated Republican turned New Dealer ex-governor. His major line of attack was to press Soapy to "debate the issues." When Williams refused, Cavanagh quipped that it was "callous to campaign like Huey Long—just smiling at people" and sneered at the "grin and call a square dance methods" employed by his opponent.[17] But Williams was well known outstate, popular with minority groups, and supported by labor in metropolitan Detroit. He was remembered, and he was loved. He defeated Cavanagh by a 3–2 margin of 146,000 in the August 2 primary.

If the task of securing a gubernatorial candidate with a possibility of winning was a grave perplexity for the Democrats, the Republicans were faced with a similar riddle: who had a chance to win the Senate seat? Romney was expected to be a shoo-in for the governorship,[18] but from the moment Williams announced his senatorial candidacy it appeared that he would beat not only Cavanagh but anyone the Republicans could put up. In Michigan the Republican party had no second-line strength to back up its star. Yet the Michigan Republicans badly needed a team victory in 1966, and if Romney was to add luster to his presidential stock it would be necessary to carry other Republicans into office. Why not start with a U.S. Senator?

Romney looked to history and found that the lieutenant governor's office had promoted Philip A. Hart to a senatorship in 1958. He approached his young lieutenant governor, William Milliken, and attempted to persuade him to make the move. But Milliken wanted to stick around Michigan until 1968 or 1970 and pick up the reins when Romney turned them loose. Since Romney had already approached Michigan State University President John A. Hannah in 1965 with no more success, he was forced to sit back and see what developed.

Insurmountable as the chore of beating Williams seemed, there were several men anxious for the opportunity: Michigan State University biochemistry professor Leroy Augenstein, State Senator Garry Brown, Grand Haven businessman Edward Meany, former party chairman John Feikens, former Detroit city councilman William Patrick, State Senator Guy VanderJagt, Grand Rapids businessman Deane Baker, and U.S. Representative Robert P. Griffin. In order to avoid the Democratic game of "I'll run; no, I won't," Republicans took steps to get behind one candidate early. On February 20 nearly two hundred district, county, and state Republican leaders gathered in an attempt to reach a consensus. The ground rules for the meet were established by Romney, who said that "at least seventy-five per cent of party leadership must support one man in order for him to win the designation of party-preferred candidate." As the meeting drew near only four men sought this nebulous distinction: Augenstein, Baker, Griffin, and VanderJagt.

Griffin had gone to the meeting as the favorite, and Guy VanderJagt withdrew in his favor the night before to give additional support. Pulling substantially more than the 75 per cent, it was Griffin, the forty-two-year-old five-term congressman, attorney, and schoolteacher who survived. But the distinction was not valued much at the time. Few were willing to wager that anyone—short of Romney himself—could defeat Soapy Williams. Griffin was a decided underdog. What happened in the next few months will be told at Republican rallies for many years to come: the story of how Bob Griffin smashed through seemingly indestructible barriers to become Michigan's first Republican senator in fourteen years.

The battle began when soundings of a private poll taken by Market Opinion Research in April gave Griffin only 23 per cent of the vote. Few people had heard of him; a tremendous recognition gap would have to be overcome. On April 30, Griffin received a boost of gigantic proportions: seventy-one-year-old Democratic senatorial incumbent Patrick V. McNamara died. Griffin was already the party-preferred candidate, and it came as no great surprise when Romney named him to serve on an interim basis until December. Now a U.S. Senator, Griffin could use his new forum and title in the coming election. In July the new senator trailed Williams by a slim 43 to 42 per cent in a poll released by the Detroit *News*.

In mid-August Soapy Williams made his first contribution to Griffin's campaign: he underwent an operation and was forced to remain in the hospital more than a week and spend several days recuperating at his Grosse Pointe home. He was sidelined for nearly five weeks and four days, and by the time he stiffly started campaigning again, a September 19 *News* poll indicated that Griffin now led him by a 51–48 margin.

Now Soapy pulled out his political shotgun, fired both barrels, and scattered charges all over Griffin's ten-year congressional career. Delivering his first major address since the operation, he made it obvious that major attention would be focused on Griffin's voting record. Speaking before the AFL-CIO Committee on Political Education (COPE), he tagged his opponent as "anti-progress, anti-people, anti-city, and anti-labor." He insisted that Griffin had "voted against widows, orphans, school kids, college students, urbanites, and businessmen . . . against cutting your income taxes, against surplus food for the hungry, against decent housing for the disadvantaged, and against a living wage for the workingman." As if noting that his broad assertions might sound a bit extreme even to his pro-Democratic audience, Soapy added, "He actually did that, and more. It's no distortion!"[19] The absurdity of Williams' accusations was his second contribution.

The third Griffin boon for which Williams was directly responsible was modification of his position on the Landrum-Griffin Act. The piece of disputed legislation came about as a result of public outcries against corrupt union practices (financial mismanagement and conflict of interest) in 1959. Labor-reform bills were introduced in both houses of Congress. Senate legislation was sponsored by two Democrats: John F. Kennedy and South Carolinian Samuel Erwin; while a similar House measure was drafted by Democratic Representative Phil Landrum of Georgia and Robert Griffin. When it became evident that a compromise would be needed, a conference committee was formed, chaired by Senator Kennedy. The legislation finally agreed upon became known as the Landrum-Griffin Act. It passed the Senate on a 95–2 vote and the House by 352–52.[20]

When the campaign began, Williams held steadfastly that Griffin "would have some explaining to do about his role in that act." But Griffin turned the liability into an asset by tirelessly explaining the benefits of the Act to the average union member. He called it "a workingman's Bill of Rights," and for proof he turned to Democratic sources, pointing out that the final bill was supported by John F. Kennedy, Hubert H. Humphrey, and Lyndon B. Johnson. Williams decided to soft-pedal the issue. That was his fourth miscalculation.

Instead of letting the issue drop out of the campaign, Griffin now became the aggressor. He had no intention of abandoning the argument. He took the Williams phrase, "I can live with it—I'm neutral" and made it work to his advantage: "When they call the roll in the U.S. Senate, you vote aye or nay. The clerk doesn't register a response of 'I am neutral,'" he said plainly. And his publicity on the issue was a master stroke. As the campaign came down the home stretch full-page newspaper ads showed Bob Griffin speaking comfortably with Senator Robert Kennedy. The ad came on the heels of a Kennedy sojourn to Michigan, and large printing read: BOBBY KENNEDY TRAVELED A LONG DISTANCE. DID HE SET SOAPY STRAIGHT ON THE LANDRUM-GRIFFIN ACT? The advertisement went on to delineate Democratic support for the effort and the Williams switch and included a quotation lauding the Landrum-Griffin Act from Kennedy's book *The Enemy Within*. By implication Kennedy was in Griffin's corner.

A number of smaller factors combined to give Griffin momentum. First, August Scholle put Griffin on page one of the Detroit *Free Press* when Griffin attempted to crash a Cobo Hall COPE meeting in September. Griffin wanted an opportunity to answer some of the charges that had been leveled against him and challenged AFL-CIO president Scholle to a debate. Stopped by the sergeant-at-arms, Griffin waited half an hour until Aldo Vagnozzi, editor of the *Michigan AFL-CIO News,* informed him that Scholle would not honor his request. Second, Griffin turned in a splendid performance in the one direct clash with Williams. Third, in the waning days of the campaign Williams contracted a severe case of laryngitis.

Griffin was able to come up with two other crucial pieces to the victory puzzle: money and the ceaseless energetic campaigning of George Romney. Democrats had been responsible for their own economic problem. The Cavanagh-Williams primary had eaten up $700,000 in candidate donations, and that financial extravaganza could not be made up. It was a sum considerably more than the $550,000 Griffin spent in his entire campaign.

Probably the key factor leading to the Griffin victory, however, was sighted by Saul Friedman in October only days after a third Detroit *News* poll showed Griffin getting stronger with a 51–46 percentage. "Romney has committed himself to Griffin like with no other Republican ticketmate, and the sheer arithmetic of Romney's majority could defeat Williams."[21] And it was surely so. Throughout his 1966 campaign Romney spent as much time explaining the Landrum-Griffin Act, touting Griffin's virtues, and defending the voting record of his Senate appointee as he did peddling the picture of state progress under his four-year administration. One of the most frequent phrases in the Romney vocabulary during the campaign was "We need Bob Griffin in the U.S. Senate." Romney's popularity was transferable!

Finally the election drew near, and the parade of out-of-state politicians ceased. If one thing was evident, it was that Bob Griffin had closed the recognition gap. Appearing at a suburban luncheon in October, Griffin expressed his new-found fame in the form of a story. It seems that two fellows in a Detroit restaurant were wondering if Griffin could get elected. They decided to ask the waitress for her opinion. Trying to be coy, they asked, "Who's Bob Griffin?" Then, to the delight of Griffin's partisan audience, this answer came forth: "Griffin? He's the fellow running for the Senate against—what's his name," she said, snapping her fingers.

On November 9 it was what's-his-name who lost.

When Neil Staebler lost the governorship in 1964, he left the Democratic party deep in debt, and the $700,000 that Jerome Cavanagh and G. Mennen Williams ate up in the Senate primary didn't make fund collecting at all glamorous. Williams had influence and political IOU's and was regarded as a possible winner; but what about Zolton Ferency? Here was a candidate who knew he would not get the minimum $300,000 that it takes to run a statewide race. Ferency was not wealthy, he wasn't known, and few thought he had any chance of winning. At the outset he set himself a modest campaign fund of $200,000, and he didn't raise quite that much. Still, Ferency was happy to receive his party's nomination, and he set out bravely to overcome the Republican Goliath.

Who was this unknown warrior, this challenger, whom Romney chose to ignore the greater part of the 1966 campaign? Zolton Antal Ferency was the forty-four-year-old son of Hungarian immigrants. John and Mary Ferency owned a lunchroom in Detroit, and as soon as he was old enough Zolton served as busboy and dishwasher. When the elder Ferency died in 1940, the restaurant was sold, but Zolton worked his way through Michigan State University doing what he was trained to do: he waited on tables, worked as a short-order cook, and tended bar. He was drafted during World War II and served in Europe as an expert on the German order of battle. He graduated from Michigan State University in 1946, married Ellen Dwyer in 1947, and became a veterans' counselor in Detroit. Two years later he became an expert in slum clearance and urban renewal when he shifted to the city housing commission. During this time he attended night school and in 1952 graduated from the Detroit College of Law first in his class.

Setting up a law partnership in 1953, Ferency was appointed deputy director of Workmen's Compensation. Later he served as a state liquor commissioner and ran unsuccessfully for Wayne County prosecutor in 1960. In 1961 John B. Swainson hired him as his press secretary. When Swainson lost to Romney in 1962, Ferency became chairman of the Democratic State Central Committee. In that position he studied George Romney daily and did not like what he saw. When Ferency said that he wanted to take on Romney, it came from the heart.

Here was truly a dyed-in-the-wool Democrat. Here was a shrewd party pro who knew Michigan political history at least as well as Romney. He was articulate. He was young. He was energetic. He was good-looking. Yet those who knew him regarded him as a party hatchetman—a function that he fulfilled admirably. Would Ferency change his image for the campaign or would he continue the slashing style that had gained him his reputation?

Ferency answered in spades. "I know I'm blunt and direct, but if I think something's wrong and needs correcting, I'm going to speak out. That's me, and I'm probably not going to change."

As the campaign unfurled Ferency gradually gained the questionable sobriquet of "the Mort Sahl of Michigan politics." To offset his budget handicap, he invested $7,500 in a beige bus that he dubbed the Happy Warrior (the name Truman had used on his 1948 campaign train) and made witty statements. Some of his wit was directed at his Democratic running mates. Of Secretary of State James M. Hare, Ferency noted that "we give him one decision a year to make—the color of the license plates—and every year he blows it." Turning to Attorney General Frank J. Kelley, who relied heavily upon his top assistant Leon S. Cohan, Ferency asked, "Wouldn't it be a shame if Cohan died and Kelley had to become attorney general?" Even G. Mennen Williams was not off limits to Ferency sarcasm. Of the sluggish Williams campaign Ferency glibly remarked that "the only thing new that's come out of Soapy in two months is six kidney stones." These remarks were not meant for public consumption, but they bespoke an unusual breed of candidate.

He was always doing the unexpected. He was waiting for an elevator, the door opened, and he came face to face with several occupants. "I suppose you're all wondering why I called this meeting," Ferency ejected. On one of his trips through Highland Park, he used a loudspeaker on the Happy Warrior to carry his message to voters on the street. A motorcycle policeman thumbed the bus to the curb, informed Ferency of the local anti-noise ordinance, advised him to stop using his public-address speaker, and let him off with a warning. "Thank you," Ferency answered politely—over the loudspeaker.[22] Standard Republican attacks focused on Ronald Reagan, whom he referred to as "that Barry Goldwater in Max Factor makeup"; and of course Romney. "I called George Romney a Republican the other day, and he accused me of waging a smear campaign," Ferency would chuckle.[23] Another favorite Ferency needler was directed at Romney's recitation of Michigan progress in the past four years. "There are only a couple of increases that have occurred in the last few years Romney hasn't taken credit for," he would say—"Dutch elm disease and the thirty per cent increase in the consumption of alcoholic beverages!"[24]

Yet despite his ebulliency and humorous stance Ferency attempted to build a number of serious issues. He charged the chief executive with neglecting state parks, being against senior citizens, ducking the tax crisis, disregarding mental health, ignoring urban renewal, taking little action on water pollution, having presidential ambitions, and seeking the vote of bigots. Constantly looking for the vital issue he hoped would surface, Ferency tried to get under the Governor's skin. He taunted Romney by saying he was "more of a propagandist than a political leader" and even tried the failing 1964 technique of connecting his GOP foe with the Republican right wing. Still making no headway, he noted several scandals that had occurred in recent years[25] and hinted that Romney should have nipped them in the bud.

As the campaign ebbed Ferency tried three more types of assault. First, he charged that Romney had failed to show leadership in solving the problem of ever increasing strikes by public employees. But here he failed to get at the base of an issue he could have developed. The increase in strikes had been brought about by a revision of the Hutchinson Law that was signed by Romney in 1965. Second, Ferency had the two-hour gubernatorial debate before the AFL-CIO Committee on Political Education edited into a twenty-eight-minute film for television airing. The film showed Ferency's better moments and was balanced against weak appearances for Romney. Last, Ferency supporters filed a suit against publication of the third and last Detroit *News* poll on the gubernatorial race. They charged that Market Opinion Research Company, the Detroit *News,* the Republican party, and the Governor had conspired to present Romney as the obvious winner, thus influencing public opinion. Wayne Circuit Judge Harry J. Dingeman, Jr., dismissed the suit the day before the election.

Throughout the campaign only two major issues developed, and Ferency couldn't directly blame Romney for either: educational penny pinching and the veto of the one-week waiting period. On educational spending, Ferency could truthfully say that most of the financial increases were due to Democratic legislators. But with Romney asserting daily that "we've increased school aid by 55 per cent," how was he going to get that point across to the public? After all, Romney had signed the budget and could therefore claim some credit for the increases, even though he opposed them on the ground of fiscal responsibility. And during the election the Governor made no mention of his thin requests for educational enrichment. No, sir; now it was something he was glad he had approved!

To counter the weakness Ferency recognized in the waiting-period veto, Romney had to shift ground. And whereas Williams had made a terrible blunder, Romney did a skillful job. In his veto message Romney had said he nullified the bill because it was "a major move toward making employment security a welfare program." He said the suggested change would not encourage those out of work to get out and look for a job. When the astute Ferency noted a fallacy (automobile workers idled because of model changeovers), Romney mellowed. His new position was that while such men should not have to wait a week for compensation, he was forced to reject the whole bill, the good with the bad, because he couldn't exercise an item veto. Now automobile workers could blame the poorly drafted legislation instead of the Governor.

That was one of the things Ferency hated about Romney—his ability to change position or give ground without any feelings of guilt. And although he knew that Romney was often inconsistent (at least on a surface level), he was shocked when Romney's new position evolved at their COPE debate. The dialogue between the two men went like this:

FERENCY: I just want to say one thing: In Flint, on Tuesday, Governor, you said you vetoed that bill because you didn't want to make it "a one hundred per cent welfare program." That's what you said.
ROMNEY: I didn't say that in Flint.
FERENCY: That's in Flint. That was on television. You should have seen yourself.[26]

Romney later said that this was a distortion of his position and that he did not have time to give all his reasons for the veto. Poor Zolton Ferency never convinced the electorate that he had an important issue.

With a record of unparalleled progress tucked safely in his pocket, George Romney formally announced on May 25 that he would seek a third term as governor. For four consecutive years Michigan had enjoyed an uninterrupted boom that changed it from a problem state in 1962 to a problem-solving state in 1964. With only nine months of 1966 expansion accounted for, planned investments within state borders were running $190,000,000 ahead of 1965 (which was topped only by 1964). Nearly a thousand industries found it desirable to expand their facilities, and Michiganites were busier and wealthier than ever. The unemployment rate of 1962 had dropped by 60 per cent, and 322,000 more people were working. Michigan's treasury boasted a $167,000,000 surplus. Romney was king. Here was a Republican ruler who not only had found a way to weave straw into gold but had managed to share it with his subjects.

Romney held other trump cards. He had performed admirably with both a Democratic and a Republican legislature. He was facing a political unknown, while the Romney name was on every Michigan tongue. He could boast a huge financial war chest. An added undercurrent was that Michigan voters wanted to have a presidential contender—they had had only one before, and that was over a hundred years ago.[27]

Several aspects of the 1966 campaign distinguished it from 1962 and 1964. In 1962, Romney had run mainly as an independent. He relied heavily on novice personnel and the Romney Volunteers. He ran as a loner; he had to because the Republican label in Michigan was no asset. He spent nearly $600,000 and managed to squeak by John B. Swainson with 70,000 votes.

In 1964 the Republican label within state boundaries had gained new prominence. But the nomination of Barry Goldwater made it necessary for Romney to disclaim direct endorsement. Although the word Republican was found more often, Romney stressed its state association and meaning. Spending only $300,000, he achieved added stature by being the lone survivor on the Republican state ticket.

In 1966 everything was coming up roses. The Goldwater albatross was gone, and the Republican party had a new and vigorous image (shaped to Romney likeness). With complete control of his party,[28] Romney hand-picked candidates and made them a part of his Action Team. Casting off all independent garments, he kissed every Republican in sight. He ignored his Democratic opponent and put his image on the line in behalf of almost every person on the GOP ticket, giving special attention to Robert Griffin. For the first time other Republicans spent more money than the Governor, who spent roughly $200,000.

And there were other telling changes. The flocks of Romney Girls dressed in blue and white now became G.O.P. Girls. The large volunteer groups of 1962 and 1964 were not utilized, and instead the campaign was run by a tight group of professionals. There was no longer any doubt about it. George Romney was a full-fledged Republican, with a capital R—but he represented what he thought a Republican should be!

Although there was no doubt about his reelection, Romney launched his 1966 campaign on August 17, three full weeks earlier than in 1964, and pledged to wage his most energetic battle. His twin purposes for the early opening were to allow ample time to work for lengthy political coattails that would put Republicans back in control of the state legislature and to build Romney's presidential prospects.

Romney went all out. He blitzed the state with the story of progress, spending little time on himself, while begging, coaxing, and cajoling the Michigan electorate to anoint his entire Action Team. Rarely was Robert Griffin, a marginal congressional candidate, or a state legislature hopeful the object of gubernatorial neglect.

Romney never forsook this strategy as the lifeless campaign dragged on. As successive Detroit *News* polls[29] announced the landslide Romney victory, the only real issue of interest concerned the Governor's Senate appointee. Could Romney carry Griffin into office? Romney continued to ignore his foe, refused a Ferency-suggested series of debates,[30] and seldom bothered to refute the wild charges that in the past had made his blood boil. He was in complete command of his campaign. In 1966 he waged a smooth, professional war, and the Democratic mortality rate was like that at Hiroshima after the bomb.

Nobody expected an eighteen-seat gain in the state House or the defeat of all five freshmen Democratic congressmen swept into office in 1964 by the Johnson tidal wave. But George Romney had turned the tide, and the undertow tugged at every key race with such force that only two Democrats kept their heads above the water. (Even these two, Attorney General Frank Kelley and Secretary of State James M. Hare, won by the narrowest margins of their career.) As for Romney and Griffin, all had gone well. Romney amassed the second largest plurality in state history—530,000—while Bob Griffin utilized the Romney magnet for a 270,000 margin of his own.

It was a Republican victory greater than any political observer had dared expect. Faced with the task of proving that he had the ability to pass on his strength to others on the ticket, Romney passed the test with flying colors. No wonder, then, that he was flooded with requests that he seek the nation's highest office in 1968. No wonder, then, that he received financial donations and offers of support. No wonder, then, that the sincere, dynamic and popular Michigan leader said that he would ponder the path—the path to the White House.

8

Measuring Political Success

IN late February, 1966, a Gallup poll reported the answer to this
question: "From what you have heard or read, what kind of a
person is George Romney?" Of the 43 per cent who could identify
the Governor, only 8 per cent characterized him in negative terms
("over-ambitious," "egocentric," "not presidential material.")
Favorable commentary found him to be "honest," "sincere," "religious," a "good administrator."[1] Romney had arrived at political
success—the generation of a favorable personal image.

Since then the number of people who know the Romney name
has been increasing daily, and as the GOP nomination for 1968
narrows down to a handful of possibilities (if not only two) many
more Americans will demand to know more about Michigan's
governor. The data quest will closely follow individual motivation.
Anti-Romney segments will seek out all materials relevant to errors
the Governor has made. They will have some measure of success but
will not stop there. They will stretch the truth over the entire gamut
and spread all sorts of stories with no basis in truth whatsoever.

On the other side of the fence, the pro-Romneyists will seek out
all successful actions the Governor has executed, catalogue them,
and spread the word that Romney is the man for 1968. They too
will stretch the truth, and in their enthusiasm will peddle non-
truths. The myth that Romney can walk on water will not seem
too remote to such ardent supporters.

Somewhere in the broad middle will be the independent,
borderline Republicans, the borderline Democrats, the Republicans
who feel that Romney is not the best choice, and the large masses
of American people who still have to make up their minds. It is

to this last and largest group of voters that my analysis is directed.

If George Romney is to walk on water, you may be assured that it will have to be well frozen. Not since Christ has a man on this earth been able to lead a flawless life. That is true on the personal level and in the political arena. No member of the Kennedy team while that brilliant American was in the White House would say that JFK never made an error. Not one Eisenhower-team member would say it about America's beloved Ike. George Romney, too, is human.

When he was a rather naive political candidate in 1962, a number of his actions clearly indicated the truth of this observation. In June, 1962, he came close to legal transgression in his nominating-petition drive. When he arrived at the Secretary of State's office to file his signatures, he had well over 70,000. This was more than he could legally file, because under Michigan law a candidate cannot "willfully and intentionally" procure more than 4 per cent of the vote cast for his party's nominee for secretary of state in the last election. Romney was 12,000 in excess of his legal number and could have been charged with misdemeanor and punished with ninety days in jail or a five-hundred-dollar fine. Justification for the law is that a citizen may sign only one nominating petition for each office, and therefore without such a limiting stipulation a candidate could conceivably collect enough signatures to make it difficult for his opponent to qualify. An alert state officer brought the law to Romney's attention, saving him embarrassment at the last minute. Romney simply filed fewer signatures.

One well-protected (and therefore not widely known) slip of the tongue occurred early in the campaign. On a speaking appearance in the upstate area, Romney heaped verbal torment on his opponent John B. Swainson. At the height of his oratory Romney concluded, "And I tell you that John Swainson hasn't got a leg to stand on." It was a figure of speech, to be sure. Romney hadn't realized he'd said it, and certainly did not mean to evoke the image of Michigan's present Governor who had lost both legs below the knee in World War II. It was a poor choice of words which Romney would never use again; an unintentional remark that when twisted out of context could hurt his credibility severely. Still, it was a true indication of his amateur status.

At present Romney is regarded as a man who can articulate his position with relative ease. In truth this is so only when his practice has been extensive on the issue he is presenting. The first television debate between the two gubernatorial candidates in 1962 found Romney not nearly so fluent as he might have been. The Governor recognized this himself. As he left the studio he looked toward three of his aides: "You don't have to tell me what you thought," he said; "it's apparent on your long faces."[2]

Another indication of Romney's political virginity was his handling of the Durant affair (see Chapter Four) in Michigan's Fourteenth Congressional district. As Damon Stetson warned in the *New York Times* on August 19, 1962, Romney was exposing his "political naïveté" in assuming that Durant's resignation from the John Birch Society was a complete severance. (Durant is still an active supporter of the society.) This error in judgment was first compounded when he put his prestige on the line and asked the Fourteenth District to reject Durant as a leader, and compounded again by the weak Communist-infiltration label he tried to pin on the Democratic party to offset the Bircher in his own party. The final irony of Romney's anti-extremism efforts was that the files of the U.S. House of Representatives listed Romney as having contributed a hundred dollars to the extremist Americans for Constitutional Action in 1960. Unable to deny the charge, Romney weakly remarked, "I know nothing about the organization and would have contributed only because of knowing someone in the group who had recommended a contribution."[3] All four actions were political gaucheries.

Another mark of Romney's amateurishness in campaigning was his sharp tendency to digress from his real opponent. Fortunately for the Republican candidate, this mistake was isolated by John Swainson in early June. At that time the Democratic Governor unwittingly assisted Romney by asserting, "From what I read, I wonder whether Romney isn't running against Gus Scholle. Every year the Republicans make the same mistake—they campaign against Gus Scholle or Walter Reuther and lose every time. They'll never learn!"⁴ Romney dropped his direct attack on labor leaders for the remainder of the campaign. He was learning by trial and error, but he was learning fast.

But the errors did not stop when Romney became Governor. Frank Kelly, Democratic attorney general, is fond of this story: Upon seeing Kelley for the first time after the election, Romney walked up to him and asked, "What exactly does an attorney general do?" When he learned that Kelley's power extended over eighty lawyers in Detroit and Lansing, he seemed to have made a great discovery. "Why, you've got more power than I have!" the new governor remarked. "As a matter of fact," adds Leon Cohan, deputy attorney general, "Romney originally viewed the role of the attorney general not as one who interprets law but as one who interprets law so that the governor of a state can do what he feels is right. He's had to learn that that just ain't so!"

Then there were the little things that a man paying strict attention to learning the business of state government had to let slide. In his early rush for economy Romney had all sorts of experts figuring out how to cut corners; yet he made the error of running a $30,000 deficit in his own office (and this in spite of the fact that the legislature had increased his staff budget for 1963 by nearly 25 per cent). This left him wide open to Democratic charges that his claims and promises of spending reform and fiscal integrity were nothing but a false front.

On one of his outstate trips to Ohio during his first year Romney again had trouble articulating. Addressing a Republican fund-raising dinner in Columbus, the heart of Buckeye land, the new governor stated, "I believe you have a football team here, Ohio University. (Ohio University is in Athens, Ohio, and strictly bush didn't know that he was speaking in the home town of Ohio *State* University. (Ohio University is in Athens, Ohio and strictly bush league.) He compounded the error once again by saying, "I'm not so sure we've had a team up our way lately," declining to mention whether his remark was directed to the University of Michigan at Ann Arbor or to Michigan State University at East Lansing. His attempted common tie of football between himself and the audience was a complete dud. If anything, he had convinced them that he knew nothing at all about the game. (Although he played high-school football, Romney probably still thinks Bobby Lane or Tobin Rote is the quarterback for the Detroit Lions. He has no time to keep up with such things.)

Throughout his career as governor of Michigan, George Romney has been a backer of traffic safety. For four successive years he has argued for "implied consent," by which as a condition for a license a driver would render his consent to a chemical drunk-driver test at the scene of an accident; yet his own driving record leaves something to be desired. As governor, Romney has four state troopers serving as his chauffeurs; but in prepolitical years Romney received several moving violations: speeding (1954), speeding (1957), improper passing (1957), and running a red light (1958). Democrats joke that Romney (who doesn't use his middle name or initial) should try this label: George Foyt Romney. (A. J. Foyt is an Indianapolis 500 winner.)

The Governor is one to point with pride to the historic past of the state. Michigan was 128 years old on January 26, 1965; but there was no proclamation forthcoming from the Governor's office. Romney had forgotten all about it. The following January, however, a grinning Romney greeted his regularly scheduled 9:30 news conference with a melodious "Happy Birthday," and then he explained whose birthday it was.

In July, 1965, Romney was in further trouble with the police. The East Lansing police log recorded an "illegal watering" of a lawn at 1045 Rosewood. This is the Governor's rented home in East Lansing. At the time there were summer sprinkling restrictions in effect, and Romney simply wasn't aware of them.

Then there was the time Romney showed up at Detroit's Sheraton Cadillac Hotel a bit early for an appointment. He calmly asked the hotel manager where he was to meet British Consul General Sir James Easton. Something was amiss; no registration card could be found for Sir James. Romney gained permission to use the hotel phone and soon located his supposed contact. The Governor was a month early; the appointment was for October 13, not September 13!

One of the Chief Executive's more serious political transgressions occurred immediately after his smashing victory in November, 1964, when he failed to see the swelling dissatisfaction with the party leadership of Arthur G. Elliott, Jr. On November 11, Charles E. Harmon (Romney's soon-to-be-appointed press secretary) reported in his Booth newspaper column, "State Republican Chairman Arthur G. Elliott, Jr., was given a vote of confidence here Tuesday night by 40 congressional district and county chairmen." The meeting had been called by Elliott in a response to comments on the heavy losses of state Republicans despite the gubernatorial landslide. Romney attended the meeting and asked district and county leaders for complaints. He didn't hear many; and apparently he didn't realize that his presence would put a damper on criticism, for after all, everyone present knew that Romney and Elliott were close personal friends. Romney left the meeting feeling that he had defended his friend and put an end to the matter. He told reporters, "Art Elliott has done an outstanding job under very difficult circumstances."

But the matter wasn't settled. It lay dormant for nearly two months, until two Republican senators quietly dropped a bombshell at the State Central meeting on January 15. Senate Minority Leader Emil Lockwood and Lansing Senator Donald Potter announced that they would back Elly Peterson for party chairman unless the Governor fully intended to keep Elliott. Just that morning Peterson had been named a special assistant to the Governor.

The Lockwood-Potter statement had been prepared to spearhead a drive for Elliott's replacement. Since the November meeting criticism of Elliott's leadership had circulated among GOP leaders but had not reached the Governor.

On Friday morning, shortly after he had announced Peterson's new relationship with his office, word reached Romney that an anti-Elliott coalition was forming and that some sort of announcement concerning the movement would be made at the State Central meeting later that day. Romney couldn't believe he had heard right. "After all," he quipped, "I asked the party leaders for their objections personally!" But investigate he must, and the Governor swung into action.

His first inquiry was directed to his top office aides in a series of private conversations. From them he learned that Elliott was being blamed for many problems hampering the smooth functioning of the State Central Committee. With this new general image of Elliott in mind, Romney contacted as many county and district leaders as he could. Dissatisfaction with Elliott was far beyond Romney's worst fears. That evening came the Lockwood-Potter announcement.

By Saturday morning, less than twenty-four hours after he had first gotten wind of the rumors, Romney was ready to act. He had cleared his proposal with congressional leaders. Elliott would step down, and Elly Peterson would take over the party reins. Romney met with Peterson, Elliott, and then Peterson again. Finally, at a 3 P.M. press conference Elliott and Romney made a joint announcement. Elliott said that he would not seek re-election. Romney announced that he would recommend Peterson for the state chairmanship at the February 19 party convention.

Romney insisted that he had had knowledge of the Elliott dissatisfaction for a long time, but that simply was not fact. He had initiated exploration at the moment he was made aware of party disgruntlement, but he did not even suspect anything until one day before he acted. If he had known on Saturday that Peterson might be the new party chairman, he certainly wouldn't have announced on Friday that she was becoming a special assistant. Romney recovered nicely by taking swift action, but he had made a mistake.

Throughout his years as governor of Michigan, Romney has been charged with favoring business over labor. Specifically, labor charges four flagrant special-interest fouls: negative-balance legislation, equalization of property-tax standards, the Chrysler law, and adoption of a quick depreciation schedule on machinery.

The negative-balance legislation was passed in 1963, Romney's first year of office. The term refers to the unemployment-compensation fund from which laid-off workers are paid: a negative balance occurs when more money is paid out to the unemployed workers of a company than is contributed by that company. Since American Motors stood to profit from negative-balance cancellation by several million dollars and since Romney had thousands of shares of its stock in trust, Democrat Joseph J. Kowalski cried, "Special-interest legislation!" Was the charge justified? Not on the basis of past state actions.

First, Romney's negative-balance cancellation had had some Democratic precedent. G. Mennen Williams canceled $117,000,-000 in negative balances in 1955 and 1956. Second, as Romney pointed out, it really is not a debt in the usual sense of the word. The negative balance is used merely to determine what rate employers will contribute to the unemployment fund in the future. It is not a debt the state could collect. A company with no such balance would have to contribute less than one with a balance or one that took the legal option of canceling its negative balance.

The second major special-interest charge was written into "Mr. Romney's constitution," which was ratified on April 1, 1963. A provision stipulated "a reduction in the property taxes paid by business. . . ." The stipulation was not limited to business-property taxes but applied to all property owners. It meant not only that businessmen in Michigan would be given a tax break, but that property-tax inequities that had existed on the local level for many years would be erased. Favoritism by local officials would be corrected, and all property taxes in the state would be levied on a uniform basis. There is no disputing that many homeowners profited from the act as well as many businessmen.

The so-called Chrysler law stemmed from a threat served up by the Chrysler Corporation relating to property taxes on tools, dies, jigs, and fixtures. Chrysler had threatened to make its expansions outside the borders of Michigan if a tax exemption on such property was not forthcoming. Romney went to bat for appropriate legislation, and it was passed. Labor bosses again screamed "special interest," but Detroit Mayor Jerome Cavanagh joined with Romney in seeking the legislation, because he wanted Chrysler to expand not only in Michigan but in Detroit. Chrysler subsequently pleased both politicians.

Finally there was the charge that Romney had vetoed the Straight-line Depreciation bill. The bill was passed in 1966, with support from Joseph Snyder, a Democratic representative from

St. Clair Shores. The accelerated-depreciation schedule in use, originating with the State Tax Commission, reduced the amount of taxes to be paid by industry throughout Michigan. When Romney vetoed the bill to outlaw such rapid depreciation, the *Michigan AFL-CIO News* headlined, "Governor Okays Fourth Business Tax Bonanza."[5] Romney argued that passage of the bill would have "wiped out years of work to develop greater justice in our property-tax assessments in Michigan" and that "instead of producing a tax bonanza for business, my veto prevented hundreds of thousands of individual citizens in many parts of our state from paying increased property taxes on their houses."[6]

In the final analysis, measuring Romney's success in defending himself against these four charges comes down to a conflict in philosophy. It is a basic labor charge that the GOP favors big business and neglects labor. It is not a just complaint in Michigan—at least not under the Romney administration. There is actually legitimate room for big business to complain that Romney has favored labor over industry. When Romney took office in 1962, Michigan had no minimum-wage law, no construction-safety law. Workmen's compensation benefits were among the worst in the nation, and public employees did not have the right to organize for collective bargaining. Today Michigan has a minimum-wage law, a construction-safety law, and attractive workmen's compensation legislation; and public employees have a right to collective bargaining.

Romney's philosophy was the right one for Michigan as it faced an economic and business slump in the early 1960's, because the greatest need in Michigan was jobs. Major employers were making their plant expansions outside the state, and few new industries were moving in. Romney reasoned that Michigan had to be made a more attractive place to do business, and all four of the "tax bonanzas" to business were concessions in that direction. As a matter of fact it was the business concessions and the consequent economic boom within the state that allowed passage of many of the labor gains mentioned above. Any labor legislation without these concessions to business would have made Michigan an even less favorable place for business. And Romney's blueprint for image changing did work: there were 322,000 more people working in Michigan in 1966 than in 1962.

Now the next question will be, Didn't the national economic boom have something to do with Michigan's progress? Certainly. When the nation can buy nine million automobiles rather than six million, it's bound to affect Michigan's economy. But as seen in Chapter Three, the decentralization of automobile production (plant expansion outside state boundaries) could have continued at a rapid rate if concessions favorable to business had not been made. Not only was the decentralization trend stopped, it was reversed. The percentage of automobile employment in Michigan has increased under the Romney administration; and in 1964 and 1965 more than $3,000,000,000 was invested in Michigan business expansions.

Ever since his first barrier-breaking act of crashing the Labor Day parade in Detroit in 1962, young and old alike have admired Romney's courage. It takes courage to appear where you are not only not invited but plainly not wanted. There was, however, at least one such appearance that the Governor might better have done without. In January of 1965, he turned up unannounced at a union-sponsored senior citizens' meeting in Lansing. He was allowed to speak briefly and promptly put his foot in his mouth. He told the audience of several hundred that he recognized the problems of Michigan's senior citizens, and he announced that he had appointed a special study commission to render proposals granting property-tax relief to those over sixty-five. Then a retired automobile worker asked the fatal question.

"My wife and I get one hundred and seventy-six dollars a month. I have had two bad heart attacks, and I have to pay five hundred dollars a year taxes. When are you going to pass the relief law?"

"We are going to get it this year," Romney replied.

"Well, hurry it up. We've got to eat every day," the man said.

"You don't look like you're starving to me!" Romney shot back.[7]

It was a spontaneous remark, but one showing lack of tact and certainly not fitting the situation. Recognizing his mistake, Romney later tried to excuse it: "I meant that there were things other than the material to be considered," he said. The Governor's hoof-in-the-mouth disease had struck again!

In almost a direct apology to all senior citizens Romney recognized an error in his tax plan of 1963 and swung full-scale to the other side of the question. In late February, Romney stated a concept that he couldn't seem to understand during his 1963 tax fight: "Most older people went to leave their children the fruits of their life's work. Often savings or fixed incomes just aren't enough to cover the necessities during their final years. I recommend that the lean provisions on medical assistance and old age assistance be repealed, and I am convinced that tax relief on the homes owned and occupied by our senior citizens is desirable."[8] His 1963 position had been that property-tax relief for senior citizens involve both a lien and interest upon their death.

In January, 1966, Romney issued a statement that seemed in step with the future—as far ahead as 1984. It was a "big brother is watching you" type of directive dealing with news releases for the nineteen newly reorganized state departments. Bud Vestal and other capital reporters played up a section of the statement so much that a modified statement was issued a month later, and the managed-news charge against Romney promptly faded. Controversial paragraph 10 in the before and after stages are compared below:

January 21 Version

Department heads are directly responsible for reviewing and approving all department public relations. All press releases are to be cleared through the department head or a designated representative. The executive assistant for public information or his representative should be kept informed of all public relations efforts undertaken by departments.

February 16 Version

Department heads or designated representatives are responsible for departmental public relations. The executive assistant for public information is available for consultation and coordination. He should be kept informed of public relations efforts other than routine matters, particularly those which may have a bearing on the executive office.[9]

Was Romney attempting news censorship? He pointed out

shortly after issuing version one that the issued statement was "neither an official nor a final document" but "a preliminary paper sent to the department heads for comment." This technique is a regular Romney tool, and Democrats are sometimes justified in saying that anything getting poor public reaction is "only for discussion" or "not final." Romney has used the technique with great success.

Romney seldom speaks about the Williams era in Michigan history without blaming Williams for the payless payday. Yet Romney is responsible for at least one payless payday of his own. In July, 1966, a temporary hold was put on state pay checks because Romney had neglected to sign a $65,000,000 general-appropriations bill that had been on his desk for more than a week. There is no comparing the setting for the payless payday of 1966 with that of 1959; but Zolton Ferency missed a beautiful campaign issue.

Other than having a good many appointment troubles and often chiding Democratic legislators for spending too freely, Romney did fairly well with his Democratic-dominated houses throughout 1965 and 1966. There was one occasion, however, when he started to go astray. On June 19, in Cadillac, Michigan, he spoke to the Republican State Central Committee and chided the Democratic-controlled legislature. He accused Democrats of failing to take action on county home rule, traffic safety, refunding of the Mackinac Bridge, water pollution, and tax reform. He charged that if the Democrats had had complete control, they would have "sent us back to bankruptcy, big debt or exorbitant taxation."

The consensus of opinion was that Romney had begun his attack too early. Possibly his words could be excused, as they were uttered at a partisan gathering to party leaders. But Romney kept up the attack in a press conference until many of his own party expressed dismay over his poor timing. With the regular session due to be adjourned within days, Romney seemed to have no good reason for jumping the gun. Finally realizing that his remarks might have damaged the possibility of tax-reform consideration at the fall session, he reversed himself. On June 26,

Romney congratulated the Seventy-third Legislature on a "job well done." He went so far as to say that "the end product of this sitting of the legislature must be placed in the credit column of our state's ledger," and maintained that the Democratic House and Senate had achieved a "batting average of about seventy to seventy-five per cent, a high mark for legislative action in any one session" of a state legislature. "With some major exceptions," he concluded, "I am pleased with the results of this session."[10] Romney had again seen the adverse press and party reactions and had modified quickly. Interestingly, the condemnation speech before the GOP State Central body was omitted from his speech mailing list.

Another major mistake occurred during the 1964 campaign. Romney limited himself to one out-of-state bigwig visit and made only one out-of-state sojourn in return. The exchange was arranged with Negro Attorney General Ed Brooke of Massachusetts. Brooke arrived in time to hold an early-afternoon news conference at Detroit's Sheraton Cadillac Hotel, stating that Romney would be "at the top level of GOP leadership if the national ticket lost in November." After the quiz period Brooke was rushed to the Alpha Phi Alpha legal fraternity house on Wayne State University's campus. There he waited, and waited, and waited for Romney. Brooke was visibly disgruntled.

Finally Romney arrived, at about 8 P.M. After a few minutes of polite chitchat Brooke and Romney dashed off to a rally at Calvary Baptist Church that drew less than two hundred people. Brooke again was disappointed. It was clear that he felt his talents were not being put to maximum use. After this fiasco the party went to a Highland Park Republican meeting that scraped together almost three hundred people. Brooke must have thought, "Wow, what a crowd!" Someone on Romney's scheduling committee had passed up a golden opportunity to shore up the Negro vote: during a twelve-hour stint Brooke spoke to no more than six hundred people. It was a waste of his time that he resented. After all, he was campaigning too! (The vastness of the Romney error is underlined effectively by a short sketch of Romney's return visit to Massachusetts: On October 26, Associated Press reporter Al Sander noted that Romney addressed a crowd of 1,100 at a birthday dinner honoring Brooke, and 700 students at a meeting sponsored by Harvard Young Republicans and the Public Affairs Forum.)[11]

Then there is the matter of the National Guard scandal of 1964. Romney handled it so poorly that he had to spend ninety-three hours of his precious time serving as judge and jury. Romney had first acted October 8, 1964, on the advice of representatives in the attorney general's office, on unanimous recommendation of the State Military Board, and on a year-in-the-making investigation of the state military establishment submitted by Billie S. Farnum, Democratic auditor general. He dismissed Major General Ronald McDonald, state adjutant general; Brigadier General Carson Neifert, quartermaster general; and Lieutenant Colonel Versel Case, Jr., the quartermaster's executive officer, for eleven state-law violations and more than thirty auditing errors.

On November 2, almost Election Eve, Frank Kelley, Democratic attorney general, ruled that Romney did not have the authority to take such action. Romney therefore reinstated the officers on November 6 and promptly suspended them pending proper procedure. Finally, on May 20, 1965, some eight months after his original move, the Governor was able to take action legally. Through his haste—not checking with Kelley and getting approval in writing—he had fallen into a political booby trap. Shortly after the election top aides from Kelley's and Romney's offices worked out "the truce of Lansing," so that such a communication error wouldn't happen again. Kelley and Romney have gotten along much better since that time, but Romney still feels that Kelley stabbed him in the back.

Another major flaw of Romney's was his failure to procure ADC-U (Aid to Dependent Children of the Unemployed), during his first year of office. In February, Lieutenant Governor T. John Lesinski placed the cost to Michigan's taxpayers at $12,000,000. By October, Democrats had placed the cost at nearly $20,000,000. What is the true story behind Romney's failure to procure federal funds that were available?

Aid to Dependent Children of the Unemployed legislation was

first passed by Congress in 1961, on a one-year trial basis. Eligibility (determination of what constitutes an "unemployed parent") was left to the states. In 1962 the law was expanded to a five-year basis, and Romney wanted to take advantage of the federal funds. When he assumed office, he asked the state Social Welfare Department to compose a bill that would qualify Michigan for this money. When the bill had been drafted, the Welfare Department checked with the Chicago regional office of the Department of Health, Education and Welfare to be sure that the phrasing would allow the bill to qualify. They were assured that it would.

The Michigan House passed the ADC-U bill and the Senate was about to follow suit, when a wire from the U.S. Health, Education and Welfare Department questioned Michigan's definition of "unemployed." The 1961 law said that the definition was to be "determined by the states," and so Romney urged that the Senate go ahead and approve it. They did. Within hours the Secretary of Health, Education and Welfare sent Romney a telegram saying that the new Michigan legislation was "discriminatory" and that he would not grant funds under it. Romney traveled to Washington to investigate and returned feeling even more justified in his original advice; but by that time his arch-rival Kelley had some interesting legal advice: he had declared the new state legislation unconstitutional. Clearly the rules had been changed to embarrass Romney.

Finally there was what most people still regard as the crowning failure of Romney's years in Lansing—his fiscal-reform flop in the fall of 1963. There are those who say that he was too inflexible in his demands. They are wrong. There are those who say that he approached Republicans when he should have approached Democrats. They too are wrong. If Romney made any error, it was an error of timing. Perhaps the first short session of 1963 was the time for fiscal reform, when Romney pushed through most of what he wanted and got his new constitution adopted in April. But he waited until September to seek out fiscal changes. This assessment is supported by T. John Lesinski, Democratic lieutenant governor: "His timing was off. He should have presented his tax program at the start of the legislative session, when his popularity was at its highest."[12] And State Revenue Commissioner Clarence W. Lock also put his finger on the crucial timing factor: "We just collected too much money," he said. The state deficit of $85,000,000 had melted to $20,000,-000 when Romney initiated the biggest push for tax reform, and legislators weren't at all sure that the money was needed badly enough for them to become fixed in the public mind as "the income-tax legislators." If Romney failed, he certainly learned from his experience. He didn't try such a one-man approach again while the state coffers continued to swell to a surplus of $167,000,000 on July 1, 1966.

Romney, then, has been accused of making numerous miscalculations in judgment, executing strategic misplays, and exhibiting occasional lack of insight. Some of these liabilities were refuted, some substantiated. Some were seen as minor, a few could be called serious, but many others fell somewhere between. Romney has also pulled off some political shrewdies and shown that he has developed true political savvy. One of his major plus factors is that he is a political realist. He has a keen sense of what is possible and what is not. Most political pros insist that Romney is too idealistic, and this, they say, is one reason that Romney may have difficulty getting the 1968 GOP nomination. Romney's record simply does not bear them out.

After failing to achieve fiscal reform in his one-man effort in 1963 and after bypassing attempts in 1964, Romney tried a bipartisan approach in 1965, reasoning, "I'm political realist enough to know that any revenue needed will have to be raised this year. Next year is election year."[13] Efforts at tax reform were not pushed with great gusto in 1966 after the collapse of fiscal-reform bipartisan support in the fall of 1965, and Romney accepted that for the time being. The probability of passage in 1966 was nil.

This sense of the possible and probable, Romney has had from the start of his political career. Knowing he was on shaky ground with the Republican-controlled legislature in 1963, Romney played it cagy. He wouldn't specifically say which bills he wanted passed and which he didn't. Detroit *News* writer Anthony Ripley summed up Romney's strategy beautifully in March of 1963: "He [Romney] has a group of top priority bills that he is counting upon and the administration is backing. But the office isn't specifying what they are . . . the beauty of the system is that it allows the Governor to take credit or duck."[14] Thanks to this strategy, Romney received rave reviews on his first session's performance.

When the Democrats took control of the legislature in 1965, Romney again recognized that the possible would be achieved through a Democratic majority. Immediately after the 1964 election he started the bandwagon rolling. "I'll do everything in my power to promote bipartisanship," he said. About a week later he warned the minority GOP legislators "to conduct themselves in a way that merits Democratic cooperation in the legislature." Developing some of his idealistic philosophy in justification, he continued, "With some exceptions I have found that people will respond to the kind of treatment they get." He underlined this harmonious approach in his second inaugural address and met with Democratic legislators before the session started, in mid-January. He knew where the votes were.

Romney met with such success in legislative requests in 1965 (again with the exception of tax reform) that the Democrats decided to get the jump on him for the 1966 session. The Democrats and Romney wanted many of the same things. On January 7 the Democratic majority announced a program of Progressive Reform that was to expand state services while not increasing taxes and maintaining a balanced budget. It sounded little different from Romney's Total Michigan Progress unmasked some six days later. Romney was leading by following; and since it is the Governor who takes the credit for progress or lack of progress in a state, he had made the possible probable.

Romney performed such astute political trickery that Democratic Senator Joseph D. Tydings commented in *Harper's* on "the most productive session [in Michigan] since the 1930's."[15] One of Romney's maneuvers was the appointment of AFL-CIO president August Scholle to the State Conservation Commission. Scholle had served as a commissioner in 1961–62 and was well qualified, but Scholle and Romney were bitter enemies. Under government reorganization Romney had to appoint a Democrat anyway, so he appointed Scholle. It was a move that Democrats had to applaud.

Then there was the growing public relationship between Frank Kelley and Romney. ("Public relationship" is the correct phrase, for the two men are far from being friends.) After the truce of Lansing, Romney seemed to go out of his way to get legal advice from Kelley's office before acting on even relatively routine matters.

In July, 1966, Romney signed a $1,400,000 appropriation bill calling for the three-year construction of a road in Ontonagon County to be used for mining purposes, but only after being assured that the initial funds would not be authorized without an opinion from Kelley. His fingers burnt on ADC-U and the National Guard scandal, Romney was not about to be taken in again. By the middle of 1966, he had made such use of the Attorney General's advice that the two men were able to join together in a war on crime.

Romney also made sure that he was not personally blamed for failure to obtain a fiscal-reform package in 1965. When a House Democratic caucus decided not to discuss the plan that Romney had labored on throughout the summer months, Romney had an out. He had held conferences with a handful of legislators of both parties and even held a two-day meeting at Mackinac Island; and since several of the legislators were Democrats, the Governor unleashed a flurry of abuse when the caucus made its announcement. "Democratic legislators must accept responsibility for whatever financial crisis develops in the next few years," Romney stated. "It should be clear now that the Democratic party to a large extent has become the reactionary party in Michigan in terms of fiscal responsibility."[16]

One of the clearest indications of Romney's realization of the possible as separated from the impossible and the thing that sets him off from the Socratic-idealist image is his appetite for a good compromise. He executed one at the 1961–62 constitutional convention when he accepted the "accommodations agreement" offered by the D. Hale Brake faction (see Chapter Four); and he has executed at least three major ones while working with the Democratically controlled legislature. In March of 1966, he was negotiating possible legislation for veterans' property-tax exemptions, when he remarked, "This is not our final offer." He was willing to compromise. In general he is more willing to compromise than most people think. The only things he won't compromise are his deepest convictions. But he can and will compromise, and has compromised, on legislation that does not involve such deep-rooted concerns.

The first major compromise between Democrats and Romney involved government reorganization. Romney had been condemning Michigan's "administrative monstrosity" long before the constitutional convention of 1961–62 made provision for paring down the 144 departments into fewer than twenty. He declared that the 1908 administrative system resembled "a twenty-mule team, harnessed in the dark by a blind one-armed idiot!" "I am not Michigan's chief executive," he would say. "Michigan has no chief executive. I'm talking about an executive who has the power to carry out the administration of this state. I'm just one of a number of executives who have some powers, and I'm the fall guy!"

During the fall session of 1965, Romney and Democrats became involved in a bitter dispute over the structure of the new departments. Romney wanted each department to be headed by one chief executive, while the Democrats wanted a commission at the helm. Each side held for as long as it could, until June 25, when a compromise was reached. Of the nineteen new departments seven were to be led by commissions, and the other twelve would be headed by chief executives. Romney had allowed the possible to intrude on what he considered to be the ideal; he had therefore gotten action. "Sure, it would have been better to get all nineteen departments under a single leader, which would eliminate buck-passing," he reasoned, "but I got more than half of what I wanted. It was a good compromise which prevented stalemate."

A second successful compromise was worked out in county home rule. County home rule is simply government for more efficiency. Theoretically it allows every county to set up a government suited to its peculiar needs, much like a city charter. Michigan has weak home rule now, and there is much waste and overlapping of services among its township governments. There was great controversy concerning the size of governing boards and the authorship of district lines, but Romney and the Democratic-controlled legislature passed a County Home Rule bill in 1966.

Third, there is Romney's action on the legislative pay raise issue. Michigan's legislators have had vast pay increments in the past sixteen years. As recently as 1948 a legislator got only $3.00 a day. From 1949 to 1952 the annual salary was $2,400 with an expense allowance of $1,000. The base salary was raised to $2,900 in 1953 and to $4,000 in 1955. In 1961 both the base salary and the expense allowance were raised, to $5,000 and $1,250, respectively. In 1963 the base salary took a $2,000 jump. By 1965 the base salary had risen to $10,000 and the expense allowance was $2,500. It looked like a give-away program of a kind, but believe it or not, the legislature wanted another raise for 1967—and they asked for $5,000.

In June, 1966, Romney engineered a deal with Democrats seeking a raise. He had often said that he would not support a raise as large as $5,000, and it was general knowledge that he wasn't too keen on any raise at all. But in June he approved a $2,500 raise in exchange for two things: a conflict-of-interest law that would bar legislators from moonlighting; and pay raises for top-ranking state bureaucrats and for members of the governor's staff. Romney had sought both of these for a long time, and he seized the opportunity to get them. The result is that full compensation for Michigan legislators is now $15,000, but at least department heads and governor's staff are paid on a scale competitive with industry.

Another area of political success has been public relations, for Romney is a super salesman when selling a product, or himself. It could be said that he is image-conscious or that he is a master propagandist, depending upon who is making the observation, but the fact cannot be denied.

As a 1962 gubernatorial candidate he faced up to the problem that many people were already thinking in terms of the White House as a suitable hitch. He passed the word that such talk was premature and insisted that his press secretary be called press assistant. This action was to spike the charge of White House ambitions that, he speculated, Democrats would toss his way.

When he crashed the Labor Day parade in 1962, he made sure of adequate press coverage. The Lonesome George picture that got such wide circulation was photographed by an expert who knew exactly what the Governor wanted.

Then there was the obvious, which Romney did not overlook. His fame and fortune had come through American Motors, but a clear severance would have to be made with the company. Soon after assuming office he chose a black Chevrolet as his official automobile. (To be sure he resisted temptation, he studied competitive bids from Ford, Chrysler, and General Motors only.) It was a small thing, but it underlined the fact that Romney was not to be a partisan governor.

In the 1962 campaign Romney had promised that he would listen to the voice of the people. To carry out his promise— or to make it appear so—he inaugurated a policy of allowing about two hours on Thursday mornings for citizens of the state to drop in and chat five minutes each with the Governor about whatever they wished. Democrats, Independents, and even some Republicans sneered at the obvious publicity stunt.

In March of 1964 Romney nipped a public-relations blunder in the bud. Bernard M. Conboy, director of state economic expansion, planned to use Romney's picture in a twenty-four-page New York *Times* newspaper supplement boosting Michigan. Romney vetoed the idea, realizing that he would be open to charges of using state funds for personal-image projection.

Then there was the first visit to Michigan of Lyndon Baines Johnson. Romney knew that the large crowd at the University of Michigan commencement in May of 1964 and the presence of the President of the United States would provide moments rich in publicity. He arrived at the airport a full forty minutes before the President was due, and after a tug-of-war with Detroit's Mayor

Jerome Cavanagh, was the first in line to shake the President's hand. Maintaining that he was there "to represent all the people of Michigan," Romney stuck to the President like glue. Because he had come prepared with academic robes and all, he even got a seat next to the President on the speakers' platform, while non-uniformed Democrats were not allowed to join in the ceremonies.

In March of 1965, Democratic State Central Chairman Zolton Ferency blistered Romney's public-relations techniques by indicating that Romney had "established what appears to be a propaganda ministry." He expounded that the Governor was the beneficiary of some vast news-media deal that would saturate the air waves with his activities. The object of Ferency's scorn was a new device called "the instant interview," dreamed up by S. John Byington, a gubernatorial aide. It had first been used during the 1964 campaign to get the Governor on record as fast as possible. If he was not near Lansing or Detroit, he would call his comments in; these would be recorded and passed on to appropriate news agencies. By the latest instant-interview twist Romney was available for direct comment on almost any issue by simply dialing an unlisted number.

The Governor's public image has also benefited considerably from personal sacrifices. Several times he has canceled out-of-state junkets because of the press of state business. In March of 1964 he cut his Hawaiian vacation short by a week to attend to the apportionment crisis. It was his first vacation in some fourteen months of intensive work, and this action could not help but boost his image in the eyes of Michiganites. When Democrats later complained that he had spent too much time outside Michigan borders in 1965, Romney responded, "I question whether the people of Michigan can be served adequately by a governor who feels that his state's business ends at the state line."

One of Romney's biggest and most successful public-relations efforts was Operation Christmas. It is not uncommon for government officials during the Christmas holidays to take advantage of the warmth of the season and offer good cheer to all citizens who might vote for them, and Romney has taken full advantage of that tradition, often walking the pavement in front of Detroit's J. L.

Hudson Company to grasp hands. Yet Romney rose to an admirable new height in sending some extra Christmas cheer to a place where it was badly needed in 1965—Vietnam. On November 26, Romney launched his program: "On my recent trip to Vietnam, I learned that several thousand Michigan boys are members of our armed forces there and will spend this Christmas thousands of miles from home. Since returning, I have sought some manner of indicating to these sons of Michigan that their state has not forgotten them and will be especially thinking of them during the holiday season. I have determined that this can be accomplished by sending a representative gift package to every Michigan GI we can identify and locate in South Vietnam."

Romney requested of all Michigan citizens that names and addresses of Michigan men and women serving in Vietnam be forwarded to: "Christmas in Vietnam, c/o George Romney, State Capitol, Lansing, Michigan." Michigan businessmen, farmers, and manufacturers were asked to contribute goods and money to the effort; and Booth Newspapers, Inc., which operates a chain of nine newspapers in the state, promised to deliver the packages to Vietnam.

It was a massive effort—and a smashing success—and George Romney holds it dear to his heart. In twenty-six short days some 76,000 pounds of gifts had been put into 7,600 personally addressed packages and were finding their way to Michiganites in Vietnam.[17] "That," says George Romney with a smile, "was Voluntary Cooperation at its peak!"

A last important ingredient in any public-relations effort is timing, and this, despite the 1963 tax-reform error, is also a Romney forte. Throughout the 1966 gubernatorial election Romney had to refrain continually from embracing support for the presidency. First there was the Rockefeller endorsement in New York; then there was the Scranton boost from Pennsylvania. Finally there was the invitation for a national tour of the breadth and scope of Richard Nixon's. But Romney knew that the time wasn't right. He knew that his only hope of achieving the White House rested solidly on a large plurality in Michigan while dragging in some other state Republicans with him. Consequently he stayed home. But when the time *is* right, George Romney will move toward every politician's dream.

Another area deserving exploration in attempting to measure his political success is the Governor's influence on the direction of the state GOP. It will be recalled that Romney started with much less than a complete party endorsement in his 1962 race, and that one of his stated objectives at the time was that he would "change the image of the party." After four years in office, therefore, the question, "Has he?" would seem to be a natural one. The record reveals that Romney was a take-charge guy right from the start and has grown stronger with the passing months.

At the Republican convention in Grand Rapids on February 16, 1963, Romney had been in office only six weeks and sorely needed party support. Attending his first party meeting as governor, he asked for things he had espoused during the campaign, including fiscal reform that the GOP had rejected for years. Detroit *News* reporter Robert A. Popa capsules the result: "Governor Romney's program for Michigan became the Republican Party's program here this afternoon as the two marched in step toward identical goals." And commentator Glenn Engle seems to agree: "The GOP State Convention was marked by unity behind Governor Romney."[18]

Just a year later Romney's leadership was again tested. The occasion was the Republican State Convention of May 7, 1964. On March 27, a three-judge federal court had ruled that the districting law adopted by the state legislature in 1963 was unconstitutional. It further ruled that no election could take place under the 1963 districting and that an at-large election would have to be held if new lines of apportionment were not drawn.

Over the protests of Governor Romney, ten Republican senators formed a coalition with ten Democratic senators and rammed through a complete legislative redistricting plan. Romney was disturbed. "The worst error of all made by these Republicans is that they made a bad deal. They sold out unnecessarily. They agreed to Democratic gerrymandered congressional districts and traded away the Massachusetts ballot and who knows what else.

And in exchange they got nothing. For that, they must answer to the people," he warned.[19]

And Romney, true to the Republican elephant image, did not forget. Two weeks later he went before the Republican convention at Grand Rapids and made an appeal that those senators be "dealt with accordingly." His commentary went something like this: "The wonderful record of progress made by the Republican majority in the legislature in the last two years has been all but smothered by the antics of a few irresponsible legislators in recent weeks . . . these political quislings[20] who sold out to the opposition. We have those in Lansing who sat in our party councils as leaders and then ran straight to the opposition to disclose our programs and plans and conspire with the opposition to undermine the very programs and plans they helped to make."[21] The party primary on September 1, 1964, rendered defeat for five of the "quislings": Lester O. Begick, Bay City; Harold B. Hughes, Clare; John P. Smeekens, Coldwater; Kent T. Lundgren, Menominee; and Paul C. Younger, Lansing. When the Senate convened in January 1965, only one "quisling", Emil Lockwood of St. Louis, remained. Romney's injury had been vindicated.

In February of 1965 the Governor was called on to make it three state conventions in a row at which his will would prevail. Fiscal reform had been a topic of interest and discussion in Michigan since G. Mennen Williams had first been forced to consider it a possibility before the 1959 payless-payday crisis. One week end before the GOP convention in Lansing, the state Democratic convention had gone on record as advocating complete and immediate fiscal reform. The question was, What would the Republican State Convention go on record as favoring?

The Governor's staff had submitted a carefully worded reform resolution to the convention, but Romney's old foe from the Fourteenth District, Richard Durant, proposed an amendment that would have put the party on record as being against any income tax not approved by a referendum. A voice and show-of-hands vote revealed that the delegates were about evenly divided on the question. Enter George Romney. He strode briskly to the rostrum for an unscheduled speech. The situation is re-created vividly by Robert Longstaff: "The convention hall was filled, and attention was riveted on Romney. Delegates moved in from the lobbies and lined the walls. Few seats were empty. Romney did not mince words. 'Adopt the amendment,' he argued, 'and you can kiss goodbye to the future of the Michigan Republican party."[22] A roll-call vote immediately following had 1,279 backing Romney and only 239 opposed!

At the fall, 1966, GOP state convention it was a similar story. The Grand Rapids *Press* headlined on August 28, "Michigan Republicans Unite Behind Romney." Not only did Romney get his own hand-picked candidates nominated, but he beat back right-wing assaults on Vietnam and fiscal reform. It was certainly a growing pattern of power!

The image-changing going on at the state conventions was only part of the story. During these four years Romney had also succeeded in fighting off a growing John Birch Society threat that constantly sought to enlarge on its Fourteenth District home base. In public statements he waged war on extremists of all types. He saw to it that the first vice-chairman of a major state party was a Negro. He saw to it that Goldwaterism and Romneyism were separated. He saw to it that when Everett M. Dirksen rejected the civil-rights bill of 1966, Michigan's GOP was clearly not implicated. In four years George Romney had completely revamped the Republican party of Michigan—and it was a tailoring job well done!

National columnist Ralph McGill made an observation on January 25, 1962, that many analysts regarded as not completely accurate. McGill said that Romney was "so plain-spoken as to be called naive—which he is not!"[23] It should now be evident to the reader that McGill knew what he was talking about. But wait, there's more! Witness the great aura of suspense that Romney created when he took two full months to decide if he would run for public office or not. Romney received thousands of letters from citizens begging him to run. It was a smooth political masterpiece.

Then there was the matter of polling. The first Republican polls in the state of Michigan were conducted under the auspices of George Romney. The Governor has Walter DeVries, an outstanding man, to rely on in this area. Ever since 1962, polls have told the Governor what issues to develop before and during campaigns, as well as measuring the success of such pitches when the contest ended. Most of the time they have been quite reliable; but one unsatisfactory piece of advice was served up before the make-or-break 1963 fiscal-reform try. A private poll done by Market Opinion Research Company of Detroit (the folks who do most of the Romney polling under the direction of DeVries) pointed out that Romney was "riding a crest of voter approbation matching the national popularity of President Kennedy" and that a fiscal-reform package including an income tax might win support if properly explained."[24] Romney thus took his program to large numbers of people.

The bipartisan approach that Romney followed after suffering this major defeat showed the operation of a skilled political mind. Benefiting from the repeated failures of Soapy Williams, Romney explained why he didn't resubmit his tax plan in 1964 or 1965: "Only a dumb governor would try again with a program that had failed twice under previous Democratic administrations and again during his first term."

During the gubernatorial campaign of 1964, Romney came up with a couple more artworthy actions. During the first Romney-Staebler debate at the AFL-CIO convention in Grand Rapids the Governor was challenged on the Massachusetts ballot. Labor leadership charged that this ballot would not allow voters to elect a straight party ticket. Speaking before a 90 per cent plus Democratic union group, Romney executed a master stroke. He produced a copy of the AFL-CIO constitution and read a simple sentence: "Every voter in a local union election is entitled to vote for any individual for any office and he is improperly influenced when presented with a slate of candidates in the nature of a party ticket."

The second shrewdie may well have been responsible for Romney's successful stand against the LBJ tidal wave in 1964: it was how-to-split-your-ticket propaganda.[25] Two groups published two versions of such information shortly before the election. The first group was led by Dr. John Eagan, a Detroiter who had made a bid for Republican congressional nomination. Dr. Eagan and his followers were responsible for distributing 200,000 leaflets illustrating "how to split your ticket for Johnson and Romney." The literature was violently objected to by Citizens for Goldwater-Miller, who blamed the Romney Volunteers. Not so. The Volunteer literature (which Romney had direct control over) simply illustrated "how to vote for Governor Romney." It did not say whom else the voter might choose to vote for, although it was clearly aimed at fighting the Goldwater albatross. Romney had no control over the Eagan group, and the Volunteers had done no direct wrong. And the happy result was that 40 per cent of Michiganites voting for LBJ voted for Romney also. It was a piece of political geninus.

A number of other political Rembrandts could be cited, but perhaps only three more need be mentioned: Romney's dealings with the "big spenders," vetoing of legislation that could be upheld, and the "Get Griffin Going" conference in the Governor's office.

The big spenders in Michigan's history (as well as nationally) have been the Democrats. They have always gone in for deficit spending, copious social legislation of all sorts, and general philanthropy, whether the money was in the treasury or not. Romney, on the other hand, does not like deficit spending. During their first budget encounter in 1965, the Governor pulled the wool over Democrats' eyes. He estimated state revenues for 1965–66 at only $756,000,000—more than $75,000,000 under actual collections. So even though Democrats spent more than Romney liked, the state surplus grew.[26]

Although Zolton Ferency in 1966 accused Romney of having vetoed sixteen pieces of legislation that hurt the people of Michigan, only four of the vetoes were challenged: tax relief for senior citizens who rented housing, cancellation of a one-week waiting period to become eligible for unemployment compensation, a supplemental money bill for small colleges and universities, and legislation dealing with property-tax exemption for disabled veterans. Romney's control of his party is seen in the fact that only one Republican House vote was needed to upset a governor's veto, yet in the House as well as the Senate the vetoes were upheld.

Last there is the "Get Griffin Going" conference of April 22, 1966. Shortly before the death of Democratic U.S. Senator Patrick McNamara, Bob Griffin, carrying the designation of preferred GOP nominee, was summoned to Romney's office. For nearly an hour he was thoroughly castigated for not campaigning hard enough. It was Romney's chance for the big campaign in 1968, and he was going to be sure that nobody botched it!

In the summation of William McLaughlin, Michigan Republican vice-chairman: "The Governor has grown up and learned a lot. I think we all recognize that he was not a politician to any great extent when he was elected in 1962. He's really been educated over the years." McLaughlin might well have added that George Romney has become a political pro.

9

Romney the Man

THROUGHOUT the 1966 gubernatorial campaign Democratic candidate Zolton Ferency repeatedly sounded this battle cry: "If I can get the real George Romney to stand up, I think I can knock him down." Ferency had set himself a difficult task, because presenting the "real" person—no matter who he may be—would seem to be impossible. The Democratic challenger could have learned from a popular educational movie called *The Eye of the Beholder*.

The Eye of the Beholder concerns six people who observe aspects of the behavior of Michael Girard, an artist. Each person perceives Girard from a different point of view. His mother sees him as a good boy, his landlord sees him as a looney, the cab driver views him as a hood, the night-club waiter believes him to be a ladies' man, the nosy old cleaning lady thinks he is a murderer, and the model he supposedly kills thinks he is a square. All six persons do not realize that they cannot see the "real" Michael Girard.

The one-sided viewpoint from which we perceive our environment and the two-party context in which our political wars are waged allow George Romney to be seen in at least as many ways as Michael Girard. Witness the three men whom Romney defeated for the governorship in 1962, 1964, and 1966. John B. Swainson labels Romney a parrot and elaborates upon this designation: "He has an adeptness for taking popular causes and making popular decisions. I'm not absolutely sure he has any deep political thoughts. I sometimes feel that it's whoever speaks to him last that's the most influential." Neil Staebler, casting his eyes forward to 1968, does not mince words either. The former congressman feels that Romney's traits "would be a catastrophe at the national level." And the most recent wound licker, Zolton A. Ferency, sincerely believes that Romney "may have a psychological problem."

Other perceptions of Romney are most praiseworthy. Pennsylvania's former governor William Scranton regards Romney as "one of the Republicans who can do the party the most good." Democratic Secretary of State James M. Hare says flatly that Romney would be the "best Republican candidate for 1968," and General Dwight D. Eisenhower also speaks favorably: "I don't believe any man can say that George Romney is incompetent to be president!"

With such wide testimony regarding Romney, is it at all possible to present a picture of the "real" man? Probably not. But a man in presidential contention must be explored and examined for the benefit of the voting public. Fully realizing that it is only one assessment of the man and fully cognizant of the limitations imposed, I offer the following commentary in answer to the question, What is the man really like?

Michigan's forty-first governor is an amazing physical specimen at fifty-nine. About ten years ago he read a phrase on a gymnasium wall that has stuck with him: "It isn't the amount of exercise, but the consistency of it." He has maintained a steady diet of early-morning runs, exercise, and long walks ever since. When the weather permits, his sporting instinct takes the form of golf. He plays alone and briskly, scarcely allowing for taking aim at the next hole. Usually he plays an "executive nine," hitting three balls at a time for three holes. When he takes his time he can shoot in the middle eighties.

His athletic five-foot-eleven-inch frame is firm, if not hard. There is no telltale middle-age bulge, and Romney weighs a trim 175, filling a size 42 suit perfectly. His hair, which started to gray when he was forty, has nearly completed the transition. He is handsome—looking so distinguished that *Newsweek* commented in 1962, "If Central Casting were to pick the ideal Presidential Candidate, Romney would be it."[1] His light-hazel eyes are made even less prominent by large, bushy gray brows that make a sharp downturn as they head outward. His chin is firm, although less so than it once was. Indeed, the often-used phrase describing him as jut-jawed must have been coined during the late 1950's, although there is a definite lingering of that characteristic.

His hair is parted more or less down the center, and his side-burns do not come down the full traditional length. His lips are small and blend almost unnoticeably into his face. His nose is not small, but teams with his other features to make him look the rugged outdoorsman that he is. He has an expressive face that mirrors his feelings well.

His favorite color is blue, and more often than not you will find him in a dark-blue suit, a conservative tie (during elections he uses one with several small elephant heads) and white shirt (without button-down or tab collar) complete with cuff links. The only other jewelry is his gold wedding ring and watch, both worn on the left. His hands are strong, meaty, and lightly freckled. His nails are trimmed short. He never wears a hat, but was named one of the "Ten Best-Hatted Men" of the year in 1962. He dresses neatly, but buys most of his suits right off the rack (he has also been named to the "Ten Best-Dressed" list by the Custom Tailors Guild of America).

His usual image is one of correctness. One time during the 1964 campaign a reporter was riding with the Governor on a hot September day. "Why doesn't somebody roll down a window?" he asked a Romney aide. "Psst," the aide said; "the Governor's hair might blow!" His vanity is shown more clearly in the fact that he would not be seen in public in his glasses for more than two years after he started using them—and even then he used half-glass frames that drew attention to themselves because they were so unusual.

He is self-reliant to a high degree, although he will usually ask others for their opinion before taking action. Once when he was to appear on a news program, a series of questions was presented to his office. Romney summoned an aide, and the aide immediately proceeded to give the Governor a briefing. "Never mind the answers," Romney snapped; "give me the questions!"

And this self-reliance is made possible by his independent monetary means. It was no accident that Romney had his own fortune when he got into politics. "I wouldn't want to get into a position where I felt money or services were being given that involved any personal obligation," he says. "When I was down there [serving as a Washington representative for the aluminum industry], I said that if I got into public life, I'd be in a position where I didn't have to depend solely on public income or political funds for a living." Other words that seem to characterize the broad-shouldered Romney are intense, hard driving, determined, clean-living, and a man of boundless energy.

He is a self-made man in the fullest American tradition. Starting with no family fortune, he acquired his first million in 1960 and was working on his third when he assumed the governorship of Michigan in 1963. He has, however, never been one to waste money, be it private or public. Back in 1959, while well on the way to that first big million, Romney was stricken with a bad cold. He was due to travel to Cleveland, and with Howard Hallas and John Conde he decided that he had better treat his cold with a couple of large cans of tomato juice. When he told the driver to pull over to a chain store so that he could make his purchase, his two aides pointed out that he could get all the juice he wanted on the train. "Oh, no," Romney replied. "They rob you blind!"[2]

Usually he is a man in a hurry. When motoring himself he often tries short cuts, and when being chauffeured he is quite apt to give directions: "You can get over," "Can we go any faster?" or "We've got to be there at five-thirty!" When serving as Con-Con delegate in 1961–62, he was so concerned with making use of every minute that he kept a pair of pajamas in his chauffeured Rambler and would slip into them in Lansing, tilt his reclining seat, and sleep the ninety miles back to Bloomfield Hills. (This novelty was the butt of many a joke, but none better than the witticism of Democratic Lieutenant Governor T. John Lisenski, who burlesqued, "I'm sorry I'm late, but my pajamas got caught in the door of my Rambler.")[3]

The time factor proved to be one of Romney's chief complaints when he assumed the governorship, and one close staff member after the January, 1963, inauguration, gave this report: "Romney accepts his responsibility but that doesn't mean he has to enjoy it. I don't think he was prepared for the demands upon his time. He can't get away to study or think. He has been surprised by the pressures. He doesn't like the ceremonial aspects of the job."[4] Lenore Romney says this language is a little strong, and takes issue particularly with the "ceremonial" comment. "George doesn't mind the ceremonial side of his job. In fact, he looks upon meeting with the Boy Scouts, Girl Scouts, Beauty Queens, or whatever as a welcome relief. What he does mind is a whole day's schedule of that kind of thing." Romney has always considered all accomplishments a race against time. He is intent on the job at hand and always has a business goal in his head. He is not one to make polite chitchat. "We see too much of the attitude 'take it easy, goof off, enjoy yourself," he often says.[5]

The keenest insight into what motivates George Romney was shown by Stewart Alsop in 1962: "The more you see of George Romney, the more you realize his religion is the key to the man. If he does something unusual, you can be pretty sure he's just doing what the *Book of Mormon* says."[6] Romney himself, writing in a February 15, 1959, Detroit *Free Press* article, expounds his religious reliance: "My religion is my most precious possession. It teaches me the purpose of life and answers life's greatest questions: where we come from, why we are here, and where we are going. It provides me with yardsticks for life based upon eternal values."[7]

In his usual commencement address the Governor typically serves up this three-part recipe for success: "Search diligently, pray always, and be believing." First, he asks students to step into life and work hard. Second, he tells them to pray, and that prayer is no substitute for work. "Prayer," he says, "is a means used by people who have worked so hard that they find defeat unbearable." Last, he advises them to have faith in their decisions once they have been made. The advice can be traced to one of the Mormon resolutions—the *Doctrine and Covenants:* "Search diligently, pray always, and be believing, and all things shall work together for your good."[8] It is not uncommon for Romney to pre-

face a remark with, "The Bible tells us . . ." Oftentimes the Bible
he is speaking of is the *Book of Mormon.*

Second only to his religion in his family. His lovely wife,
Lenore, is without doubt his most treasured earthly possession as
he himself points out: "I crossed the continent six times just to be
in her dust. It was the best sale of my life when I convinced her to
become my wife." His enthusiasm for a happy home life is
contagious. Shortly after the Romneys were married, the Governor
came home from work with his face all aglow. When he saw his
wife in a sad mood, his broad smile faded away. "I can't possibly
stand for you not to be cheerful," he said, touching her shoulders.
Realizing that his happiness, as he said, depended on her, Mrs.
Romney promised herself "that ours was going to be a cheerful
family in a home he would adore to come home to."[9] After all
these years he will go to almost any lengths to spend the night
at home with his wife and family.

The family has always seemed to Romney an important
nucleus in shaping a youthful personality. "If you put the man
together right, the rest will take care of itself," he says; and while
his own children were growing up, he made sure that they got the
needed love and attention. Every Monday night was set aside as
family night, when members would sit and talk, sing, pray, and
pop corn. In 1966 he went so far as to urge a series of "strengthening family ties" conferences on a statewide basis. "Family problems
are the cause of many of our other public problems," he reasoned.
"The family is the basic unit in society, and when one family in
three is broken up, many other troubles follow. There is an
obvious need to reverse the trend."[10]

His home is his castle, and he enjoys the privacy of it
to the fullest. At home his public world vanishes, and he is
able to relax completely, often in slacks, slippers, and a long-
sleeved sweater. He enjoys talking with his children and grand-
children. He likes to give presents and sometimes celebrates
his birthday by giving the whole family gifts. Both of his sons-
in-law received Rambler station wagons in 1962.

George Romney is also a very able handyman and sportsman.
He can cook (he makes his own breakfast when rising early and

likes Cream of Wheat). He is an excellent carpenter, mechanic, painter, gardener, and landscape designer (witness the shrubbery around his Swiss-chalet home). He is a good dancer. He swims, golfs, rides, and plays ping-pong—only if time permits, which it usually doesn't.

Most of these homey activities have been omitted on account of demands on the Governor's time. Lenore Romney says that the transition from business to politics worked a great hardship on usual family patterns in general and on a husband-wife level in particular. "Probably the most difficult thing for me as a woman was the fact that everyone owned my husband. Everybody wanted a piece of him. When he went on a trip, for instance, it used to be that he and I would sort of chat together on the plane and get off and maybe go to a theater. But that has completely changed. When we're on a plane, either a stewardess or someone else is kneeling down beside him or kids are getting autographs. And when we get to where we're going, there are reporters there. I'm constantly trying to find out where he is going to be, and I often end up in another car and wonder when he's going to be back at the hotel. He's constantly sending me messages and trying to keep me informed, but it isn't the same. We could be dancing on the dance floor as we did right after the first campaign—we went to California for a week—and women would come up and dance with him, leaving me standing there on the floor."

Over the years Romney has contracted a number of nicknames. In high school he was called Gas. As the leading proponent of the compact car he became known as The Giant Killer. At his Ontario cottage he is known simply as The Brick. The latter name is fitting for an older man who is at least as active as men twenty-five years his junior. To caddies on the Bloomfield Hills golf course next to his home he is known as The Ghost, because he plays at wee hours in the morning when no one else is on the grounds. There are few people who are allowed to use these forms of familiarity, however, and it is rare for someone to address him as George. Most aides and pressmen refer to him as Governor when in his presence.

Romney is a "big ham" to those who don't like him, but he is thoughtful and compassionate to those who do. Once while at American Motors in 1958, he broke into tears while condemning excessive concentration of power in business and unions.[11] Another time he returned to England to visit with friends he had made while a missionary. Such things as soap and candy bars were hard to get, so he took along a generous supply and really enjoyed playing Santa. When he goes to Utah, it is not at all uncommon for him to call old friends and ask how they are, and the Governor will often go out of his way to search for salt and pepper shakers for one of his two maids, Mrs. Elizabeth Boyd. (She now owns over three hundred sets.)

A most telling incident occurred after the 1964 Goldwater rally in Detroit's Cobo Hall. It involved seating arrangements. After he had shaken hands with numerous supporters, Romney and his party of four (Mrs. Romney, Scott Romney, Don Faber, and a young graduate student from Purdue) made their way to the white Rambler. Jay Kennedy, one of the Governor's bodyguards, would drive; but where would the five passengers sit? Without a moment's hesitation George Romney slid to the center of the front seat, over the hump, and Mrs. Romney was given the extra leg room on the right front side. It was really quite a sight, the Governor of Michigan sitting hunched with his elbows on his knees in the middle of the small car. The Purdue student mused, "This Romney is really quite a guy!"

And the basic goodness and humility come across to the voter. Louis Cook captured the effervescent good will in 1962: "George Romney looks and acts very much like a type of fellow who would gladly help little boys put together their electric trains and assist elderly ladies across busy intersections. He puts out good will as naturally as a spring does cool water."[12] His image is enhanced further by his abstemious personal habits. He has long been identified as a man who will not compromise on his fundamental beliefs and convictions. It is one of the blood-racingest expressions in the English language when Romney takes a firm stand, with his determined jaw put forth, his face taut, and his right hand raised, to aver, "To this point in my life I have not compromised any of my moral principles, and I'm not going to start now, no matter what the prize!" He says it with total conviction, and most folks who have seen him say it believe he means it.

Even John F. Kennedy was impressed by the downright goodness of Governor Romney. Paul B. Fay, Jr., reported in the August, 1966, issue of *McCall's* that Romney was the one man Kennedy did not want to run against in 1964. "That fellow could be tough," Kennedy said. "No vice whatsoever, no smoking, no drinking. Imagine someone we know going off for twenty-four hours to fast and meditate, awaiting a message from the Lord on whether to run or not to run. Does that sound like one of the old gang?"[13] No, it did not. Is Romney too good to be true? Are there any chinks in his armor?

One of the most serious charges leveled against Romney is that his temper is short, that he is sometimes incapable of making rational decisions. Naturally, the Democrats have attempted to build this into a glaring issue. Democratic Deputy Attorney General Leon Cohan has this to say regarding Romney's emotional balance: "I know that LBJ is supposed to be very excitable, and I've read up on some of the other presidents, but never have I read anything approaching what I have seen with my own eyes. On the basis of what I've seen, I wouldn't want the nation's future to be in his [Romney's] hands." Is there any truth to the charge?

As was pointed out in Chapter Four, Romney's temper was one factor that kept him from becoming Con-Con president—but it was only one factor. For another, he was regarded as a marginal Republican by many of the Old Guard. Then, too, he was not a politician, had no real knowledge of constitution writing; and many felt he simply wouldn't know how to lead a political group.

During the 1962 campaign Romney visited the Detroit *Free Press* and submitted to a group interview. When he accused a reporter of being biased against him, Managing Editor Frank Angelo would have none of it and told Romney it was "a damn lie." Romney was offended and promptly stormed out. In the hallway momentarily he calmed down, and he came back for more questioning.[14]

During that first gubernatorial campaign Romney crossed

lances with August Scholle in a bitter winner-take-all joust. Here both knights had a reputation for a low boiling point. Each was expected to need his beaver, as the gauntlets were surely going to fly. The crowd of more than a hundred cheered, each for his own, as Scholle and Romney battled for the microphone: "If I lied, you lied," said Scholle, raising his voice. "These are your figures!" "You're not lying," cooed Romney, "you're just fabricating the facts!" "No, no, you said I was lying," the Michigan AFL-CIO president maintained. The debate was a toss-up, but George Romney had protected his greaves—he had passed the temper test![15]

During the 1964 campaign Romney got into an altercation with a runt of a laborer in Flint. The little man egged Romney on by calling him every name in the book. Romney took it pretty well for a while, but the workman became so filthy and vulgar that Romney turned beet-red and took a step toward him. His lips curled, and his voice was tense. "You're a despicable, dirty little man," he said as his state trooper stepped between them. Observers felt that not only had Romney held his temper well in view of the torrents of abuse, but indeed, he had taken it better than they would have!

During his four years as governor he has learned a great deal in terms of temper display. A real mark of his amateur status for the first year or two was that he wanted to answer every charge leveled against him. He was offended at every negative word and wanted to "set the record straight." The very fact that he found it necessary to defend himself made it appear that many of the charges contained a germ of truth. Gradually he learned that his counter-arguments would be heard more clearly if he answered only the important charges. As William Kulsea noted in 1965, "the education of a political pro was taking place."[16]

The only people who see the Romney wrath (which he refers to as "intensity") are those who come into daily contact with him: staff, legislators, and reporters. In early December, 1965, Romney and Zolton Ferency were commenting on open-housing legislation in an aide's office when emotions began to flare in full view of the Greater Lansing Coordinating Council on Human Rights. "You let me finish," the Governor said several times to Ferency.

Finally he brushed by Ferency standing in the doorway and strode on out. That afternoon he was asked about the "shoving match" that had occurred in the morning, and he erupted. "I did not have a shoving match with Mr. Ferency. I did not touch Mr. Ferency except to walk out of the room when the meeting was over. To call it a shoving match," said the Governor, becoming more intense, "is a complete inaccuracy."[17]

Yet there are times when his intensity can easily be taken for anger. During the 1964 campaign Romney was barnstorming the lower-thumb area of Michigan and pulled into Algonac. He (like most gubernatorial candidates) did not know the names of the many local candidates and depended on an aide to write their names on a small pad. When it came time during his brief talk to mention the local candidates, he looked down at the pad, but nothing was forthcoming. The handwriting was so bad that he couldn't read it. He looked down coldly from the platform and told his aide to write the names more clearly. "I'll do it next time," the aide promised. "No, you won't," snapped Romney, "you'll do it here!" The aide was embarrassed, but Romney knew that it was a one-shot appearance, and he had to ask for support for the local candidates right then. There is no doubt that the aide thought Romney was angry, not just intense.

The distinction between his anger and his intensity is a hard one to make for most people, and it is a fault that Romney clearly recognizes. "People tend to confuse my intensity for anger. This apparently is a family trait. It even took three or four years for Lenore to get over that."[18] There are those who have worked near him for long periods who wish they knew the difference. As John Conde, a Romney speech writer for several years at American Motors, comments, "One thing you learn early is that you don't volunteer negative reactions."

Even if he is angry and not just intense, Romney has a habit that shows him to be bighearted. Shortly after a heated exchange he will look up the other person, put his arm around him, and apologize in an oblique way that eases working relations and usually wipes the incident from the mind. That being done, Romney holds no grudges, and indeed forgets that the incident ever happened.

Another supposedly negative Romney trait is his stubbornness in refusing to admit that he is wrong. He can, in fact, be most determined, but he will admit his error if he finds a good reason for reversing a previous opinion. Back in January of 1959 he admitted that he had erred in assuming that the Detroit school system was asking for money needlessly: "I went into this study with the idea that we could get the things we need through more efficiency. I have now reluctantly concluded that we must increase Detroit school taxes."[19]

In a December, 1961, New York speech Romney accused General Motors of intending "to use its facilities abroad for importation of components into the United States." On January 3, he admitted that in the verbatim account of his press-conference statement on December 15 there were serious inaccuracies: "I was wrong in these specific assertions," he said.

After the 1962 Con-Con "accommodation agreement," Romney acknowledged that he had goofed in disclosing the plan. "It's my own fault . . . I've learned a lesson. We were so intent on trying to arrive at an understanding and a desire to produce a better document that we didn't provide the proper reporting of the whole development to the press and everybody in the state."[20]

One of the most disputed Romney traits is his sense of humor. Some commentaries—from people who should know—would lead the average person to think that humor is not a personal plus with the Governor. Howard Hallas, number one speech writer for Romney at American Motors for eight years, gives this opinion: "He has a good sense of humor, but is just not a good storyteller. He gets so wound up he runs right through the punch line." Richard Evans, one of the twelve Mormon apostles, sheds more light: "George has a good sense of humor, but will go only so far when laughing at himself." John Conde adds that although he "appreciates a sense of humor in other people, he lacks humor within himself." Again, the testimony seems to be contradictory.

Although it would be difficult to fill a volume on the Romney wit, he does like to tell a good humorous story. One of his most successful concerns his father-in-law, Harold A. LaFount. LaFount had moved to Washington after being appointed to the Federal Radio Commission (now the Federal Communications Commission) and thought it would be proper to thank President Coolidge personally. He contacted the White House and was told by the President's secretary, Everett Saunders, that he would have to appear in formal morning clothes. "Now," Romney says, "my father-in-law didn't have any formal morning clothes, so he rushed to the tailor and paid a hundred and seventy-five dollars to have a tailcoat and striped trousers made." When LaFount got to the White House the next morning and he was ushered into the President's office, Coolidge was working at his desk. Finally the President looked up. Harold LaFount thanked him for the appointment, and Coolidge said nine words: "When in doubt, read the law. Good day, sir!"

He is at his best, however, with ad-lib comments. When involved in Con-Con in 1961, he was putting every minute of his time to use. He was serving as Stake President of the Detroit branch of the Church of Jesus Christ of Latter-Day Saints, running an automobile company, and playing constitutional author. One day as he breezed into Lansing with a bulging briefcase, he dashed from his chauffeured automobile into the Jack Tar Hotel, and someone asked if he was pressed for time. "Oh, it's not so bad," Romney replied, "I've been so busy that I've had to drop all my activities except this convention, my company, my church, and my family."

Midway through Con-Con, Romney announced that he was considering running for Governor, and the American Motors board of directors suggested that he should not enter the race. A reporter asked him if this acted as a dampener. Romney paused for just a moment, his forehead knitted, and this answer came forth: "Well, did you ever stop to think how I might feel if they *wanted* me to get into it?"

Soon his affirmative decision was made, and he made the most of the fact that he was stepping out of a million-dollar-a-year job (salary, bonus, and stock options) to seek the few-thousand-dollar position as governor. He always got a roar or round of applause when he referred to himself as "an unemployed businessman looking for a new job" or when he made the casual observation, "I don't know why I got into this thing; I've already got a fairly good job!"

And the Governor's humor is not lacking when he encounters the enemy. On a Grand Rapids factory tour in 1962, Romney encountered a band of ardent Swainson supporters who fired a variety of point-blank remarks in his direction. One female employee carried a large sign reading, "Georgie Porgie is all through." She walked to within a few inches of the Governor and leaned forward so that she was practically breathing in his face. "Hello, millionaire," she gibed. Without batting an eyelash, Romney coolly commented, "Why, I'm poverty-stricken compared to John Kennedy!"

When Massachusetts Attorney General Edward W. Brooke visited Michigan in October of 1964, Romney told a Highland Park Republican rally, "Massachusetts has the kind of attorney general we would like to have. I would be willing to make a trade—and toss in the entire Democratic Administrative Board to boot!" The remark met with thundering approval.

In February of 1964 Governor and Mrs. Romney were departing for a three-week vacation (their first since the 1963 inauguration), and Democratic legislators criticized this move severely. "It's a bad time to take a vacation," Democratic Senator Raymond Dzendzel argued, "budget hearings are on and we've got to take care of the budget before we get into other spending bills." But again Romney showed himself to be well equipped with words. "I'm pleased that the Democrats feel my presence here is so vital," he smirked.[21]

When in 1960 Romney was serving as chairman at a Citizens for Michigan board of directors meeting, the discussion turned to required qualifications for study-committee chairmen, and a former president of the Michigan League of Women Voters went on record for not making the standards too rigorous. "After all," she said, "a chairman doesn't have to be a great brain." Loud laughter worked its way through the group as all eyes turned toward Romney. He had been laughing just as loudly as the others, but stopped to say: "It didn't hurt so much to hear the remark as to hear how everyone roared."[22]

He has mockingly asked for "aid to underdeveloped parties" when noting the Democratic party had finance troubles. And he has hit back at Alabama's Governor George Wallace. In July of 1966, Wallace was quoted as saying that Romney couldn't carry Alabama if he ran for president in 1968. Noting that Wallace might himself become a 1968 candidate for the White House, Romney mused over Wallace's comment that the southern governor would "do well in Michigan." "Good," said Romney. "When they come to Michigan to run, I'll run Lenore against Lurleen."

Romney's typical speaking habits include a humorous pattern. He will always begin with a little joke or two before getting down to business. More often than not he will use jokes that have become quite stale to those who have often heard him speak. Many of his campaign speeches in 1962, 1964, and 1966 were prefaced by the same stories.

One of his favorite openings concerns the politician who is being heckled by a voter. "I wouldn't vote for you if you were St. Peter himself!" the citizen shouts. "That's all right," says the politician. "If I were St. Peter, you wouldn't even be in my district!" The joke is a crowd pleaser, and Romney tells it well; but most jokes have got to be tested before he will try them before a crowd, and even if he plans a new one the old and familiar stories have a way of slipping out anyhow.

And there is more of Romney's speaking that varies no more than the humor—the quotations that brand him as the moralist that he is. These quotations, for the most part, may be traced back to his years at American Motors. They are pretty pieces of language that Romney feels get at the core of the democratic process and the Continuing American Revolution. They are often criticized by intellectuals as trite generalizations, but Romney has a way of putting the commonplace into living expressions that make the blood pound. He can take a tired expression as "Honesty is the best policy" and make you believe it.

Some of the key Romney quotations you will be hearing as the gray-haired evangelist makes his way toward Washington are: "Power tends to corrupt, and absolute power corrupts absolutely" (Lord Aston); "To surrender what you are, and live without belief, is more terrible than dying" (Maxwell Anderson in *Joan of Arc*); "The only thing necessary for the triumph of evil is for good men to do nothing" (Edmund Burke); "Our chief want in life is somebody who shall make us do what we can" (Emerson); "There is one thing stronger than all the armies in the world: and that is an idea whose time has come" (Hugo); "If we could first know where we are and whither we are tending, we could better judge what to do and how to do it" (Lincoln); "Nothing is more needed than a consummate power of articulation, both in thought and action, with respect to the fundamental things" (Charles Malik); "Our spirit of enjoyment was greater than our spirit of sacrifice. We wanted more than we wanted to give. We spared effort, and we met disaster" (Marshal Pétain at the fall of France); "All things are ready if our minds be so" (Shakespeare); "Not by reason of force, but by force of reason" (Max Ways); "The most powerful force in the world is the spontaneous co-operation of a free people" (Woodrow Wilson).

From Thornton Wilder's *Skin of Our Teeth*, Romney selects these words: "I know that every good and excellent thing in the world stands moment by moment on the razor edge of danger and must be fought for." From Whitman's *Leaves of Grass* he recites words similar in meaning: "It is provided in the essence of things that from any fruition of success, no matter what, shall come forth something to make a greater struggle necessary." From a speech made by Daniel Webster before the U.S. Senate in 1834 he has committed these words to memory: "Nothing will ruin the country if the people themselves will undertake its safety; and nothing can save it if they leave that safety in any hands but their own."

A favorite Shakespearean quotation is from *Julius Caesar*: "There is a tide in the affairs of men, / Which, taken at the flood, leads on to fortune; / Omitted, all the voyage of their life / Is bound in shallows and in miseries. / On such a full sea are we now afloat, / And we must take the current when it serves, / Or lose our ventures." But probably no quotation is more characteristic of Romney the man than what Thomas Jefferson wrote in a letter to William Jarvis in 1820: "I know of no safe depository of the ultimate powers of the society but the people themselves; and if we think them not enlightened enough to exercise their control with a wholesome discretion, the remedy is not to take it from them, but to inform their discretion."

This capsule anthology of Romney quotations provides much more than a choice collection of wise words to the man himself. He has internalized each generalization to such degree that he has become the one offering the counsel, not the great statesmen and authors of yesteryear. To the Governor these wise words embody the guts of the American being.

The philosophy inherent in the handful of favorite quotations would be lackluster indeed if it were not for the forceful speaking of which Romney is capable. He places a high regard on saying things with precisely the right words, and sometimes will spend hours in his favorite chair working with pencil and sketch pad, deleting, adding, clarifying, specifying. It is not uncommon for him to call on his speech writers at odd hours of the night to report a new idea or phrase that he thinks ought to be utilized, and important speeches go through several drafts.

After hours of work the Governor will sometimes throw away the script and speak extemporaneously (this upsets his speech writers, but they have come to realize that Romney is much better when speaking off the cuff). "I'm not a very effective speaker unless I believe in something strongly myself," he says, and he couldn't be more correct. In general, the more emotionally wound up he gets in what he's saying, the better he says it, and if he's on familiar ground, has a good audience, and is in the proper frame of mind, you won't find a much better public speaker anywhere.

When Romney is "right," he becomes a highly convincing speaker. He makes a good first impression, and that impression does not grow stale quickly. It is hard not to believe what he is saying. His delivery is dynamic and tense. He is forceful, energetic, magnetic. His sincerity comes through almost overwhelmingly. His voice is deep and full. His facial expressions change constantly, and his eyes seem to pierce right through you. At times he will lean forward and drop his volume to make a special point; then again, he will plant his feet as if to brace himself for a fight with words.

What, then, is Governor George Romney really like? He is independent, stubborn, hard-working, persuasive, courageous, quick-tempered, generous, religious, humorous, statesmanlike, gentle, firm, warlike, peace-loving, determined, yielding, a family man. He runs the gamut of descriptive language. Probably the best phrase was served up by the Governor himself during his first campaign: "George Romney is far from perfect, and he has some faults. But every day he battles to do better tomorrow."[23]

Romney's Image of America

THOSE who think that the New Frontier slogan originated with John Fitzgerald Kennedy will be surprised to learn that twelve years before the phrase became the rallying cry of the national Democratic party, Romney used it in a Founders Day Address at the University of Utah.[1] And Romney went Kennedy several better. He spoke of seven frontiers: waging peace through the United Nations, correcting outdated economic policies, curtailing federal encroachment, curbing excessive industrial and labor power, stabilizing the American economy, mobilizing more citizen participation in politics, and activating more teamwork.

Now, a generation later, Romney is still battling for these same frontiers. His goals for America's destiny have not deviated from his 1949 statement. What has changed is the working vocabulary used to expound his beliefs, quotations from famous statesmen who support his ideas, and the dynamism with which he presents his program.

Ever since Romney's name was placed in serious contention for the 1968 presidential nomination, some factions have raised questions concerning his political depth. Does he have any new ideas? Has he analyzed the *unique* American system of government? Does he have any new solutions for "old problems"?

George Romney has learned his political lessons quickly: he has a good grasp of the American political and economic systems; and he has definite ideas as to where this country should be going. He is a much deeper thinker than most people give him credit for being.

Long before 1949, Romney had come to grips with a basic

problem confounding the nation's leaders: the necessity of identifying national problems and trends. Taking the words of Abraham Lincoln to heart, "If we could first know where we are and whither we are tending, we could better judge what to do and how to do it," he continually read, discussed, and recorded personal experiences, crosschecking for answers to such questions as: Where are we? Where are we headed? Are there any roadblocks? Are we headed in the right directions? Why not? What can be done to change trends or speed development? And by 1949 Romney had isolated his seven frontiers. During his years at American Motors he proceeded to build upon this bedrock, and three major themes emerged in the late fifties as he discussed far more than American Motors policy before audiences all over the United States. Romney's speeches made people think; and this made him think too, more deeply.

All this was prepolitics. In 1962, when he decided to run for governor of Michigan, his speeches were naturally more concerned with state problems than with national affairs. It was not until early 1965 that Romney again began developing the national plans that he had been advocating so diligently before entering the political arena, and the old Romney themes of the Unfinished American Revolution, Excessive Concentration of Power, and Individual Responsibility once again asserted themselves. In the late 1950's Romney was well known as the Rambler man who had made it big, but few people knew of his personal image of America.

Of the three basic themes, the roots of Romney's philosophy are deepest in his concept of the Unfinished American Revolution. "I believe that the Declaration of Independence and the Constitution are divinely inspired documents, written by men especially raised up by their Creator for that purpose. I believe that the hand of God has shaped, guided, and preserved this nation. I believe that God has a purpose for this nation, and a plan for every individual in it," Romney says.[2] He believes that the world has been the object of only one authentic revolution, that started by Jesus Christ; and he views our Declaration of Independence and Constitution as an extension of that revolution. Why? Because men and women had fought and bled for centuries for spiritual freedom and the separation of church and state. Americans, therefore, are the living benefactors.

He believes that all of our material wealth and abundance has come about as a by-product of four principles contained within these twin documents of our heritage: our belief in God, acknowledgement of our divine origin, and recognition of our brotherhood with mankind; delineation of a policy of government by consent, complete with a system of checks and balances to ensure maintenance of that policy; the concept of universal education, that our citizens shall be able to render an informed opinion; and the principle of economic freedom in choice and opportunity.[3] Though all of these convictions were stated in principle, it would take years, even centuries, to fully perfect our system. Starting with a base of religious freedom, the principles of political, economic, and social freedom would need time to evolve.

Reviewing our progress on the political front, Romney traces the development in this country of the right to vote. When the Constitution was adopted, in 1786, the franchise was limited to male property owners, with the result that only 5 per cent of the people could vote. Gradually the right was extended to male non-property owners, and with the passage of women's suffrage in 1922, the voter ratio jumped to three in ten. Negroes did not gain full voting rights until 1964. Thus our revolution continues. What there was in political principle took nearly two hundred years to reach its present state of realization. Romney believes that our home-front revolution will not have been completed until each and every American is in full possession of his four freedoms: religious, political, economic, and social.

But Romney envisions far more than merely taking care of America. To him our principles are universal in application and can be accepted by all peoples, tailored to fit their cultures, and still yield the same results—freedom from bondage. Although we have not completed the job at home, we must start spreading the foundations of our economic abundance, not just the wealth itself. "It is our destiny to aid men everywhere in freeing themselves from religious, political, economic, and social bondage of all forms. Where are we? Just in the early stages of the Unfinished American Revolution."[4]

It is his further conviction that we are locked in a struggle for survival, the fourth in our country's history. The first battle for survival was the Revolution itself, the second occurred when it became apparent that the Articles of Confederation would be too weak and the Constitution was devised, the third was the Civil War. But the struggle is in a new form this time. The world is gathering around two poles: democracy and communism. He cites the rapid growth of communism since World War II and illustrates this with a comment by Dr. Charles Malik:

> The Communist is a man who has received a tradition and honors it profoundly and believes in it and therefore is willing to propagate it. You [Americans] are a bit different. Many of you don't know your own tradition. My deepest fear . . . is that you don't know the infinite values that you have at the basis of your own civilization, and you don't believe in them enough to put them strongly to the rest of the world.[5]

Malik, whom Romney regards as the most perceptive non-American speaking on America, is a Christian Arab educated at the American University in Beirut. He is a past-president of the U.N. General Assembly and taught several years at Harvard.

Another non-American authority Romney relies on frequently is Father R. L. Bruckberger, a Frenchman who in 1958 wrote *Image of America*. The most often quoted passage:

> Americans, return to the first seed you sowed, to that glorious Declaration of Independence in which, for the first time, the rights of man . . . were explicitly defined and defended. . . . What ill luck, how great a misfortune it is for all, that it should be the ideology of the Communist Manifesto, and not that of your Declaration of Independence, which is now conquering so large a part of the world. You Americans have been too ready to look upon the Declaration of Independence as a document designed for yourselves alone, and not for other nations. How fatal an error. . . .[6]

Romney concludes that we are losing the struggle because we do not understand the spiritual, moral, political, and economic principles that made us what we are. There is too much fuzzy thinking about our unique society. Even those who should be articulate in describing our system are sometimes found lacking. One of the Governor's favorite illustrations of this is a story about General Eisenhower; intending no personal affront, he repeats it merely to show that fuzzy thinking is a significant problem. At a July, 1957, press conference, President Eisenhower related that at the end of World War II he was confronted by Russia's Marshal Zhukov with the argument that communism was more idealistic than democracy because while democracy lets everyone do whatever he wishes, communism requires each individual to subordinate himself to the state. Eisenhower's response? "When you run up against that kind of thing . . . you run against arguments that almost leave you breathless . . . you don't know how to meet them."[7]

Setting these examples before us, Romney explains how our revolution differs from all others. Whereas the European revolutions consisted of conflicts over who was going to rule the state, with the state still ruling the people, our revolution placed ultimate power over the state in the hands of the people. Ours, therefore, is unique—the only authentic revolution.

Next, Romney attempts to isolate the reasons why Americans seem to lack conviction in their revolutionary principles, and careful reflection has yielded this conclusion: "I think this lack of conviction and understanding results from the fact that a growing number of Americans are suddenly finding themselves enjoying all the good things of our way of life without the sense of having earned them; therefore they do not understand them nor do they appreciate them. I am convinced we do need to rediscover the basic principles of Americanism."[8]

His solution is to educate the average American in the meaning of his country's founding principles and ultimate God-given goal. A favorite Romney device is supplying an answer for the Zhukov challenge: "The facts are that we are not free to do whatever we want. The fundamental premise of Americanism is that we are children of a Creator and that we have a supreme obligation, which we cannot escape, to comply with the principles enunciated by our Creator as we individually understand them. Furthermore, as children of God we are also brothers and sisters. We also believe we have the obligation to obey the laws of the federal, state, and local government that we created to preserve order and freedom under law. The obligations that we have in freedom make the obligations of the communists look puny indeed."[9]

Whatever other subject Romney may be dealing with, his underlying belief in America's destiny should be remembered. This worldwide vision forms the basis for all his other themes. Without this base his ideas might not make sense. With it, they reveal a clear-cut philosophy of American destiny.

A thorough understanding of Romney's second major theme, Excessive Concentration of Power, will entail a fresh orientation toward the American economic system. Romney believes that the American people as a whole are "woefully ignorant of the unique character of our economy and the revolutionary changes which have taken place within it."[10] Most are so uninformed that they still describe their economy as capitalistic, and Michigan's governor believes this is unfortunate, for two reasons. First, in our battle for the minds of men in the developing nations of the world we help the communists by perpetuating a word that has acquired derogatory meanings and connotations. Second, "capitalism" is at least sixty years out of date in terms of how our economy operates.

In support of point number one, Romney tries to warn us concerning the real meaning of the word "capitalism." He cites Karl Marx (although not by name) as the first person to speak of it as a system in which the masses are exploited for the benefit of a few. Even our present-day dictionaries define capitalism in Marxist terms, Romney adds. Typical examples are *Webster's New International Dictionary*: "The power or influence of capital, as when in the hands of a few"; and *Funk and Wagnalls College Standard*: "A system that favors the concentration of capital in the hands of a few." "By continuing to use the enemy's terms to describe our system," Romney says, "we are inadvertently but foolishly helping the Soviets sharpen a major propaganda tool for use against us."[11]

The second reason that "capitalism" should not be used has reference to the famous Khrushchev boast "We will bury you."

Pointing out that this was an economic threat, Romney maintains that Khrushchev had set himself an impossible task, because we have succeeded in burying the capitalistic system ourselves. With the rise of the industrial revolution, economic power concentrated more and more in the hands of a few. But toward the end of the nineteenth century, with the passage of the antitrust laws, we stopped our drift toward European-type cartelism and capitalism. By dividing economic power, just as we had divided political power, we put the consumer in the driver's seat. Our economy should therefore be described as Consumeristic." Just as we vote for a person in the political sense, we vote economically by buying a certain product rather than another. Since business seeks our vote, we receive goods suited to our taste, of better quality, and at lower prices. Benefits are not for a few at the expense of the masses, but for all.

Taking this "consumeristic" label as his point of departure, Romney delves into the intricacies of our economy, explaining that we have proved four economic principles: competition, cooperation, distribution of economic progress, and reward based on contribution.

The principle of competition allows enterprises to compete with one another for customers. It offers people a choice and allows them to rule the market place. The antitrust laws were passed so that monopolies could not dictate what customers should receive. Since competition in its purest form would produce jungle-law conditions, it behooves businessmen to cooperate voluntarily to solve problems relating to their industries. Thus auto safety is a common concern of Ford and Chrysler, while each would still vie for larger sales.

Romney credits Henry Ford I with thoroughly establishing the third principle—distribution of economic progress among customers, workers, and owners. Ford was the first to really share progress with customers and workers, by building a dependable low-priced automobile, giving cash rebates, and doubling workers' wages to five dollars a day. In 1922 Ford's stockholders took him to court because they felt that profits should be shared with no one other than investors. Ford lost the trial, but he bought his stockholders out and continued along the lines of progress sharing. He soon proved that allowing the workers to make enough to become customers was the biggest boon to business possible.[12]

Last, the principle of reward based on contribution provides incentive. Those who invest must see a possibility of making money. They take a great economic risk and therefore are entitled to great financial reward.

Put the four principles together, and you have Romney's idea of the unique operation of the American economy. It is a consumeristic system that has evolved from the principles stated in our Declaration of Independence and Constitution.

But do not be deceived into thinking that the consumeristic society has evolved completely. It has not. Furthermore, it has not been easy to get it as far as we have. Powerful interests have always tried to dominate our economy. Sometimes they have succeeded. (In the early thirties business and industry succeeded in passing the Smoot-Hawley tariff bill in exchange for the McNary-Haugen Bill, and farm subsidization began. And in 1935 the Wagner Act unleashed union power.) At other times they have clashed with powerful presidents—Roosevelt, Taft, Wilson. These men led the antitrust crusade that resulted in the Clayton Act of 1914. And the battle for control is not over.

Speaking out in February, 1958, before the subcommittee on Antitrust and Monopoly of the U.S. Senate, Romney named four indications that our consumeristic society was in danger:

1. Since World War II we have had a periodic repetition of the wage-price spiral.
2. The merger of A.F.L. and C.I.O. has increased collaboration between affiliated international unions on collective bargaining, thus further concentrating union power.
3. A mounting attack on our profit-and-loss system has resulted from lack of public understanding, and the use of excessive union power has narrowed profits down to a dangerous level.
4. An increase in business mergers resulting in a decline in the number of separate firms in most basic industries has increased economic concentration of industrial power.[13]

Teeing off on problem number one, Romney says that inflation is only the symptom of a much deeper problem: excessive concentration of power. "We don't even have true inflation," he says. "True inflation exists where too much money is chasing too few goods." He maintains that our inflation has been artificially created by three factors: the "compensatory theory" adopted in the 1930's, the development of a labor monopoly and greater industrial power concentration, and excessive reliance on monetary controls.[14] Singling out the major area of the three, Romney attacks the excessive power concentration in both unions and management. "There is a fundamental conflict in our economic policy. Our labor laws are based upon the principle of monopoly, and our industrial laws are based upon the principle of competition. If the national labor policy is going to permit unions to concentrate their power without limitation, then you can't keep a competitive system because manufacturers and employers are going to have to organize their power to offset that power."[15]

Being still more specific, he designates excessive concentration of union power as the number one cause of inflation and for proof points out that wage and benefit settlements since 1955 have exceeded the increase in national productivity. If labor makes up 80 per cent of cost, as Romney maintains, then prices will rise sharply as labor goes up, up, up. The result is runaway inflation. And union monopoly makes it possible for collective bargaining to become collective bludgeoning. A case in point: the United Auto Workers versus one of the Big Three.

UAW bargains on a one-company-at-a-time basis in order to make maximum use of its power. The union presents its requests to one company, and if demands are not met, it strikes. Knowing that competitors will make economic hay while their company is idle, management must give, give, give. After one company has given in, the process is repeated. But the price isn't the same further down the line. Since the smaller companies can least afford a strike, they are forced to pay additional benefits (pattern-plus bargaining). Because of its leadership position the UAW pattern then influences bargaining in all unions connected with what goes into the production of the automobile (chain-reaction bargaining). And this sets off an inflationary spiral!

In the long run there is an even greater threat posed by this excessive concentration of union power: unions and employers can shut down an industry that is vital to the economic welfare of the entire nation. We have but to witness the national airline strike in 1966 to realize how serious such power concentration can be.

What, then, should be done about this excessive union power? Should we offset it with industry-wide bargaining? No, says Romney, because it would simply accelerate power concentration into two national blocs: union versus industry. If that happened, there would be "price fixing," and the federal government would step in. That would be bad because it would stifle our consumeristic system.

Romney, therefore, makes these proposals for changing our national labor policy: a combination of national unions for common bargaining purposes should be prohibited; unions affiliated with a national union representing workers of a single large company should be permitted to combine in collective-bargaining demands; within prescribed geographical limits, affiliated unions should be allowed to combine bargaining efforts when employers have less than 10,000 workers, but those representing more than 10,000 workers of a single employer should not be allowed to combine; and no other restrictions should be placed on union cooperation. His ultimate goal is to prevent excessive concentration of power that would destroy the competitive basis of our economy.[16]

Romney urges labor and management to work together as a team. Workers should come to realize that the company can pay them what they demand only for as long as the company is making a reasonable profit. Company profits must rise before any more personal gains for the workers will be possible. In the long view, then, when a company is successful, it will be possible for employees to get better wages and benefits. The moral: instead of trying to get a larger slice of the pie for yourself, help make the pie larger so that everyone may have a larger slice!

Moving to the area of industrial concentration, Romney believes that our antitrust laws are inadequate for the intended purpose of ensuring a minimum number of competitive companies in our basic industries. First, they are too slow. (It took twenty years to terminate and disperse the Aluminum Company of America monopoly). Second, the law makes it mandatory to show that an industry intended an evil purpose or actually brought about an un-desirable result. Intent is hard to prove, and, in truth, can be proved only by demonstrating that undesirable effects have oc-curred. Romney holds that this is unfortunate and warns that "power corrupts, and absolute power corrupts absolutely."

To ensure adequate competition in our basic industries, Rom-ney proposes the principle of "economic birth." He visualizes the process as a modernization of the antitrust laws. He suggests that limitations should be placed "on firms whose size, integration, and financial strength make possible the domination of a national mar-ket." How? "When any one firm in a basic industry, such as the automobile business, exceeds a specific percentage of total indus-try sales over a specified period of time, it shall be required by law to propose to an administrative agency a plan of divestiture that will bring its percentage of sales below the specified level. Where a firm is engaged in more than one industry, the maximum per-centage of total industry sales should be fixed by law at a point lower than the percentage to be fixed for companies operating in only a single basic industry."[17] When he originally introduced the plan in 1958, Romney suggested a figure of 35 per cent as a basis for discussion. He sees that percentage as a minimum; he would rather err on the side of too much competition than too little.

The reasoning behind such a plan goes something like this. In-dustrial concentration in the basic industries has narrowed down to a few survivors in our competitive system, and the risk is now so great that no new company is likely to enter the market (for ex-ample, it would take a minimum of five billion dollars to form a new automobile company). Thus we must continually break up the most successful company (say, General Motors) into smaller com-panies (such as Chevrolet, Oldsmobile, and Cadillac).

His system would have several advantages over the existing antitrust laws. It would be faster, would be on a voluntary basis, would allow for a tax break for the new company and would con-tinue to allow for product improvement, lower consumer prices and other consumer benefits. In addition, it would no longer be neces-sary to rely on the factor of self-restraint, which Romney feels is a naive policy. As a case in point, Romney points out that General Motors could sell automobiles for such a low price that at least two of its competitors would be driven from the market. Knowing, however, that they would be faced with antitrust action, they do not improve their product or price to such a degree as to cause this drastic effect. The customers therefore do not get as much as they could; an "improvement drag" exists in our society. If this principle of economic birth were utilized to its fullest, Romney believes, we could produce goods cheaply enough to re-enter and control world markets.

And we should be concerned with world markets. Relating industrial birth and modern union legislation to our unfinished American Revolution, Romney points out that we are an island of prosperity in a hungry world. We need to realize our obligations to feed the rest of the world, because "an approach based on excessive nationalism will not only be self-defeating but possibly harmful, and prevent the development of economic relationships that could prove a pattern for the free world in its coming struggle with a highly integrated communist economic structure."[18]

Romney also proposes a revision of foreign-aid programs. Instead of government handouts, he feels that our aid should be in the form of private investment. The people-to-people and company-to-company relationship would breed fewer resentments and accomplish more. Two steps in the right direction would be management sharing when American investors establish abroad, and "trade bridges" that would allow tariff-free exchange on a company-to-company basis.[19]

The third fundamental Romney theme, individual responsibility, could be considered an offshoot of the excessive-concentration-of-power theme, because it is just that in a different sense. Romney believes that the federal government has gradually been usurping more individual freedom and that the survival of a free America depends on a proper balance among four action routes: the private sector of economic organizations such as business, industry, agriculture, and labor; the independent sector of individual action and voluntary association; the sector of state and local government; and the sector of federal government.

He firmly believes with Lincoln that "the legitimate object of government is to do for the people what needs to be done, but which they cannot, by individual effort, do at all, or do so well for themselves," and has frequently taken issue with the phrase in Lyndon B. Johnson's inaugural address, "A Great Society breeds a great people." This is not the case, Romney insists: it is a great people that makes a great nation. "You've got to start from the bottom up," he says. "We must begin with the moral decay from within," he pleads, quoting Gandhi's "Turn the searchlight inward." Can we build a Great Society on such things as 300,000 broken homes, a divorce rate of one out of three marriages, declining religious convictions, and a weakening moral code? No, these are things that government money cannot eradicate. We must begin by placing more responsibility in ourselves and in the hands of the independent sector as well as in state and local government, because "the moment we stop asking what we can do for ourselves and for each other voluntarily, and start expecting government to do it all—in that moment we have begun to lose our freedom, the source of our greatness."[20]

Romney says that Lincoln recognized and met the major challenge of his time—an excess of state sovereignty that threatened to destroy the Union—and that the problem we face today is the exact opposite. We must seek not to maintain states' rights but to save state and individual responsibilities.

Romney freely admits that many factors leading to more federal power (such as the past necessity to curb the power of the private sector, the great depression, and two world wars) were beyond state control. But one fact stands out in his mind. Looking at past records, it is evident that people have needs and that the federal government will act to meet these needs if individuals and closer units of government do not.

Romney therefore has developed a four-prong program for retrieving responsibilities from the federal government. Since it was developed from a governor's point of view, it deals with what the state can do to encourage power dispersion. States must modernize their constitutions so as to have modern tools for dealing with the problems of the people; keep or restore their fiscal integrity; meet the needs of the people; and most important, encourage citizens to meet their own needs through voluntary and individual efforts.[21]

And the federal drift (which Romney calls Potomac fever) is not slacking off. In 1966 Romney was cautioning against a "new and ominous trend in federal-state relations": federal programs were bypassing state governments and giving poverty funds directly to cities and private organizations. So Romney is not crying wolf.

One harmful effect of federal domination is that it creates personal frustration; people feel that they no longer count. "One of the best-kept secrets of our time is that Americans would rather give themselves to something great and sweat and struggle to obtain it, than to vegetate in pampered ease," he says.[22] He argues further, "People want meaning in their lives." Increasing federal power simply adds to the vacuum.

People must be encouraged to become involved and regain personal respect, he warns. They should realize that through the tool of voluntary cooperation they can be more than a statistic. Pointing to American life on the frontier where life itself depended on person-to-person cooperation, he often supports his position with De Tocqueville's commentary:

> In no country in the world has the principle of association been more successfully used or applied to a greater multitude of objects than in America. Societies are formed . . . to promote the public safety, commerce, industry, morality, and religion. There is no end which the human will despair of attaining through the combined power of individuals united into a society.[23]

Romney often notes Woodrow Wilson's "The most powerful force in the world is the spontaneous cooperation of a free people." Citing personal examples of this terrific force, he adverts to the Automobile Board for War Production, the committee on Detroit school needs, and Citizens for Michigan mentioned in earlier chapters. He defines voluntary cooperation as "a social mechanism through which individuals and groups freely join forces to solve problems which are too big for individual action." In 1959 and 1960 he went so far as to propose an American Foundation for Voluntary Cooperation and a Citizens for America organization.[24]

Long before George Romney entered politics, he realized that the issues, trends, and problems of which he spoke would ultimately reach the political spotlight. In September, 1957, he stated, "The decisions I am talking about are going to be settled in the arena of public attitudes, public knowledge and economic understanding and, finally, in the area of political action."[25] He was also aware that our political institutions virtually shape everything outside the religious sphere; and since our political institutions and resultant national policy shape our economy and social activities to a considerable extent, our national health depends on an informed electorate and the political choices offered by the two major parties.

Following this basic democratic tenet, Romney raises the question, Are the American people being informed? His answer is No. He feels that there are only two ways for citizens to become educated: through direct participation and through intelligent discussion. That the first method is not effective is supported by a study from the Survey Research Center of the University of Michigan that divided up our total adult population in this fashion: only 7 per cent attend political rallies, dinners, or meetings; only 4 per cent give money; only 3 per cent work for a party or candidate during a campaign; only 2 per cent belong to a political party. In other words, Romney points out, active participation in the two political parties in the United States is less than the membership of the Communist party in Russia! No, Americans are not being informed via direct participation.[26]

Intelligent discussion is not doing the job either, and Romney sees no major differences between the parties at election time: "The candidates have had superficial differences but not substantial ones. Both parties are headed in exactly the same direction and will reach the same destination. The difference is a question of who is going to drive and whether we are going to go at thirty miles an hour or fifty miles an hour."[27] "I think it is tragic that in this country, faced with problems of the character I have tried to touch on, we should have two political parties that are not giving the public an opportunity to express themselves on the big basic issues that are going to make or break us," he says. He points to five such problems: Whether we will have a government supported and controlled by the people or the reverse; whether we will have monopoly or competition; whether we will have a centralized planned economy or an economy based on voluntary cooperation supported by strong legislation; whether we will have collective bargaining based on conflict and power or employees and employers working as a team; and whether we will have a dispersion of all forms of power or excessive concentration in industry, union or government.[28]

Why aren't there any differences between Republicans and Democrats? For what Romney considers to be five "fundamental and legitimate" reasons. First, the primary purpose of both major parties is to win elections. They are not organized to provide thorough and thought-provoking discussion of timely and significant issues. They contend simply over who is going to be responsible for government for the next two, four, or six years while other vital considerations take a back seat.

Second, both parties draw a cross-section of Americans. This means that there are liberals and conservatives with differing opinions as to what the party should stand for. This division within the parties makes compromise the order of the day, resulting again in relegation of basic problems.

Third, the two major parties are weaker than many pressure groups of national scope. One such pressure group has more than fifteen million members as compared with the combined Democratic and Republican total of two million. The parties must heed these powerful interest groups if they are to get elected, for that is where money, volunteers, and publicity will be found. Unless you are a very rich man, you incur obligations.

Fourth, the influence of these pressure groups is growing, and that threatens to subordinate human and spiritual principles to economic interests.

And last, the very nature of a political party discourages participation by impartial citizens who seek truth and the best possible solution to any problem. As a loyal party member you are expected to conform.

So the parties are not predisposed to discuss the deep issues of our time, and that puts the issue squarely up to the individual citizen. As Americans we believe with Thomas Jefferson that an informed electorate will allow democracy to work: "I know of no safe depository of the ultimate power of society but the people themselves: and if we think them not enlightened enough to exercise their control with a wholesome discretion, the remedy is not to take it from them but to inform their discretion."[29]

Speaking before the American Farm Bureau Federation in Chicago only two months before first announcing for the gubernatorial race in Michigan, Romney gave this clue to any future presidential race in which he might be involved:

> Within our two-party system, in terms of direct participation through the parties in the political process, have we yet reached the stage in America where any group or individual who tries to deal bluntly with the issues can win effective support? The failure of our political leaders to move beyond the safety of the fringes of major controversial issues and to avoid positions that would offend the pressure groups indicates that they do not believe so.
>
> But if we are not at this state, we need to find the mechanism to get us there. If we continue to postpone our problems and our issues until events create crises and crises produce action, we are going to be too late in this world struggle.
>
> I cannot escape the conviction that if some of our leaders and one of our political parties would depart boldly from the traditional "all things to all people" approach, and dramatically place the future of this nation above winning an election, the imagination of the people would be captured![30]

The Path to the White House

WHEN George Romney accepted the invitation extended to all governors to attend the presidential inaugural festivities in January, 1965, not many were surprised. After all Romney had attended other Democratic functions—and this time he had been invited! Still, there were those who felt that this was more personal than official. One Democratic representative was understood to say, "I suspect the governor's real purpose in riding down Pennsylvania Avenue this year will be to look over the parade route for the future."

Two years later the remark seemed much more in vogue. The elections of 1966 had rebuilt most of the Republican strength that had been sapped away by the Goldwater candidacy of 1964.[1] By January, 1967, Republicans could claim three new senators, forty-seven new representatives, eight new governors, and 548 new state legislators. The immediate diagnosis was a threat to the second-term aspirations of Lyndon B. Johnson. Republican governors in the nation now equaled state executive seats held by Democrats, and the electoral vote which they represented totaled 290—*more than enough to elect a President.* As if that were not enough, a post-election Harris poll indicated that Romney held a 54-46 percentage popularity edge over the President. When eighteen Democratic governors openly blamed LBJ for the huge Democratic losses in November, Johnson had ample reason to worry. What had happened during these two short years to make this reversal possible? Some of the voters felt that Lyndon Johnson had erred in choosing basic guidelines for the economy, inflationary controls, and the conduct of the

Vietnam war. But at least a portion of this new Republican portrait was painted from within the Grand Old Party.

The axiom that feuds from within the family are more violent than those from without was to have further proof. Both wings of the party (liberal and conservative) seemed to glean totally different messages from the election results of 1964. Goldwater had lost by more than 15,000,000, but that figure seemed to escape his attention. The only number he would utilize for discussion was that he had won 27,000,000 votes. This he stubbornly held to, saying it was a real tribute to the conservative movement. He read these votes as proof that he should continue to lead. Speaking at Scottsdale, Arizona, on November 5, he stated that he would have a great deal of time to give to the party and its leadership in the future (he lost his senatorship as well as the presidency) and that he had every intention of doing so.

More impartial elements of the party, however, read the 15,000,000 vote margin in a more practical manner. Interpreters here read it as a warning that the party was going in the wrong direction—in fact headed for extinction—unless certain trends were reversed. One such person was Michigan National Committeeman John Martin. While Goldwater asserted he would serve as leader, Martin announced that Dean Burch (appointed by Goldwater that July) should resign his national chairmanship. The move was not directed at Burch; he was only a symbol. The issue involved: "Does Barry Goldwater remain as titular head of the Republican party?" If Burch could be dumped, the answer would be "no," and the rebuilding process could begin.

With the battle lines drawn, Burch quickly announced that he would not resign and Goldwater backed him: "My recommendation would be to keep him because for the first time in memory we finished the campaign in the black. He's done a very, very fine job." Nevertheless, by the end of November Martin's suggestion had started to gain support. Senator Hugh Scott of Pennsylvania noted that there was a place for conservatives in the party but not at the top. Scott pointed out that the Goldwater supporters literally stopped campaigning the last week before the election, canceling television appearances in order to build up the surplus that Goldwater mentioned. "We will have to get rid of the urn-carriers that would rather carry the ashes of the Republican party than contribute to it," he added.[2] Three days later Charles Percy, who, in his race for the governorship of Illinois had backed Goldwater, joined the "oust Burch" movement.

The position of Richard Nixon and George Romney, the two men most likely to lead the 1968 GOP, might profitably be examined. Nixon made his first post-election move on November 6, attacking Nelson Rockefeller for being "cool" toward the Goldwater candidacy (which was probably the understatement of the year). He called the New York governor a spoilsport. Rockefeller countered by labeling Nixon's remarks "a peevish post-election utterance," and pointed out, "This is a time for constructive rebuilding of the Republican party as a vital force in the mainstream of American political life. Mr. Nixon's latest maneuver is hardly calculated to advance this effort."[3]

The tact of the other future GOP leader, George Romney, revealed a sharp contrast. His steps led down the narrow path of unification. Romney chided Nixon, saying, "When you're trying to unify something, you don't begin to say things that will create greater feeling of division. You undertake to include those who are in a position to make a contribution." He called for a broadly based party, labeled the demands for Burch's resignation as premature, and even had kind words for Goldwater: "I think that Senator Goldwater has demonstrated in the past his concern about the Republican party as a whole. I don't think we should assume it's going to be necessary to find some way around him. He should be given a part of any leadership group."

Early December found the Burch issue debated by eighteen GOP governors and governors-elect in Denver, Colorado. There the Republican party and Governor Romney made two moves that would enhance their future. First the governors released a policy declaration calling for new leadership. Gov. Robert Smylie of Idaho, commenting upon the vague wording of the resolution, said smugly, "It describes the kind of guy Dean Burch isn't." The second positive step was the formation of a subcommittee that was to plan a new National Republican Leadership Council (later called the Republican Coordinating Committee). The new body was to formulate Republican policy and declare positions.

Romney was the double benefactor because he changed his image as a "loner" and served as the central focus in the formulation of the new leadership body. Up until the 1964 Denver conference many of his fellow governors had secretly felt Romney was interested in Romney—not the party. They felt that he was too "aloof" and "holier-than-thou" in his person-to-person dealings. But now he emerged from the conference clearly indicating that the other voices had been persuasive. He had gone into the discussion with fellow Republican governors feeling that the Burch ouster was premature; he had come out as part of the Republican team of governors who were after the national chairman's scalp: "Burch has become the symbol of disaster that has hit this party," he said, "I see no other alternative but to urge that he be removed or that he resign." Romney was now "one of the boys" and this was a position he badly needed to secure.

The second feather in Romney's war bonnet in terms of 1968 presidential politics concerned the new committee for establishing a national policy-making organization. True, Romney had obtained the chairmanship of that group. That was a sign of influence, but what was more important was that Romney arrived at the Denver conference with the plan to form such a leadership body. It was his brainchild and the other governors bought it. He was therefore joining the "team move" and asserting leadership at the same time. The two maneuvers were perfectly executed.

On the basis of the new gubernatorial Denver stand, Goldwater, Eisenhower, and Nixon (the three men who had carried the GOP banner in the last four elections) held a summit conference at Eisenhower's Waldorf Towers suite in New York. There Goldwater was told that his handpicked party chairman would need a clear mandate at the January 22-23 national committee meeting—not a simple majority. On December 12, after a breakfast session with Eisenhower, Romney felt confident enough to say that there was increased likelihood that Burch would be replaced at the Chicago meeting. By this time the name of Ohio's Ray Bliss had been batted back and forth in terms of Burch's replacement. Bliss had been a highly successful state chairman for years and had been mentioned as early as 1956 for the national chairman's position. He had been reelected nine times and in 1964 was placed on the national committee.

It was now clear that anti-Burch sentiment would not yield a mandate and Goldwater therefore wanted to avoid the direct snub of his party. He met with Bliss for a two-hour conference in Washington on January 8. Four days later Bliss and Burch made a joint announcement: Burch was out and Bliss was in. A vote of the 132-member national committee would not be necessary and party bloodletting would be kept to a minimum. Bliss was to take the helm in April, thus allowing Goldwater forces to save face and achieving the change in image that moderate and liberal Republicans so badly sought. A significant feature of the new Republican profile was history.

Only a week earlier a lesser characteristic was etched, when Gerald R. Ford had completed a coup under the auspices of Reps. Robert P. Griffin of Michigan and Charles Goodell of New York. On January 4, Ford had become the new minority leader replacing Charles Halleck of Indiana. This contest too was touted as a moderate-liberal victory within the party. It did not carry the thorough Goldwater stigma associated with the national chairmanship. Still, it did help to provide a new image.[4]

On March 10, the newly formed Republican Coordinating Committee opened for business. The fruition of Romney's efforts consisted of 26 members: the five living presidential nominees—Goldwater, former President Eisenhower, Alf M. Landon, Richard Nixon, and Thomas Dewey; five GOP representatives of the Governors' Conference; eleven Congressional leaders, and five representatives of the national committee. By June the Coordinating Committee had released task force statements criticizing the President's handling of the balance of payments problem, recommending more federal-state-local government interaction, accusing the Johnson Administration of failing to enforce the spirit and letter of civil rights laws, and ridiculing the absence of long-range foreign policy goals.[5]

Ray Bliss officially took charge of the national Republican

machinery on April 1, 1965. Despite the light mood indicated by the calendar date, he immediately donned his white robe, stationed his stethoscope, and applied his success formula to the national party affliction. His prescription was twofold: he made it clear that he wanted a tightly controlled fund-raising mechanism and he soft-pedaled ideological differences which had caused the deep-rooted illness in search of party unity. Bliss was acting as a skilled political physician who recognized the need for well-financed campaigns and who also feared intraparty bloodshed. He adopted a neutral position between the two warring factions and asked for a cohesive party. Money came rolling in and unity seemed to be the battle cry; the official policy-making organ of the party became the Republican Coordinating Committee.[6] When combined with the Johnsonian popularity plunge, these image-changes made possible the sweeping victory of November 8, 1966.

So the two-year period had answered the leadership question. Goldwater would not be titular head of the party. As his role faded it became clear that the Republican party had no national spokesman. There was, indeed, a GOP leadership gap—a gap that had been filled by the Coordinating Committee until a national party spokesman in the role of a 1968 presidential nominee came to the surface. Those were the rules as if Goren himself had declared them, and it was only natural that several of the major Republican victors would want to play.

Mistaking the game for "Go to the head of the class," Romney burst out after the November elections with dice in both hands. If any number could win he might as well be the first to roll the highest. At his press conference the day after the election, he acknowledged that he was highly complimented by those who mentioned his name as a presidential contender but allowed that he had made no decision. With that remark he breezed off to Washington, D.C., for a five-day trip that would include a nation-wide TV interview on *Meet the Press,* a huddle with nine national political advisers, a private conference with Dwight D. Eisenhower, and a discussion with Senator Hugh Scott, a former GOP national chairman who served as campaign manager for William Scranton's bid to the Republican presidential nomination in 1964. Romney firmly stated that the trip had no political implications and that his major reason for the junket was to speak with the federal chairman of the new Upper Great Lakes Regional Economic Development Commission, Thomas P. Francis, about plans for removing the tolls on the Straights of Mackinac Bridge, which connects Michigan's two peninsulas. Anybody believing that story was truly a political neophyte! Although Romney was not yet skating, he was out testing the ice.

Delaying his usual post-election vacation in order to attend the Michigan State-Notre Dame football game, Romney arrived at Durado Beach, Puerto Rico, on November 20. If anybody had the idea that Romney would sink into national oblivion for the next two weeks they were wrong. Promptly on arrival Romney took issue with another Republican governor who had been vacationing in the area, Nelson Rockefeller. Rockefeller had told reporters that the Republican party needed to establish a "consensus" much in line with the past Bliss theory of party unity, but Romney reacted violently to the use of that term: "I identify the word consensus with someone who has not fared too well recently [Lyndon Johnson]," he said coyly. "I think what we need is leadership." Thus Romney was breaking with the Bliss strategy and the policy-making group. He was making it clear that he was becoming the leader—the national Republican spokesman.

When public uproar concerning Romney's disagreement with Rockefeller—which was more than mere semantics—had abated, a letter that the Michigan governor had written to Goldwater captured national headlines. The letter was in response to Goldwater's December 6, 1964, written request that Romney explain why he had not backed the Arizona senator in his presidential bid. Romney had responded on December 21, 1964, but for two years the letter had lain dormant in Republican files. Now it burst like a bombshell spreading Romney's name and reasons for not backing Goldwater across the face of the nation. If the issue that Romney had "taken a walk" during the 1964 election had to be faced in securing the presidential nomination, then better now than later.

With the letter still claiming attention in *Newsweek, Time,*

U.S. News and World Report, and other media, Romney ended his "vacation" on December 4, and made two outstate forays which removed all doubt that he entertained presidential thoughts. On December 7 he addressed the 87th annual meeting of the Charlotte, North Carolina, Chamber of Commerce where fifteen hundred people frequently interrupted his speech with applause. In New York City the next day he spoke to the 71st Congress of American Industry of the National Association of Manufacturers (NAM) and delivered a multitude of attacks on the Johnson Administration.

Before the headlines in North Carolina and New York were dry, Romney wrote a letter to Burke Marshall, chairman of the National Advisory Commission on Selective Service, urging a Congressional review of the draft and headed off to the Republican Governors' Conference at Colorado Springs. Here Romney announced that he would not make a candidacy decision for at least six months but said he would not repudiate efforts of others directed at securing his nomination.

December 12 found the Michigan wayfarer in Washington for a meeeting of the Republican Coordinating Committee, and while Chairman Bliss outlined a national survey showing Republican resurgence,[7] Romney attempted to patch up his quarrel with the ultraconservative wing of the party. In a four-minute personal confrontation he offered to campaign for Goldwater's 1968 senatorial comeback attempt "if he wants me to." He referred to the recent letter release as "past history."

Four days later he arrived at the National Governors' Conference in White Sulphur Springs, West Virginia, where he was destined to play an important role as chairman of a subcommittee on national-state relations. In proposing two resolutions Romney was to clash indirectly with President Johnson, because LBJ was on record as opposing both. It proved to be the right time for passage, because Democratic governors wanted to impress the President with the fact that the huge Democratic losses were due to an anti-Administration vote. As spokesman for eighteen of his colleagues, Iowa Gov. Harold E. Hughes made a public statement to that effect, and the repercussions benefiting Romney were summarized by Bud Vestal: "Romney went into the Democratic lair and came out with all the glory and attention, while President Johnson stood short and did a slow burn. Romney won almost unanimous adoption of two resolutions calling on the federal government to revolutionize its method of financing state programs against the wishes of the Democratic president."[8] Republican Governor John H. Chafee commented gleefully, "If I were the President, I'd be darned mad."[9]

So George Romney was off and running even though unannounced. What had caused him to cast aside his Michigan mount and spur his national political steed? Two factors: his coattail strength at the November 8 election and national polls.

As early as March, 1966, political gossip within the party had handed Romney this unwritten message: "To be considered for the presidency you will, of course, have to win reelection. But the victory itself does not matter. The two items of utmost importance are (1) the size of the plurality, and (2) the number of Republicans you carry into office. The emphasis is on the latter."

In order to publicize the importance of the coattail portion, Wisconsin Rep. Melvin Laird offered this presidential entrance requirement, "If Griffin wins there is no doubt in my mind that Romney will be our 1968 nominee."[10] Although the statement sounded like an endorsement, it was not. The utterance came before Senator Pat McNamara's death when the chances of a Griffin victory were remote. When Griffin was appointed to fill McNamara's Senate seat and his victory became much more probable, Laird and other conservatives upped Romney's presidential tuition to a U. S. senator and three congressmen.

Aware that the five freshmen Democratic congressmen from Michigan had done their homework, political observers doubted that Romney could afford the new congressional requirement placing him in the electoral college. Romney himself was hopeful, but gave himself an out: "I think if they [Laird and the other stipulation makers] are going to set up handicaps for people, they ought to do it across the board."[11] But on November 8, the senatorial and three congressional requirements seemed easy indeed: Griffin won by nearly 300,000 and all five freshmen Democratic congressmen lost. Romney had even carried a gerrymandered state senate for the Republicans and equally divided an even more disproportioned state House. The Romney coattails were several feet longer that his 5' 11" frame might indicate.

The political pulse of the nation toward Romney's presidential candidacy had begun to be measured by professional pollsters in December, 1965. At that time a Gallup Poll among Republicans placed George Romney in fourth position following Richard Nixon (34 percent), Barry Goldwater (13 percent), and Henry Cabot Lodge (12 percent), with Romney commanding only 11 percent of intraparty support. When the choice was narrowed to Nixon and Romney, the one-sided score card read: Nixon 55 percent and Romney 38 percent, with 7 percent undecided.

Two months later Romney still placed fourth with Republicans by the same 23 percentage chasm, and the same Gallup Poll revealed that Independent voters favored Nixon by a 9 percent margin among the twelve men mentioned. Since even Democratic voters placed Nixon 7 percent above the Michigan governor, the Romney supporters had little to write home about.

But a Gallup Poll released in April revealed some encouraging information to Romneyites. Nixon had lost 6 percent of his support among the GOP rank and file, while Romney had gained a modest 3 percent and had risen from fourth to second in terms of party preference. Among Independents he had moved from fourth to third, but still trailed Nixon by 8 percent. Then a July cross section of the nation's voters indicated that Romney was favored over Nixon by a 45 to 43 percentage, while a survey completed before the escalation of bombing in North Vietnam placed Romney only 4 percent behind President Johnson. (Nixon placed 11 percent behind LBJ.)[12] Soon a Detroit *News* poll indicated that Romney would carry Michigan, if running against Johnson, with a 43–37 leeway.

In September a Harris survey showed Romney bowing to

Johnson in a thin 51–49 contest and told that Republicans and Independents favored Romney over Nixon. After the Michigan election boost to the Governor and the detrimental Democratic results, a new national study indicated Romney would beat LBJ. Louis Harris announced, "Governor Romney of Michigan stands a better chance of winning the White House than any Republican since Dwight D. Eisenhower. Romney now leads President Johnson by a 54–46 margin."[13]

Romney's coattail strength and the growing public support combined to make him decide that a presidential bid was a real possibility. He decided it was time to move. He would now expose himself to the national press and encourage his supporters. Now was the time to let people know that he appreciated their patronage, that he knew how to hit the headlines, and that in the near future he—George Wilcken Romney—would take the presidential plunge. Yet he was aware that two large areas of discomfiture separated him from his goal: securing the nomination and winning the election. In many respects the first task seemed the harder of the two.

Strangely enough it seemed at first glance that one of the new problems facing Romney's nomination was created by the gigantic Republican victory that November. Republicans had elected 23 of 35 governors and had received 51 percent of the 41,446,525 votes cast.[14] When this figure was compared with the 45 percent gathered by the eleven Democratic gubernatorial victors and set alongside the electoral vote power represented, it was evident that the Republican presidential prospects for 1968 were radically improved. Now the GOP was convinced that President Johnson could be defeated and they would be selective in choosing their candidate. This meant that there were any number of new and reelected faces that could gain the nod. Hence the presidential nomination prospects included Charles Percy, Ronald Reagan, Nelson Rockefeller, Mark O. Hatfield, Richard M. Nixon, and George Romney.

Yet the immediate post-election activities of the six prospective candidates would seem to demand a different interpretation. Within ten days four had withdrawn themselves from the contest. On November 10, Charles Percy, 47, and a former president of Chicago's Bell and Howell Company who claimed a 422,000 victory over Senator Paul H. Douglas, announced that he had no plans to take on Romney: "I look forward to staying with my new job," he said, "I have no plans for 1968 or 1972."[15] Second, Ronald Reagan, 55, the former actor who had defeated by nearly one million votes the man Richard Nixon was unable to defeat, let it be known that he planned to serve a full four-year term. Next came a similar statement from Mark O. Hatfield, 44, the handsome former Oregon governor who had survived a close senatorial contest with Rep. Robert B. Duncan. As for Nelson Rockefeller, 58, who had defied the polls and defeated Democrat Frank A. O'Connor in a four-way battle to gain a third gubernatorial term, there was no change of plans. The two-time seeker of the GOP nomination had taken himself out of the 1968 race in order to gain support for his reelection.

Four of the six-cylinder GOP 1966 model had ceased to function. It was possible that a little repair work by skilled party mechanics could make any one of them fire up again, but for practical purposes and as long as the vehicle moved along highway '68 toward Washington, only two cylinders would fight it out. Richard Nixon and George Romney had made no such denials. Both yearned to be the driving force that would put the party limousine in the White House driveway.

If the flood of new Republican big names had not raised a serious problem to Romney's candidacy, had the November elections created any other perplexities? No, not directly. But they had caused the Michigan governor to stave off activities that should have already been in motion. Robert Novak and Rowland Evans pinpoint one such essential in their *Inside Report*: "Romney is unquestionably off to a late start in seeing to the manifold details attendant to running for the presidency." The two nationally syndicated columnists explain their statement by telling how Romney refused to allow the groundwork for a national organization to advance (even in an informal manner) prior to his reelection. And they are quite correct. The only indications of a

Romney presidential campaign before November were constant trips taken by Robert McIntosh, a chief Romney adviser. But McIntosh was severely handicapped. He was not allowed to approach any party leaders with something concrete and openly seek their support. Consequently, as the November elections ended, Romney was in urgent need of advice. He needed position papers on national issues, he needed counsel from political pros, and he badly needed to enlarge his staff which was well and good for state purposes, but weak indeed in terms of a national effort.

Throughout his years as Michigan's chief executive, Romney had made it a practice to consult with a seven-man "cabinet" or "brain trust" whom he referred to as his "scramble boys."[10] There was no executive secretary, no second-in-command, all seven were of equal rank. It was a system Romney had worked with much success while president of American Motors and which he carried over to the governor's chair. The original seven "scramblers" appointed in December, 1962, were Walter D. DeVries, 33, a political science Ph.D. who had served as assistant to the Speaker of the Michigan House of Representatives since 1957; Richard L. Milliman, 35, who resigned to become the editor and publisher of the Mt. Pleasant *Daily Times-News* after the 1964 campaign; Robert J. Danhof, 37, a lawyer who had served with Romney during Con-Con as chairman of the judiciary committee and had run unsuccessfully for the office of attorney general; Richard C. VanDusen, 37, a Birmingham attorney who had also been at Romney's side during the Constitutional Convention and who returned to private practice in 1963; Arthur Elliott, Jr., 45, who immediately became state party chairman; L. William Seidman, 41, a certified public accountant who also ran as a Romney ticket-mate for the office of auditor general in 1962; and Glenn S. Allen, Jr., 48, a former four-term mayor of Kalamazoo, who was an unsuccessful candidate for state treasurer in 1962.

Since that time some new faces have infiltrated Romney's "Dutch Mafia." Only Danhof has remained in his former position, but all of these men can be counted on for Romney's presidential push. Most are still in close contact with Romney. The new talent added at one time or another included Lt. Gov. William G.

Milliken, 44, a former state senator and president of J. W. Milliken, Inc., department store in Traverse City; State Treasurer Allison Green, 55, a former school teacher, superintendent and seven-term House veteran; and Robert J. McIntosh, 44, a lawyer and former Port Huron congressman. Milliken and Green have been absorbed in their respective state duties, while McIntosh was appointed director of the new Michigan Department of Commerce in early 1965, and in late 1966 left state service altogether to set up machinery for Romney's presidential drive. The only other formal cabinet post belongs to Charles E. Harmon, a Booth newspaper correspondent who covered Lansing for four years before becoming Richard Milliman's replacement.

Backing up this formal and informal cabinet are five or six administrative assistants or "second stringers." Usually there are seven, but the Governor finds himself continually tapping his advisory brainpower for prominent state positions. Herbert C. DeJonge, 32, recently replaced Robert McIntosh as director of the Commerce Department. Rounding out the gubernatorial second-line assistants are Albert A. Applegate, 38, a Ph.D. candidate in political science at the University of Michigan and former college professor; Charles J. Orlebeke, 32, a political science Ph.D. of Michigan State University and former Falk fellowship holder; Nicholas P. Thomas, 32, a Syracuse University doctoral candidate in public administration; and George T. Trumbull, Jr., 38, a journalism major from Michigan State University and former reporter for the *Pontiac Press*.

This was the bulk of Romney's political advisory machinery in November, 1966. And although he could boast of his statewide staff, Romney could not be deceived into thinking that his present personnel could operate nationally. Consequently he began to make the probes that columnists and professional politicians had been advising for months.

Before appearing on his fourth *Meet the Press* show, he huddled with a group of advisers that included Leonard Hall, the GOP national chairman throughout the Eisenhower Administration; Robert Carter, former aid to Hall on the National Committee;

Virginia Rep. Joel Broyhill, an ardent supporter of Barry Gold-water in 1964; and fellow Mormon J. Willard Marriott, the motel-restaurant multimillionaire and long-time Romney friend.[17]

As the year drew to a close two prime political management prospects had apparently been considered and dropped: F. Clifton White was still too closely identified with the Goldwater movement and New York's Deputy Mayor Robert Price was vetoed by Gov. Nelson Rockefeller and Senator Jacob Javits. Still, McIntosh was at work setting up a national organization and Romney himself admitted he would soon acquire a staff of advisers to help him decide whether or not to run. Explaining his actions in terms of a home buyer, Romney made this analogy: "It's perfectly obvious that if you're going to buy a large home, you need some experts to help you determine whether or not that house represents a good investment. You like to have the electrical wiring, the plumbing, and the soundness of construction checked. If considerable financing is involved, you'd need advice on financial aspects. Well, I've agreed to explore the most important secular responsibility in the world today. No man in his right mind would do that without expert assistance."[18]

The Romney exploration (referred to by the press as GROPE —George Romney's Organization for Presidential Exploration) began with the formation of two distinct organizations: The Romney Associates and the Romney for President Committee. The Associates were men close to Romney who had aided his political rise in Michigan whereas the Washington group was a new breed of cat to the Governor's program. At first there was friction between the two groups as each tried to gain Romney's favor, but by May the vague beginning goals of each faction had been clarified. When the Washington branch officially opened on March 20 its sole goal was lining up delegates for the 1968 convention. The Associates or "Lansing Loyalists" would write speeches, research, draw up position papers, and handle public relations.

By May 1, 1967, Romney's national organization had been beefed up considerably. DeVries (who had resigned his state post on January 11th) headed up a Lansing staff consisting of S. John Byington, a public relations expert who had managed Romney's third-term campaign; Glen L. Bachelder, a young Michigan State University Ph.D. candidate who handled research for all three Romney gubernatorial campaigns; Richard Headlee, a former Burroughs Corporation junior executive; George F. Gilder and Bruce K. Chapman, the authors of *The Party That Lost Its Head*; Jack Vandenburg, former assistant to U.S. Senator Clifford Chase: Johnathan Moore, Harvard specialist in international affairs; Travis Cross, former assistant to Mark Hatfield; Hugh Morrow, a top speech writer for Nelson Rockefeller; and original "scramble boys" Siedman, Van Dusen and Milliman (Romney's favorite speech writer).

The Washington contention was headed by former GOP National Chairman Leonard Hall; J. C. Folger, former ambassador to Belgium; Max M. Fisher, vice-chairman of the Paz Oil Company (Israel's largest distributor of petroleum), director of the Marathon Oil Company, and owner of Detroit's skyscraper of the same name; Lawrence B. Lindemer, the former state party chairman who managed the 1964 presidential campaign of New York's Nelson Rockefeller in Michigan; William Murphy, former assistant to Pennsylvanian Governor William Scranton; William Prendergast a research specialist for the Republican National Committee until removed during the Goldwater disaster; and Carl Spad, New York Republican State Committee Chairman—in addition to Romney's Utah high-school chum William Marriott and original Romney for president rooter Jack McIntosh.

As the national organization began to be realized a new obstacle appeared: the conservative-liberal rift that has plagued the party since the Roosevelt candidacy in 1912. In many respects the 1968 convention battle began to look more and more like that of 1952 between Robert A. Taft and Dwight D. Eisenhower. This time Nixon had been assigned Taft's conservative role and Romney that of the moderate Eisenhower. This dichotomy has to have a curious basis, because Richard Nixon is by no means a second Barry Goldwater and George Romney is far from a protégé of the

"Eastern Establishment." How then did this forced categorization come about?

The basic dividing wedge was sunk in the party tree when Romney "accepted" but did not "endorse" Goldwater during the 1964 campaign. For this the ultraconservatives and Goldwater never forgave him. (A twelve-page letter, frankly written, could not even make Goldwater *understand,* much less *forgive.*) Nixon had campaigned for the Arizona senator and therefore had earned the right, according to unwritten political credo, to become the next nominee. When Goldwater saw that he had lost the titular leadership of his party, he publicly passed along his blessings (and he hoped his support) to the former Vice President. Even after the face-to-face meeting with Romney at the Republican Co-ordinating Committee in December, 1966, Goldwater still proclaimed Richard Nixon to be his choice for the nomination. "After all," Goldwater pointed out, "he is the best equipped."[19] Would Goldwater's advice be followed?

According to the conservative Washington weekly *Human Events,* a large number of delegates to the 1964 convention said they would neither work for nor vote for a presidential nominee who had not endorsed the Arizona senator. The survey covered about 40 percent of the delegates and alternate delegates to the Cow Palace convention of 1964. Of the 1,050 persons responding, 38 percent said they would support Richard Nixon at the 1968 convention and 25 percent said that they would support George Romney.[20]

In order to measure the significance of this poll, it is necessary to consult past history to see how many of these delegates actually return to party conventions. It can be estimated that only 35 percent to 45 percent will be held over from 1964. Thus only a few of the same delegates would be back—alternate delegates do not count—and the Romney percentage was fairly strong anyway.

When these facts are added to commentaries from party leaders who should know, the complexion of the 1968 convention would seem to be greatly improved. Senator Hugh Scott says that some of the same faces will be back, but not with the same minds, and even staunch Goldwater supporters are speculating that the 1968 convention will be no carbon copy of the conservative-minded 1964 body. One such personal ally is Arizona Senator Paul J. Fannin, who notes that 1968 will probably see a more balanced convention, while another senator feels that if Romney proves to be clearly in the lead as 1968 approaches a lot of people will move over.[21]

How is Romney to be "clearly in the lead"? He will have to follow the Kennedy route and bring a bagful of primary victories to the convention with him. Will this not be relatively easy if the polls continue to show Romney with the wide popular support he held in December, 1966? Yes and no. First, it is going to be hard for Romney to maintain the 54-46 edge he already has over President Johnson, much less improve upon it. Second, there is no such animal as a "sure" primary. The candidate campaigns in unfamiliar surroundings and before voters who are alien to him. He is used to being "known." To take an entirely new approach—introducing oneself all over again—can be an adjustment that asks too much. Presidential primaries are unpredictable; a technique that was quite successful in 1960 might prove to be the very opposite in 1968. Then there is the task of securing a suitable opponent and of picking the "right" primaries (the ones that will yield the most bargaining strength on the convention floor).

With the party convention only fourteen months away it looked very much as if Romney would be spared these last two perplexities. When asked if it would be necessary for "those being put forward for the presidency in 1968 to test their appeal in primaries," Richard Nixon replied, "Yes, I believe that the primary road is essential for whoever is going to get the nomination."[22] Only four days earlier Romney had put these words on record: "Primaries are a yardstick. They indicate the public acceptance of the people involved."[23] Although nothing had been directly stated, the meaning to political observers was as clear as if Romney had challenged Nixon to a joust and the former Vice President had bent over and picked up the glove. The formidable opponent had been found.

It also appeared that the question of which primaries to enter had been taken from Romney's shoulders. At this time foreseeable future developments did not enrich Romney's candidacy hopes. The threatened development was an indicated avalanche of "favorite son" candidates representing states where presidential primaries are usually held. There were definite signs of such developments in California, Ohio, New Jersey, Massachusetts, Florida, and Pennsylvania—all had been important fields of battle in the past. If these states moved in the favorite son direction (in effect declaring their territory off limits to outsiders), it would be hard indeed for Romney to make the calculated primary gains, but the choices as of May 1, 1967, stood a good chance of being narrowed to New Hampshire, Wisconsin, Oregon and Nebraska. If Romney really wanted to make a primary record for himself, he would have to approach privately some of these favorite son candidates and convince them to step aside. His only other choice would be to persuade them to release their delegations sometime before or during the convention.

Some political observers have insisted that primary victories are the only way that Romney can purge himself of his 1964 Goldwater neglect. No doubt a series of significant victories would erase most scarred tissue, but it might still be possible for Romney to seek successfully the nomination, primaries notwithstanding. The reasoning? First, both Ronald Reagan and Barry Goldwater have said that they will support the 1968 Republican candidate "whoever he may be." Second, the Michigan chief executive has been gaining strength in geographical areas previously known as "Goldwater territory." Third, Romney has demonstrated strong coattail support and is popular with the public. Fourth, Goldwater will be running for the U. S. Senate seat in Arizona in 1968 and cannot afford to alienate the large ten percent Mormon voting block by snubbing Romney. Fifth, there is widespread party feeling that Richard Nixon is "a loser," and as Ray Bliss, the national chairman, observed immediately after the 1966 elections, "We want a winner."

In early 1967 these additional signs pointing to Romney's nomination could be witnessed. First, the Michigan Republican State Central Committee officially endorsed Romney for the presidency. The approval was unanimous, although Michigan has a few ultraconservatives of its own. Second, the Republican governors demanded and received an increase of two on the coordinating committee. This means that they will be more influential than ever and that their voice will be heard—if not in command—when the presidential candidate is chosen. Third, two pro-Romney governors were chosen as chairman and vice-chairman of the Republican Governors' Association: Colorado's John A. Love would head the body throughout 1967 and Rhode Island's John H. Chafee would become the association's guide during the crucial presidential year.

The simple election of these two men were good omens for Romney's future, but when placed in the perspective of the previous night in Colorado Springs the choice serves as a rough index of the entire association's regard for Michigan's chief executive. On the eve of the two-day meeting, both Love and Chafee held press conferences and strongly praised Romney. "I could wholeheartedly support him," the Colorado governor said energetically, while Chafee noted, "No one has any better credentials as a strong Republican than Governor Romney." When asked if Romney would be badly hurt for his failure to endorse Goldwater in 1964, both men agreed it put "no blemish on his record."[24] Both prospective leaders had therefore tipped their hands before the election was held. The result was a big boost for Romney.

Another significant development occurred when California's George Murphy was elected as chairman of the Senate Campaign Committee (a very important position in terms of presidential elections) although there were those who interpreted this as a blow to Romney's candidacy quest. Such observers said that Senator Hugh Scott would have been a better pro-Romney man, and they were right. But Murphy was certainly not anti-Romney. He has traveled to Michigan on several occasions, has been widely welcomed, and has warmly reciprocated.

Two other significant boosts occurred when Iowa's Robert D. Ray, a man closely identified with Romney's bid for the White House, was named head of the National State Chairman's Association by GOP National Committee Chairman Ray Bliss, and in

May, when Gladys O'Donnell defeated the more conservative Phyllis Schlafly to become president of the National Federation of Republican Women. The series of events enhanced the Romney candidacy considerably.

As would be true of any candidate put up by either party, the Michigan governor has several built-in assets and some serious handicaps to overcome. He faces the enormous task of convincing the American nation that he has what it takes to run the most powerful nation in the world. The American voters will have to give any candidacy of George Romney a close look. What are some of the things that an early microscopic look might reveal?

There are obviously many things that Romney possesses which make him seem like a strong presidential candidate. He is handsome. He is articulate. He is energetic. In this modern age of living-room campaigning, he comes across well on television. He is devoutly religious. He is both honest and a hard worker. He does not smoke or drink and he yearns to expand America's destiny and continue the American dream. He is the chief executive of one of the nation's largest industrial states. He has personal magnetism that make men want to follow him. He is a strong Republican, yet not so stringent that he would be denied Independent and Democratic support. He is a self-made man and has never known the taste of political defeat.

He is healthy—at 59 he has suffered only appendicitis and a few bad colds. He has energy to burn and would be a tireless presidential campaigner. Just prior to his 1966 state campaign he passed a complete physical examination at Detroit's Henry Ford Hospital with flying colors. Dr. Herman Alvarez merely confirmed what is abundantly clear to those who have attempted to follow the brisk pace Romney perpetuates: that "Governor Romney is in excellent health."[25]

An added positive factor is that he is a contented family man and has not been divorced. His wife, Lenore, a vibrant, energetic woman of 58 is one of his greatest political assets. A hazel-eyed brown-haired vote-getter and friend-maker for her husband, she is a cordial, loquacious warm person. She has known George Romney most of her life (they met when she was a sophomore in high school) and she dotes on him with an ardor that brings a smile to the lips of close observers.

Mrs. Romney is a political dynamo who has encouraged her husband to achieve all that she knew was within him. She has internalized the Governor's goals until they have become her own. She is active in numerous societies and associations and has had more formal education that the Governor. The people of Michigan have found her such a potent force that she now claims two honorary doctorates. Since becoming Michigan's first lady she has traveled throughout both peninsulas, averaging more than one hundred speeches a year. On the speaker's platform she makes it hard not to pay attention.

When all these convictions and attributes are set side by side it becomes readily apparent that there is a multitude of factors that would make Romney a formidable candidate and a capable President. Yet there are at least three major handicaps that Romney will have to surmount: the Mormon stand on the Negro, a modest record concerning world affairs; and the possibility of a second Michigan money crisis.

In a nation where 97 percent of the citizens believe in God, where 123,000,000 claim membership in some religious body and where nearly half the population attend church services weekly, the religious beliefs of a presidential candidate attract much attention. Until 1960 it was considered impossible that anyone not of the 68,000,000 Protestant majority could be elected President. When John F. Kennedy, a Roman Catholic, overcame tradition (there are about 45,000,000 Roman Catholics in the United States), it was both a credit to the American Constitution and an encouragement for those representing smaller religious segments. The Kennedy precedent is important to George Romney because the Church of Jesus Christ of Latter-day Saints, the faith that he avows, numbers only 2,400,000.[26]

Yet the size of the Saint body is not the major problem that Mormonism presents Michigan's chief executive. Decidedly not. The real religious ramifications involve an official Latter-day Saint doctrine known as "the Curse of Cain," which denies the Negro the priesthood. According to revelation Negroes are descendants of Cain who killed his brother Abel. The dark skin is a mark of their continuing punishment; consequently they are barred from the highest posts of the church. Since the majority of the American people object to racist philosophy, the question of negative Negroism as propounded by the Church of Jesus Christ of Latter-day Saints deserves careful examination. Is this really official church doctrine? More importantly, does George Romney believe it?

The answer to the first question is "Yes." When David O. McKay, the prophet, seer, and chief revealer was asked in 1964 if he thought the doctrine barring Negroes from the priesthood would be changed, the Mormon elderly president answered, "Not while you and I are here." Thus, by saying it would not be changed, McKay had acknowledged that it existed. It is official church doctrine and it will continue to be so, until divine revelation rescinds the decree in the same fashion that the practice of polygamy was rescinded.

The answer to the second question is "No." Although this reply might seem to negate the Governor's image as a devout man, it does not. Wallace Turner in *The Mormon Establishment* clearly explains the area of latitude existent within the church on the anti-Negro doctrine: "Even among many who cling tenaciously to their belief, there is a swelling opinion that the church is dead wrong on the issue. Mormonism is unusually open to unrest in such a situation, emphasizing as it does the responsibility of every man to be a priest and to be his own repository of knowledge on doctrine. Thus it produces men who can disagree vigorously with some doctrine enunciated at the top, and yet declare themselves in equally positive terms to be faithful believers."[27]

That George Romney is such a man is proven by his record. His strongly pro-civil rights stand began to emerge more than twenty years ago when Romney was serving as director of the Automotive Council for War Production. At that stage of World War II there was a drastic shortage of workers; one reason for the sparse supply was the segregation that existed in defense housing.

Romney made public statements condemning this practice and carried the issue to federal and state officials.

In 1950, Romney appeared before the Detroit Common Council as a member of the board of directors of the Citizens Housing and Planning Council and protested further development of the city housing program on a segregated basis. He was the only industrialist who cared enough to speak out. Then, too, as president of the American Motors Corporation, he put his company squarely behind the Fair Employment Practices Act of 1955 and enjoyed exercising what the law meant long before the official command.

In 1961-62 he took a position of leadership and was largely responsible for the establishment of a new Civil Rights Commission under Michigan's new constitution. As governor he has made sure that the commission was nurtured from its modest sixteen-member, low-budget beginning to a major state agency with more than one hundred employees and a budget of almost one million dollars. The commission exercises a distinctive leadership in the nation. To date it has accepted more than 1,800 complaints of discrimination in areas such as housing, employment, education, and law enforcement, meeting with such consistent success that only a handful of cases have reached the courts.

But Romney has not been content to let the commission handle the civil-rights issue. He saw to it that Joseph Bell, Jr., was appointed as the first Negro Michigan vice-chairman in Michigan history. He handpicked Negro George Washington as a member of his "Action Team" in 1966. He was one of the first to praise the awarding of the Nobel Peace Prize to Martin Luther King in 1964 and personally led a civil-rights march in Detroit in 1965. He wrote a letter to Everett M. Dirksen asking for his support on the 1966 Civil Rights Bill and, of course, he refused to endorse Barry Goldwater in 1964 because of his segregated campaign strategy.

The Romney record speaks for itself, and the Governor does not shirk this deep personal conviction. In December, 1965, he appeared in Charlotte, North Carolina, and did not budge one iota on the question. His commitment to equal rights for all is inherent in his philosophy of the American dream and it is not uncommon to hear him proclaim, as he did in a speech before the Zion Church

Annual Conference in Detroit in 1965 that "The most urgent domestic problem of our time continues to be the civil-rights struggle. Nearly two centuries ago our Declaration of Independence declared that all men are created equal and that they are endowed by their Creator with certain inalienable rights. Among these rights are life, liberty, and the pursuit of happiness. Now either we believe the fundamentals upon which our country was founded, or we don't. Either we believe that humans are created by God, are given certain inalienable rights, or we don't. Well, I'm a believer."

These observations about Michigan's presidential contender become much more meaningful when interpolated with a few key statistics. A *Newsweek* survey of September, 1966, revealed that 79 percent of Negro voters are registered Democrats, and while the national GOP figure is normally 10 percent, in 1964 it plunged to a nadir of 5 percent. In the meantime, the Michigan Negro has been traveling another route. Romney received 10 percent of the Negro vote in 1962, 19 percent in 1964, and 34 percent in 1966. Michigan Negroes have increasingly become receptive to the Governor's constant plea: "Measure me by my actions."

Thus, in the area of the Mormon anti-Negro controversy it may be seen that Romney is not fainthearted. He has never hesitated to take the lead in the matter of civil rights. He has never directly contradicted the official church doctrine, but strongly believes in separation of church and state. He believes that religion should not be an issue in a political campaign. But perhaps his dedication to an equal chance for all may be best summed up in his own words: "They're making something of the fact that my religion does not permit Negroes in our priesthood—I will fight that too if necessary!"[28]

The second major Romney handicap is identified as an "experience gap" in world affairs. People want to know what he thinks and what firsthand experiences he has to draw upon. This is an area in which the Governor recognizes he must improve. "Now look," he says, shaking his fist and staring through the questioner, "I'm not as deficient in world affairs as some people say. I've lived abroad. I've worked in the automobile industry, a worldwide industry. I talk to people frequently about world affairs. I regularly read *Foreign Affairs Quarterly* [a scholarly American publication] and *The Economist* [an equally deep-thinking British magazine]." Then pointing to his briefcase, he will exclaim, "This briefcase is full of stuff I'm currently reading on Vietnam!"[29]

And he has a wide range of experiences that would seem to bolster his credentials as a world thinker. In addition to the two-year missionary stint in Scotland and England, Romney has served as employer delegate to the Metal Trade Industry Conference of the International Labor Office in 1946, 1947, and 1949. Romney was not politicking when, after the 1946 session in Toledo, Ohio, he brought the entire hundred delegates to his Bloomfield Hills home for a meal. He was doing something he believed in, establishing person-to-person relationships with those from other countries. After the 1947 meeting in Stockholm, Sweden, the Romneys took a six-week vacation on the Continent. The 1949 conference was held in Geneva, Switzerland.

As president of American Motors he often spoke in Canada, and as governor of Michigan he has gained world-wide firsthand experience. In 1965 he logged an additional five weeks of "world experience." In April Romney led a Michigan delegation of seventy businessmen and government officials on "Operation Europe," a trade-building tour of Western Europe including good-will meetings with leaders of six nations: the Netherlands, West Germany, Italy, Switzerland, France, and England. (In 1964 Michigan exported $134,000,000 in goods directly to foreign countries.) The ten-day whirlwind tour gave Romney first-hand contact with Walter Hallstein, president of the European Common Market; Couve de Murville, an economic expert considered to be the third man in the French governmental hierarchy; and numerous other government officials and business leaders.

In October of 1965 Romney tripled his earlier foreign junket with a three-and-one-half week Oriental sojourn including two weeks in Japan, five days in Hong Kong, and four days in Vietnam. Romney was one of ten governors making the trip to "promote mutual understandings and improve public administration," and Ryotaro Azuma, governor of Tokyo led the delegation representing all forty-six Japanese prefectures (states).

Visiting Vietnam just before returning to the States, Romney flew in a jet to Da Nang, watched flight launchings from the deck of the U.S.S. *Ticonderoga,* and visited remote camps. He lunched with enlisted Michigan men and was near enough to feel the ground shake when sky-raiders bombed a Vietcong hideout. It was an educational four days for Michigan's chief executive. He was alert every moment and constantly asked questions, measured answers, and interpolated the data he received. After returning to Michigan he made a statewide speech on the Vietnam question.

Since 1966 was an election year, Romney was not able to leave his home state for any extended period of time. But he did manage to bring many distinguished foreign leaders to the United States for a "world preview" of Michigan that May.[30] The seven-day agenda included a reception at the Romney home, a flying tour of the state, and propaganda concerning Michigan's dynamic progress. Each of the twenty guests was given a sponsor who catered to his individual interest for a three-day period. An International Dinner at Detroit's Cobo Hall climaxed the program. Although Romney already has a considerable record of international exposure for a governor, it may safely be assumed that he will use 1967 to further bridge his "experience gap." A major world tour including Thailand, the Philippines, England, France, Germany, Africa, South America, and a second visit to Vietnam is tentatively planned for the fall of the year. Exactly how extensive the tour will be depends to a great extent on the third major obstacle in Romney's presidential path: the possibility of another Michigan financial crisis.

The possibility that Michigan's financial home-front picture might serve as the trip wire to Romney's presidential hopes was gleefully voiced by Democratic State Central Chairman Zolton Ferency only a month after Romney had defeated him in the gubernatorial race: "George Romney will be an early casualty in the GOP presidential scramble," he predicted. "Romney's greatest political asset is on the verge of becoming his greatest political liability. What happens in the 1967 legislative session will sound the death knell for Romney's presidential hopes just as the 1959 legislature ended Mennen Williams' hopes. I predict there will be no fiscal reform during the coming session."

Romney had already failed to achieve tax reform in 1963 and 1965, yet, as 1966 came to a close, he had emerged as the GOP's top presidential contender. Why would the events of 1967 concerning fiscal reform change his image? For several reasons. First, there had been no major changes in Michigan's tax structure since the 1959 payless payday crisis. Instead, tax windfalls from a booming economy had temporarily solved the problem. But Bernard M. Conboy, state director of Economic Expansion predicted that Michigan's burgeoning economy was in for a breathing spell in 1967. Second, the $974,000,000 budget, which Romney had approved in July, did not accurately indicate the general fund money that would be spent. Supplemental school aid, additional contributions to the state's public school retirement fund, and the underestimated cost of the Medicare program boosted the figure by $40,000,000. Third, programs already in progress would use $90,000,000 of the 1966 surplus by June, 1967, and if no fiscal reform package were adopted by 1968, Michigan could be right back where it was when Romney was elected in 1963—approximately $100,000,000 in debt.

So the Ferency claim is a possibility, and in terms of state history on fiscal reform attempts it must be regarded as a definite roadblock. Romney has no choice, he is forced once again to seek an income tax. As he does, only three possible outcomes exist: (1) he will be successful and this will be an even bigger boon to his presidential aspirations, (2) he will not succeed and, instead will reduce services substantially (there are not enough Democratic votes in the Senate to override a gubernatorial veto), or (3) he will combine a portion of the first two.

As the 1966 legislative session came to a close in December, Romney presented this bleak financial outlook to the legislators and concluded: "Although we face no immediate financial crisis, we must agree, in the forthcoming session, upon a new revenue program in time to put it into effect by January 1, 1968. For practical purposes, this means the legislature must enact tax reform by July 1, 1967, to provide the lead time necessary for implementation. Michigan's problems of the late 1950's arose from the appropriations of substantial budget increases without also providing adequate revenue to finance their costs. We are not going to repeat that error," he warned.

Within a matter of days he had acted to underscore that fact. By executive decree he ordered Social Service Director Bernard F. Houston to withold medicare services beyond those already in effect, thereby temporarily canceling phases two and three of the program as called for by a newly passed statute. Romney noted that the appropriation of $21,000,000 fell far short of the cost of the program and said the money simply was not available for the planned increases. Again with reference to 1959 he said, "We are not going to repeat that error. I can't emphasize that too much."

The action had been calculated deliberately to show that Romney meant what he had told the legislators only a few days earlier. He did not want to cut services, but had now shown that he would. It was as if he warned the incoming Democratic lawmakers, "If you don't want more of the same you had better support my tax reform attempt," and Romney himself came close to that language in late December: "There aren't going to be any appropriations until we see the revenue. Revenue action must come first." Thus he had set his course for 1967, but once again he left himself an out. He would push as hard as he could for fiscal reform, but if it were not possible he was at least on record as being prepared to accept the ultimate decision of the legislature: "If the elected representatives of the people want to cut services, we'll cut services."

On February 2, 1967, Romney revealed his budgetary and tax reform plans. He called for a reform package which would raise $340 million in new revenue. The plan was keyed to a 2.5 percent individual, 5 percent corporate and 8 percent income tax on financial institutions. His suggested budget for 1967-68 was $1.15 billion, up $128 million from the past year. The package was defeated in the Michigan Senate on March 30 by a 23-14 vote. Six Republican Senators joined with seventeen Democrats to send Romney's proposals back to committee.

As the fiscal reform battle shifted to the House, Romney made good his threat of cutting expenditures. On April 14 he mapped out an austerity budget providing a 16 percent across-the-board-cutback in every state supported program from public schools to mental health: "I am determined to see Michigan live within its income" he reiterated. But the Michigan House, still Doubting Thomases, rejected a modified fiscal reform package on May 4 by a 57-48 margin.

As this book goes to press the wise money is on Romney. He holds all the aces. If, as seems likely, he gets his desired reform, he will be hailed as a leader who had the courage to fight for needed revenue increases and won, which will enhance his presidential stock. But if some sort of reform is not achieved by July 1, (the start of the new fiscal year) he will undoubtedly go through with his proposed budget cuts—a move calculated to please conservatives everywhere and thus aid him in his battle for the GOP presidential nomination. At the same time denying the needed dollars would alienate almost every interest group in the state (particularly the educator) toward the Democrats who would be forced to provide the wide majority of "no" votes. Although this issue is an important portion of Romney's presidential obstacle course, it appears that he will once again finish with a passing score. As one Romney aide likes to put it, "The Governor will come out smelling like a rose."

On another important matter of speculation perhaps it would be wise to ask this question: If the presidential race should narrow down to Romney versus Johnson, what would be a few crucial issues? A sampling from Romney's attacks on the incumbent administration over the past two years would indicate three broad areas of battle: Vietnam, general foreign policy, and domestic programs.

The Romney stand on Vietnam began to develop with the Governor's first utterance on the subject after the 1964 election. It came on February 8 in response to a White House announcement of retaliatory air strikes into North Vietnam: "I don't think we had any alternative but to make it clear we mean business." One month later he added that he supported the Johnson Administration's decision to bomb North Vietnam targets because "I've felt for some time that we should take a stronger stand, and I'm pleased that we are taking it."

It was not until the July National Governors' Conference in Minneapolis that Romney set himself up as a major administration critic by voting "No" on a resolution presented by Georgia Democrat Carl E. Sanders. The resolution put the governors on record as backing the President's conduct of the war. In effect, it was a blank check endorsement; only Romney and Oregon Gov. Mark Hatfield withheld such approval until they were briefed by the President the next evening. "My only point," Romney said in casting his negative vote, "was that we should have been briefed by the President *before* voting." He noted that much of the information to make such decisions was classified and available only at the White House. After a special two-hour briefing with the President and Cabinet members the next day, Romney joined the majority: "Based upon the additional information received today, I support the President's actions taken yesterday and I urge all Americans to do the same."

Romney found his November four-day Vietnam tour sobering and began a statewide televised report to the Michigan people in this fashion: "I have not been an unquestioning supporter of our government's policies in South Vietnam . . . but my major conclusion is that what we are doing is morally right and necessary." He phrased the basic question as to whether the Vietnamese war was a genuine war of liberation (a civil war) or an international communist conspiracy. His conclusion was the latter. Still, he did not give the President a blank check endorsement: "I do not know whether all the strategy and tactics being used are right or wrong, but it is wrong to give foreign aid to countries whose ships are delivering supplies to North Vietnam."

By January, Romney had devised some more advice for the President: "Vietnam is a total struggle involving every aspect of human life. I do not think it will be won via the military route. You've got to win the people. We are there to help the South Vietnamese. We should not make this an American war. We should not escalate it to the point where we are taking over for them." Romney said that he had not seen evidence that United States social, economic, and political efforts were adequate.

Four months later, before a Republican fund-raising dinner in Rhode Island, Romney said that the Johnson Administration had made mistakes in handling the Vietnam war: "I'd like to know if the people of South Vietnam really want us there," he said and reiterated his belief that the war should not become an American effort. Then, in June he made his strongest statement to date in terms of specific war conduct. He said that the United States should bomb strategic storage areas in North Vietnam because it was "inconsistent to be in Vietnam and not to do obvious things like cutting off supplies." He stated further that it "was a mistake to get involved in a land war," and that what we needed most was "a clear-cut policy in South Vietnam." Romney insisted that he was not becoming a "hawk" but merely pointing out an inconsistency in our present policy. "As far as I can see we have neither an adequate policy in terms of military results nor an adequate policy in terms of negotiated settlement. We need to make up our minds which our objective is because this ambivalent position we are in weakens both efforts."

At the National Governors' Conference in July, Romney found himself voting with the 48 governors he had refused to side with one year earlier on a similar Vietnam resolution. This time the resolution had been watered down to such a degree however that it really did little more than confirm our global commitments including support of some sort for the military defense of South Vietnam. (And this time Mark Hatfield was the only dissenting voice.)

It was at this Los Angeles Conference that Romney made the biggest blunder of his newly acquired national political career. When asked to voice an opinion on Vietnam, he responded with a statement that *Newsweek* called "so opaque that his own staffers scratched their heads in disbelief" and *The National Observer* labeled as coming "perilously close to an unmitigated disaster." His statement was vague. It was disorganized. It went around in a circle and arrived nowhere. It was certainly not the type of statement a presidential contender should be making.

Partly due to that costly blunder and partly due to the oncoming elections in Michigan, Romney became rather quiet on the Vietnam issue until after his reelection. Then on *Meet the Press* in mid-November he served up this commentary: "As far as I am concerned, the Vietnamese conflict is the most far-reaching, complex, and meaningful problem facing the nation. It not only involves what we are doing in Asia and our relationships there but also our relationships around the world and our domestic programs. I have never taken a specific position, and I have never made any specific proposals. I have done a good deal of studying of the problem. I have had the opportunity to visit South Vietnam. I have talked with people in our government. I have been briefed by the President and by military and diplomatic officials. I have talked with some foreign representatives from foreign nations. But I am concerned about certain aspects of this conflict about which I have not been able to secure sufficient information to make specific proposals. Now I expect to take the time to dig into those aspects and to get the information I need before taking a specific position. I expect to get into it in depth, and when I do I will make such proposals as I think will be meaningful."

On December 10 he said that the Johnson Administration was not doing the job in Vietnam, said he thought the American people had a right to know what he thought about the subject, and promised that he would speak out in the future. As the year came to a close it appeared that Michigan's governor had set the course he would follow until late 1967, he would study and gain all the information he could. When the time was right—according to his presidential timetable—he would step forward and ask the people to accept his formula for victory. "Appeared" is indeed the correct word, for the time to speak out on Vietnam came much quicker than Romney and his advisors dared contemplate.

In February, as Romney made his first presidential wind testing tour, through six Western States, he began in Anchorage, Alaska by unleashing a bitter general attack on Lyndon Johnson's

Vietnam policy calling it "clumsy, ill-timed and poorly co-ordinated." This type denunciation of LBJ did not sit well with the forty odd newsmen accompanying Romney on the trip. They began pumping him for specifics. Romney was irritated and at Pocatello, Idaho, made another Los Angeles circle-type comment. The result was that the national press, fellow GOP concern and a mild plunge in national polls pressured Romney into speaking out much earlier than he had planned. While on a trip to Washington he casually announced that he would make a major speech on Vietnam at Hartford, Connecticut, on April 7. The statement flabbergasted his aides, but Romney had decided the time was right, and that was that.

The decision, although impulsive, proved to be sound for two reasons: First, with national attention riveted on his Vietnamese stand, very few reporters seemed concerned when his income tax plan failed on March 30, and second, his basic stand on Vietnam came off like silk on a spool. The thirty minute speech was interrupted eight times by applause. It put him firmly on record, showed that he understood what was going on, disarmed his critics, allowed him future flexibility, and most important of all, brought him time to research further.

In terms of general foreign policy Romney has continually chided what he calls the "defensive" or "containment" policies of the Johnson Administration. "We conduct our foreign affairs on the basis of reaction and mere survival when what we need is a definite positive foreign policy based on our national purpose, divinely inspired constitutional principles, and proved social and economic principles," he often says. His conclusion is, "We need a drastic, total upheaval and reshaping of American foreign policy."

Last there is a whole gauntlet of domestic issues that date back to Romney's 1945 "Seven Frontier" speech. Specifically, Romney will take exception with the Keynesian principals, which he labels "grasshopper economics": excessive concentration of power in the hands of big labor, big business, and big government; the "credibility gap," which exists under President Johnson; the anti-missile lag; the loss of individual responsibility; the decline of American morals; crime, urban affairs; air and water pollution; transportation, and many others.

And to Romney these areas of debate will not be mere vague word differentiations. He has grasped the real meaning of America, and he has the foresight and the will to lead the nation. Some time in 1967 he will consolidate his piecemeal attack into a broad program package. Whether he offers an "American Deal" or "Total American Action" or a "Generation of Progress" will make little difference. What will make a difference is the presentation of that program and the resultant verdict of the American people.

Notes

Index

CHAPTER 2

1. "Rambling Into the Fray," *Copyright, Newsweek, Inc.,* Dec. 18, 1961, p. 28.

2. Edward S. Corwin, *The President, Office and Powers* (New York: New York University Press, 1962), pp. 31-32.

3. "Romney—Republican Hopeful for 1968?" *U.S. News & World Report,* Sept. 5, 1966, pp. 54-61.

4. Corwin, *op. cit.,* p. 33.

5. Joseph N. Kane, *Facts About the Presidents* (New York: Permabooks, 1960).

6. Thomas F. O'Dea, *The Mormons* (Chicago: University of Chicago Press, 1965), p. 22.

7. *Ibid.,* p. 42.

8. This entire portion relies mainly on the O'Dea manuscript.

9. "The Dinosaur Hunter," *Time,* Apr. 6, 1959, p. 86.

10. "Island of Prosperity," p. 2. Address before American Farm Bureau Federation in Chicago, Dec. 12, 1961.

11. "The Citizens' Candidate," *Time,* Nov. 16, 1962, p. 22.

12. *L.D.S. College Catalogue, 1927–1928,* p. 12.

13. Associated Press Biographical Service, Bulletin No. 138.

14. *The "S" Book, 1925,* p. 50.

15. *The "S" Book, 1925,* p. 67.

16. *The "S" Book, 1926,* p. 31.

17. Tom Mahoney, *The Story of George Romney* (New York: Harper & Brothers, 1960), p. 73.

18. W. Tuohy, "Dark Horse: Off and Running," *Copyright, Newsweek, Inc.,* Feb. 19, 1962, p. 25.

19. Detroit *News,* Oct. 13, 1954.

20. Address before Los Angeles Junior Chamber of Commerce, Nov. 19, 1964, p. 8.

21. Mahoney, *op. cit.,* p. 75.

22. *Ibid.,* p. 90.

23. Earl Mazo, "My Husband George Romney," *Good Housekeeping,* June, 1962, p. 57.

CHAPTER 3

1. Mitford M. Mathews, *American Words* (Cleveland: World Publishing, 1959), pp. 18-19.

2. *The History of the Republican Party* (Washington, D.C.: Republican National Committee, 1962), pp. 7-9.

3. John P. White, *Michigan Votes: Election Statistics, 1928–1956* (Ann Arbor, Mich.: University of Michigan, 1958); also the 1958 and 1960 Supplements.

4. George H. Mayer, *The Republican Party, 1854–1964* (New York: Oxford University Press, 1964), p. 475.

5. *U. S. Census of the Population, 1960,* Vol. I, Part 24 (Washington, D.C.: Govt. Printing Office, 1963), p. 39.

6. William Haber, Eugene McKean, and Harold Taylor, *What's Ahead for Michigan?* (Kalamazoo, Mich.: Upjohn Institute, 1959), pp. 9-25.

7. Daniel R. Fusfeld, *The Michigan Economy: Prospects and Problems* (Kalamazoo, Mich.: Upjohn Institute, 1962), p. 15.

8. Willis F. Dunbar, Michigan: *A History of the Wolverine State* (Grand Rapids, Mich., 1965), pp. 631-39.

9. Clever Bald, *Michigan in Four Centuries* (New York: Harper and Row, 1961), p. 476.

10. Gordon E. Baker, *Rural Versus Urban Political Power* (Garden City, N. Y.: Doubleday, 1955). The eight states were Georgia, Florida, Maryland, Delaware, Connecticut, Rhode Island, New Jersey, and California.

11. Judith Laikin, "What Made the Mess in Michigan?" *Reporter,* Mar. 31, 1960, pp. 33-35.

12. James Reichley, "Michigan: Labor's Love Lost," Chap. II, *States in Crisis* (Chapel Hill: University of North Carolina Press, 1964), p. 33.

13. Frank McNaughton, *Mennen Williams of Michigan* (New York: Oceana Publications, 1960), p. 9.

14. *Ibid.,* p. 10.

15. *U.S. News & World Report,* May 11, 1959, p. 102.

CHAPTER 4

1. Detroit *Free Press,* Feb. 16, 1959.

2. A. W. Baum, "The Man Who Surprised Detroit," *Saturday Evening Post,* Dec. 20, 1958, pp. 14-15. © 1958, The Curtis Publishing Company.

3. Tom Mahoney, *The Story of George Romney* (New York: Harper & Bros., 1960), p. 101.

4. "The Dinosaur Hunter," *Time,* Apr. 6, 1959, pp. 84-89.

5. Mahoney, *op. cit.,* p. 120.

6. *Time,* Apr. 6, 1959, p. 88.

7. Detroit *Free Press,* May 3, 1946.

8. Mahoney, *op. cit.,* p. 127.

9. *Ibid.,* p. 135.

10. *Ibid.,* pp. 181-84.

11. "Romney: Man to Watch for '64," *Business Week,* November 17, 1962, p. 96.

12. Eric Sevareid, "The Two-Family Car," *Reporter,* June 28, 1956, p. 13; also "Detroit Missionary at Large," *Newsweek,* Feb. 24, 1958, pp. 83-85.

13. Speech before National Parking Association, Detroit, June 5, 1957.

14. R. A. Smith, "Will Success Spoil American Motors?" *Fortune,* Jan., 1959, pp. 99-100.

15. Detroit *Free Press,* Dec. 27, 1958.

16. S. S. Harrison, "Romney and the Republicans," *New Republic,* Mar. 5, 1962, pp. 17-28.

17. Albert L. Sturm, *Constitution-Making in Michigan, 1961–1962* (Ann Arbor: University of Michigan, 1963), pp. 25-26.

18. Detroit *Free Press,* Jan. 10, 1962.

19. Detroit *Free Press,* Feb. 11, 1962.

20. Detroit *Free Press,* Mar. 16, 1962.

21. *State Journal,* Mar. 25, 1962.

CHAPTER 5

1. Detroit *Free Press,* Aug. 31, 1962.

2. Detroit *Free Press,* June 10, 1962.

3. *Newsweek,* Dec. 18, 1961, p. 28.

4. Detroit *Free Press,* Sept. 1, 1962.

5. Detroit *Free Press,* Feb. 12, 1962.

6. Detroit *News,* Aug. 5, 1962.

7. Detroit *News,* Aug. 5, 1962. None of the percentages of agreement were less than 63, and the Romney staff felt that the one item that was that low was worded poorly. Most were in the 80 or 90 bracket.

8. Detroit *Free Press,* July 10, 1962.

9. Norman C. Thomas, "Politics in Michigan!" *Papers of the Michigan Academy of Science, Arts, and Letters,* Vol. XLVII (Ann Arbor: University of Michigan Press, 1962).

10. Detroit *Free Press*, Sept. 25, 1962.
11. Detroit *Free Press*, Oct. 2, 1962.
12. Hugh A. Bone, *American Politics and the Party System*, 2d ed. (New York: McGraw-Hill, 1955) p. 445.
13. Daniel R. Fusfeld and others, *The Michigan Economy* (Kalamazoo, Mich.: Upjohn Institute, 1962), p. 33.
14. *Ibid.*, p. 15.
15. Detroit *Free Press*, Sept. 24, 1962.

CHAPTER 6

1. Detroit *News*, Apr. 27, 1963.
2. The groups represented were Council of College Presidents, Michigan Education Association, Michigan Association of School Boards, Michigan Association of School Administrators, Michigan Table Toppers Association, Michigan AFL-CIO, United Automobile Workers, Building Trades Council, Michigan Trucking Association, Michigan Railroads Association, City of Detroit, Wayne County Board of Supervisors, Michigan Association of Supervisors, Michigan Municipal League, League of Women Voters, American Association of University Women, State Chamber of Commerce, Michigan Junior Chamber of Commerce, Detroit Board of Commerce, Michigan Medical Society, Michigan Association of Osteopathic Physicians and Surgeons, Michigan Bar Association, Michigan Manufacturers Association, Michigan Bankers Association, Michigan Retailers Association, Michigan Association of Certified Public Accountants, Michigan Farm Bureau, Michigan State Grange.
3. Governor's Message to the Special Session of Michigan 72d Legislature, Sept. 12, 1963, p. 9.
4. "State GOP Slaps Romney," *Business Week*, Nov. 16, 1963, pp. 80-81.
5. *State Journal*, May 31, 1964.
6. Robert D. Novak, *The Agony of the G.O.P. 1964* (New York: Macmillan, 1965) pp. 156-66.
7. *Ibid.*, p. 165.
8. Theodore H. White, *The Making of the President, 1964* (New York: Atheneum, 1965), pp. 130-161. See also Novak, *op. cit.*, pp. 416-38.
9. *State Journal*, July 13, 1964.
10. *State Journal*, July 22, 1964.
11. The new state constitution had provided for an eight-member bipartisan Apportionment Commission. The intent of the commission was to keep gerrymandering by the legislature under control. The

constitution provided that in the event the Apportionment Commission could not agree, the State Supreme Court would pick a plan from those submitted by members of the commission. This is precisely what happened in Michigan in 1964. The matter was compounded by the fact that the State Supreme Court was forced to revise a decision made earlier when the U.S. Supreme Court ordered both houses of a state legislature to be based on population. The result in Michigan was that the plan adopted was a Democratic gerrymander.

12. *State Journal,* July 13, 1964.

CHAPTER 7

1. This was only the third time in Michigan history that Democrats gained control of both houses. The other times were in 1890 and 1932.

2. Grand Rapids *Press,* Nov. 5, 1964.

3. Grand Rapids *Press,* Apr. 28, 1965.

4. *Michigan AFL-CIO News,* June 9, 1965. A technical flaw in the wording of the bill helped Romney to secure the compromise.

5. The seven departments to be headed by commissions were civil rights, state highways, education, civil service, conservation, correction, and agriculture. The twelve super departments to be headed by single executives included state, attorney general, treasury, administration, state police, military affairs, commerce, licensing and regulation, labor, mental health, public health, and social service. Romney signed the bill on July 23, 1965. *(State Journal,* June 25, 1965.)

6. *State Journal,* Dec. 16, 1964.

7. Grand Rapids *Press,* Feb. 27, 1965.

8. Flint *Journal,* Mar. 3, 1965. Romney also felt that mental health could use additional funds.

9. The first bill would have made the four-year registration mandatory on a statewide basis, whereas the second allowed for this stipulation on a local-option basis. Swainson vetoed seventeen bills.

10. Grand Rapids *Press,* Dec. 10, 1965.

11. Detroit *News,* Mar. 30, 1965.

12. Grand Rapids *Press,* Sept. 22, 1965.

13. Governor's Message to the 73d Legislature, Second Session, Jan. 13, 1966.

14. Formal burial ceremonies came about a week later.

15. There were two-day sessions held on August 22-23 and October 11-12 before the sine die meeting in December.

16. Grand Rapids *Press,* Jan. 10, 1966.

17. Cavanagh also saw to it that the party vignette on the ballot

that had included the Williams likeness for the past decade was altered to contain only the likeness of Franklin D. Roosevelt. The Republicans took this opportunity to add the Romney image to that of Lincoln.

18. Romney gave serious thought to the possibility of running for the Senate himself. G. Mennen Williams was faced with a similar choice in 1958. Williams chose another gubernatorial team and lost a shot at the vice-presidency in 1960.

19. Detroit *Free Press,* Sept. 27, 1966.

20. Grand Rapids *Press,* Oct. 25, 1966. As explained by William Cote.

21. Detroit *Free Press,* Oct. 15, 1966. Friedman also compares the "lagging" Soapy with the "sharp, imaginative" campaign of Griffin.

22. Grand Rapids *Press,* Oct. 28, 1966.

23. Detroit *News,* Oct. 30, 1966. Robert Popa provides an excellent profile of the Ferency wit.

24. Detroit *Free Press,* Oct. 5, 1966.

25. The scandals that Ferency listed concerned malpractices at Fairwood Hospital, the failure of the Public Bank in Detroit, and conflict-of-interest charges against former Insurance Commissioner Allen Mayerson. He did not mention the drunk-driving record of one Democratic legislator, the morals conviction of a second, or the identity scandal of a third Democrat. It is not likely that Romney or anyone else could have done anything before these incidents were made public.

26. *Michigan AFL-CIO News,* Nov. 2, 1966.

27. Thomas E. Dewey was a native of Owosso, Mich., but when he sought the presidency in 1944 and 1948 he was governor of New York. Lewis Cass was the earlier effort, in 1848. He was a Democrat.

28. At the very start of his campaign Romney dealt with a minor uprising within the ranks of the conservative Republicans of the state GOP. Speaking personally at four county and district conventions where John Birch factions were threatening, he succeeded in keeping moderate Republicans in leadership positions in all but Macomb County. Of course, Richard Durant still controlled the 14th District on Detroit's northeast side.

29. In July, Romney held a 3–1 margin over Ferency. Sixty-two per cent of those interviewed said they would vote for Romney, 21 per cent for Ferency, 13 per cent were undecided, and 4 per cent said they would not vote at all. A September poll gave Romney a 60–37 edge. By October 9 that edge had grown to 64–33. Two days before the election the last poll hit close to actuality: Romney 61, Ferency 36.

30. The two gubernatorial candidates did meet on the same platform on three occasions. They made a joint appearance before the

Michigan Municipal League and debated twice in Detroit. The first debate was at the COPE AFL-CIO convention, the second before the Detroit Economics Club.

CHAPTER 8

1. Philadelphia *Sunday Bulletin*, Feb. 27, 1966, p. 17.
2. Detroit *News*, Nov. 7, 1962.
3. Detroit *Free Press*, Sept. 24, 1962.
4. Detroit *Free Press*, June 10, 1962.
5. *Michigan AFL-CIO Journal*, Apr. 13, 1966.
6. Address before state AFL-CIO Conference at the Civic Center, Lansing, June 1, 1966.
7. Detroit *News*, Jan. 28, 1965.
8. Detroit *News*, Feb. 23, 1966.
9. Grand Rapids *Press*, Jan. 22, 1966.
10. Detroit *News*, June 27, 1965.
11. *State Journal*, Oct. 27, 1964.
12. Detroit *News*, Nov. 19, 1963.
13. Detroit *News*, Mar. 27, 1965.
14. Detroit *News*, Mar. 6, 1963.
15. Sen. Joseph D. Tydings (Md.), "The Last Chance for the States," *Harper's*, Mar., 1966, p. 77. This article does not directly deal with Romney's role in Michigan politics; its major concern is with the Supreme Court's "One Man—One Vote" decision of 1964.
16. Grand Rapids *Press*, Sept. 22, 1965.
17. Grand Rapids *Press*, Dec. 21, 1965.
18. Detroit *News*, Feb. 17, 1964.
19. *State Journal*, Mar. 24, 1964.
20. Vidkun Quisling was a Norwegian traitor who sold out to the Nazis during World War II. When the Governor first used the strong language, he was greeted with scattered *Oh no's*. By the end of the speech the audience was solidly Romney's, and he was given a long standing ovation. It was one of the finest speeches Romney has ever given.
21. The other five senators involved were Clyde H. Geerlings, Holland; William L. Leppien, Saginaw; Emil Lockwood, St. Louis; Elmer R. Porter, Blissfield; Lloyd A. Stephens, Scottville.
22. Grand Rapids *Press*, Feb. 22, 1965.
23. *State Journal*, Jan. 25, 1962.
24. Detroit *News*, Sept. 12, 1963.
25. Michigan historically has had a rather high percentage of split-

ticket voters. It is not at all unusual for the results to announce a governor of one party and a president of another.

26. Grand Rapids *Press*, July 1, 1966.

CHAPTER 9

1. "Dark Horse: Off and Running," *Copyright, Newsweek, Inc.,* Feb. 19, 1962, p. 23. In a cover story *Newsweek* quoted someone else.

2. A. H. Raskin, "A Maverick Starts a New Crusade," *New York Times Magazine,* Feb. 15, 1960, p. 42. Romney was getting $150,000 in salary alone at the time.

3. Detroit *Free Press*, May 1, 1962.

4. Detroit *News,* March 7, 1963.

5. "Here Comes the Rambler Man," *Life,* Feb. 9, 1962, p. 39.

6. S. Alsop, "George Romney: the GOP's Fast Comer," *Saturday Evening Post,* May 26, 1962, p. 16. © 1962, The Curtis Publishing Company.

7. Detroit *Free Press,* Feb. 15, 1959. His was the first of a series of Lenten articles written by leading Detroit citizens.

8. *Doctrine and Covenants,* 90:24.

9. Earl Mazo, "My Husband George Romney," *Good Housekeeping,* June, 1962, p. 57. An excellent article on Romney.

10. Grand Rapids *Press,* Feb. 17, 1966.

11. "Why a Big Businessman Hit Big Business," *Business Week,* Feb. 15, 1958, p. 37.

12. Detroit *Free Press,* Oct. 1, 1962.

13. Grand Rapids *Press,* July 21, 1966.

14. *Time,* Nov. 16, 1962, p. 22.

15. Detroit *News,* Jan. 10, 1962.

16. Grand Rapids *Press,* Nov. 12, 1965. Kulsea gives background material that supports this point.

17. Grand Rapids *Press,* Dec. 8, 1965.

18. Detroit *Free Press,* Oct. 25, 1962.

19. Detroit *Free Press,* Jan. 29, 1959.

20. *State Journal,* Mar. 25, 1962.

21. Detroit *News,* Feb. 27, 1964. The Governor was absent for only two weeks instead of the three he had planned, however.

22. © 1960 by The New York Times Company. Reprinted by permission. (*New York Times Magazine,* Feb. 15, 1960, p. 44)

23. Detroit *Free Press,* Jan. 14, 1962. There are some other good insights into Romney given in this article.

CHAPTER 10

1. "The West and Today's Frontiers," pp. 8-14. Speech at University of Utah, Feb. 26, 1949.

2. Speech before Lincoln Day fund-raising dinner in Des Moines, Iowa, Feb. 10, 1965, p. 3.

3. "Flight Toward Reality," p. 7. Speech before Kiwanis International Convention, Miami Beach, June 30, 1960.

4. "Can America Keep Its Rendezvous With Destiny?" p. 6. Speech before Executive Club of Chicago, Jan. 16, 1959.

5. *Ibid.,* p. 1.

6. R. L. Bruckberger, *Image of America* (New York: Viking Press, 1959), p. 276. There is a good description, on page 266, of why Romney's term "consumeristic" should be adopted.

7. "The Message and the Example of America," p. 12. Speech before National Management Association in Detroit, Oct. 23, 1959.

8. "Individual Freedom vs. Concentrated Power," p. 9. Speech before the Anti-Defamation League of B'nai B'rith in Detroit, Sept. 26, 1959.

9. "Bridge of Freedom," p. 7. Speech before Honolulu Chamber of Commerce in Honolulu, Jan. 5, 1961.

10. Speech before Associated Press annual meeting in New York City, Apr. 19, 1965, p. 2.

11. "Individual Freedom vs. Concentrated Power," p. 5.

12. Speech before Associated Press annual meeting in New York City, Apr. 19, 1965, pp. 3-5.

13. Statement before subcommittee on Antitrust and Monopoly of Committee on Judiciary, U.S. Senate, Feb. 7, 1958, p. 7. (Only four of six indications are listed.)

14. "The Importance of New Ideas," pp. 4-5. Speech before 34th annual meeting of New England Council in Boston, Nov. 20, 1958.

15. "The Nation's Number One Problem," p. 10. Address before National Association of Life Underwriters in Detroit, Sept. 19, 1957.

16. Statement before subcommittee on Antitrust, p. 30.

17. *Ibid.,* pp. 13-14.

18. "Bridge of Freedom," p. 12.

19. "The International Bridge of Freedom," p. 17. Speech before joint meeting of Empire Club and Canadian Club in Toronto, Canada, Jan. 26, 1961.

20. Speech before Lincoln Day fund-raising dinner of Middlesex Club in Boston, Feb. 12, 1966, p. 3.

21. Speech at Valentine dinner salute to John and Ann Love in Denver, Feb. 14, 1966, p. 3.

22. Speech at All-American Cities Award Banquet in Michigan City, Indiana, May 13, 1966, p. 5.

23. "The Force of Voluntary Cooperation," p. 4. Speech before American Society of Association Executives at Boca Raton, Fla., Nov. 17, 1959.

24. *Ibid.*, p. 1. See also "Flight Toward Reality," p. 20.

25. "The Nation's Number One Problem," p. 14.

26. "Flight Toward Reality," p. 8.

27. *Ibid.*, p. 9.

28. "America's Internal 'Somethings,' " p. 9. Speech at annual meeting of American Petroleum Institute in Chicago, Nov. 10, 1958, p. 19.

29. "Island of Prosperity," p. 20. Address before American Farm Bureau Federation in Chicago, Dec. 12, 1961.

30. *Ibid.*, p. 22.

CHAPTER 11

1. In 1964, Goldwater cost the GOP one Senate seat, three House seats, and 485 state legislative seats. The GOP gained one governorship.

2. Grand Rapids *Press*, Nov. 30, 1964.

3. Midland *Daily News*, Nov. 6, 1964.

4. For an accurate and detailed account of the Ford-Halleck battle see Henry Z. Scheele, *Charlie Halleck* (New York: Exposition Press, 1966), pp. 243-59.

5. *State Journal*, June 2, 1965.

6. *From Disaster to Distinction* (New York: Ripon Society, 1966), pp.84-98.

7. The survey indicated that a downward trend of Republican popularity had been reversed. Before the 1966 election, 25 per cent of the population regarded themselves as Republican, 45 per cent Democrat, and 30 could be labeled independents. Now these figures were 29, 43, and 28 per cent, respectively. The downward trend had been in motion for twenty years.

8. Grand Rapids *Press*, Dec. 17, 1966.

9. *National Observer*, Dec. 19, 1966.

10. *Time*, Mar. 18, 1966, p. 29.

11. Grand Rapids *Press*, Oct. 1, 1966.

12. Philadelphia *Sunday Bulletin*, Feb. 5, 1966, Apr. 9, 1966, and July 10, 1966.

13. Detroit *Free Press*, Sept. 19, 1966, and Nov. 20, 1966.

14. Detroit *News*, Dec. 21, 1966.

15. Detroit *News*, Nov. 10, 1966.

16. Most of this material was gleaned from the Michigan State

library biographical collection, although two fine articles by Bill Kulsea (Aug. 22, 1965) and Robert Longstaff (June 5, 1966) in the Grand Rapids *Press* augmented these files.

17. Detroit *Free Press,* Nov. 12, 1966, and Nov. 19, 1966. There is an excellent article on Romney's performance in the Nov. 14, 1966, Detroit *News.*

18. Detroit *Free Press,* Dec. 18, 1966.

19. Detroit *News,* Dec. 14, 1966.

20. Grand Rapids *Press,* Nov. 29, 1966.

21. Grand Rapids *Press,* May 16, 1966.

22. Detroit *Free Press,* Nov. 17, 1966.

23. Grand Rapids *Press,* Nov. 13, 1966.

24. Detroit *News,* Dec. 9, 1966.

25. Grand Rapids *Press,* June 7, 1966.

26. This data was compiled from a series of articles on United States religious bodies: *Time,* Apr. 29, 1966, Apr. 8, 1966, and Jan. 14, 1966, and *U.S. News & World Report,* Jan. 17, 1966.

27. Wallace Turner, *The Mormon Establishment* (New York: Houghton Mifflin, 1966), p. 246.

28. *Saturday Review,* Mar. 3, 1962, p. 5.

29. *National Observer,* July 11, 1966. This is a caustic article on Romney's Vietnam statement.

30. The guest list included J. F. Helder, Netherlands, secretary of the World Poultry Association; Sir Mobolzji Bank-Anthony, Nigerian industrialist; Tom Normanton, Manchester, England, industrialist; Professor Hermann Doerner, University of Heidelberg, Germany; Dr. Eni Njoku, vice-chancellor, University of Nigeria; John Rose, Birmingham, England, industrial executive; Alf Sanengem, Central Institute for Industrial Research, Oslo, Norway; Carlos Velasco, National Society of Spanish Chemists, Madrid; Gerald F. Ludovici, merchant-broker, London, England; Chandralekha Pandit Mehta, New Delhi, India, daughter of Indian writer and political figure Madame Pandit; Dr. H. J. Kuhlmeijer, rector of Foundation for Business Administration, Netherlands School of Economics; Manuel Travares, corporation president, Santo Domingo, former government leader of Dominican Republic; Carl Andersen, power executive, Denmark; Sheikh Michel al Khoury, president of Lebanon National Council of Tourists; Father Andrew C. Varga, S. J., general assistant of Society of Jesus, Rome; Dr. Jose Meiches, secretary for public works, Sao Paulo, Brazil; Father R. L. Bruckberger, Jesuit priest from France; M. Strack, director of Society of Explorations, Seine, France; Goren Ahrsjo, Stockholm, Sweden, businessman; Rainer Van Fieandt, immediate past-governor, Bank of Finland; Mrs. ReJane Iossif, president of Greek National Tourist Association; and Carlos Ovidiom Lagos, editor of La Capital, Rossario, Argentina.

Index

Abernathy, Roy, 56

Action Team, 4, 6, 145, 234

AFL-CIO, 64-65, 85, 122, 132, 138, 142, 173

Aid to Dependent Children of the Unemployed, 99, 114, 116, 160-61, 164

Alcoa, 47-49, 53, 93, 203

Allen, Glenn S., 233

Aluminum Wares Association, 48

American Motors Corporation, 50-59, 73, 75, 90-91, 98-100, 103, 111, 153, 167, 182-88, 190, 195, 223, 234-36

Anti-missile gap, 244

Applegate, Albert A., 224

Augustine, Leroy, 3, 135-36

Austerity Budget, 237-38

Automobile Manufacturer's Assoc., 46, 49, 50, 52

Automotive-Civic Golden Jubilee, 52-53

Automotive Council for War Production, 50-53, 61, 207, 233

Automotive decentralization, 35, 156

Axe the Appointee, 132

Bachelder, Glen L., 226

Bagwell, Paul D., 32, 39, 42-44, 61-64, 70-72, 84

Barcus, Norman, 90

Bartlett, Lynn, 124

Beaux Arts Ball, 49

Berrien County, 84

Bliss, Ray, 70, 214-18, 229-30

Blondy, Charles S., 94, 97

Bone, Hugh H., 33, 88

Book of Mormon, 13, 16, 180-81

Boosters Club, 22

Bowman Bill, 76

Brake, D. Hale, 67-68, 74, 165

Brooke, Edward, 11, 159, 189

Broyhill, Joel, 225

Bruckberger, R. L., 197

Burch, Dean, 212-15

Burke, Bill, 99

Burning Tree Country Club, 48

Bury the Budget, 131

Business Activities Tax, 36, 44, 79

Byington, S. John, 168, 226

Cass, Lewis, 29

Cavanagh, Jerome, 65, 97, 133-35, 139, 154, 167

Chafee, John H., 219, 230

Chase, Clifford, 226

Chihuahua, 17

Chrysler Law, 153-54
Ciceronia, 21-22
Citizens Advisory Committee, 59-60
Citizens for America, 208
Citizens for Michigan, 59-63, 72-73, 189, 207
Civil Rights Commission, 234
Clayton Act, 201
Cohan, Leon S., 141, 150, 184
Collins, Joe, 66, 82, 110
Colonia Dublan, 17
Colonia Juárez, 17
Colorado Springs Conference, 218
Committee on Political Education, 137-38, 142
Compact car, 56, 58, 59
Conboy, Bernard, 110, 167, 238
Conflict of interest, 166
Constitutional Convention, 59, 64-68, 72, 74-75, 164-65, 184-88
Construction safety legislation, 95, 155
Consumerism, 200
Continuing American Revolution, 190, 195, 197
Council of the Twelve, 15
County home rule, 165-66
Coup de grâce, 125
Cow Palace, 107
Credibility gap, 244
Cross, Travis, 226
Curse of Cain, 233

Danhof, Robert J., 223
Deacon (rank), 23
De Jonge, Herbert C., 224
Dempsey, John, 75
De Tocqueville, Alexis, 207
Detroit Board of Education, 59-60

Detroit school needs, 59-60, 207
DeVries, Walter, 6, 91, 119, 173, 223, 225
Dewey, Thomas, 215
Dinosaur symbol, 58-59
Dirksen, Everett, 173, 234
Doctrine and Covenants, 13, 180
Drummond, Roscoe, 87
Durado Beach conference, 217
Durant, Richard, 81, 93, 149, 171
Dutch Mafia, 223
Dzendzel, Raymond D., 122, 130-33, 189

Earmarked Fund, 36-37
Economic birth, principle of, 204-5
Edinburgh, 26
Eisenhower, Dwight D., 32, 66, 104-6, 148, 177, 198, 214-16, 221, 224, 226
Elder (rank), 24
Elliott, Arthur Jr., 72, 75, 94, 118, 152-53, 223
Engle, Glenn, 83, 133, 170
Essex Wire strike, 104
Evans, Rowland, 222
Excessive concentration of power, 195-204, 244
Executive reorganization, 123, 165
Experience gap, 235-37

Fair Employment Practice Act, 234
Farnum, Billy, 177, 133, 160
Favorite son candidates, 229
Ferency, Zolton, 6-10, 110, 128, 133-34, 139-45, 168, 174-77, 185-86, 237-38
Fiscal reform, 127-29, 161-63, 237-39

Fisher, Max M., 226
Folger, Cliff, 102
Ford-Canton legislation, 114-15
Ford, Gerald, 215
Foreign travels, 235-37
Friedman, Saul, 139

Gallup Poll, 100, 147, 220
Gateway Amendment, 63-64
General Fund, 36-45, 76, 110-11, 124, 129, 131
Generation of Progress, 245
Goldwater, Barry, 74, 102-8, 111-13, 118-20, 141-45, 172, 174, 183, 211-34
G.O.P. Girls, 145
Governors' Conferences, 103-5, 213, 218, 229, 241-42
Governor's veto, 126-28
Great Society, 206
Green, Allison, 94, 224
Griffin, Robert, 4-11, 136, 138-39, 145-46, 174-75, 215, 219-20
GROPE, 225

Hallas, Howard, 58, 179, 187
Hall, Leonard, 224, 226
Halleck, Charles, 215
Hare, James, 7, 32, 63, 96, 133-34, 141, 146, 177
Harmon, Charles E., 6, 152, 224
Harris Poll, 211, 220-21
Hart, Phillip A., 135
Hatfield, Mark O., 11, 221-26, 241-42
Haun's Mill Massacre, 14
Hawley-Smoot tariff bill, 46, 201
Headlee, Richard, 226
Higgins, George, 111-12
Holland Tulip Festival, 78

Humphrey, Hubert H., 138

Implied consent, 151
Individual responsibility, 195, 205, 206, 245

Javits, Jacob, 225
Jefferson-Jackson Day Dinner, 78, 133
John Birch Society, 81, 108, 149, 172
Johnson, Lyndon Baines, 39, 102, 118, 138, 146, 167, 173-74, 206, 211-21, 228

Kelley, Frank, 7, 117-18, 133-34, 141, 146, 150, 160, 164, 183-84, 194, 228
Kennedy, David, 23, 25, 56
Kennedy, John F., 7, 32, 39, 69, 95, 101, 107, 110, 137-38, 148, 173, 183-84, 194, 228
Kennedy, Robert, 138
Keynesian economics, 244
Khrushchev, Nikita, 199
Know-Nothing era, 109
Knudsen, W. S., 46
Kowalski, Joseph J., 94, 97, 120, 122, 125, 129-30, 134, 154
Kulsea, William, 121, 185

Labor Day parade, 156
LaFount, Harold A., 188
Laird, Melvin, 219
Landon, Alf M., 215
Landrum-Griffin Act, 137-39
Lansing, truce of, 160
Latter-Day Saints, 13, 18, 21, 24, 188, 233

League of Women Voters, 62-63, 189

Legislative pay raise, 166

Lesinski, T. John, 67, 96, 160-61, 179

Lincoln, Abraham, 109, 191, 195, 206

Lindemere, Lawrence B., 226

Lindsay, John, 11

Lock, Clarence W., 162

Lockwood, Emil, 152-53, 171

Lodge, Henry Cabot, 107, 220

Longstaff, Robert, 171

Love, John A., 230

McClean bill, 77

McDonald, Ronald, 160

McGill, Ralph, 172

McIntosh, Robert, 223-26

McKay, David O., 233

Mackie, John C., 133

Mackinac Bridge legislation, 158, 217

McLaughlin, William, 175

McNamara, Patrick V., 136, 175, 219

McNamara, Robert S., 133

McNary-Haugen bill, 201

Mahoney, Tom, 52

Malik, Charles, 191, 197

Market opinion research, 136, 142, 173

Marriott, J. Willard, 100, 102-3, 225-26

Martin, John, 212

Mason, George, 53-56

Massachusetts Ballot, 116, 170, 173

Mayer, George H., 32

Medicare (reduction of funds), 239

Metal Trade Industry Conference, 53, 236

Metropolitan, 54

Mexico, 12, 14, 16-17

Michigan economy, 109-11, 155-56

Midget team, 21

Milliken, William G., 4, 11, 127, 135, 224

Milliman, Richard L., 38, 106, 223-24, 226

Minimum wage bill, 95, 114, 155

Monday Club, 49

Moore, Johnathan, 226

Mormons, 13-17, 67, 180, 187

Mormon stand on the Negro, 232-35

Mormon War, 14

Morrill Anti-Bigamy Law, 16

Murphy, George, 230

Murphy, William, 226

National airline strike, 203

National Association of Manufacturers (NAM), 218

National Fair Campaigns Practices Committee, 82

National Federation of Republican Women, 231

National Guard scandal, 104, 114, 117, 160, 164

National Press Club, 48, 100-104

Nauvoo, 14-16

Neanderthals, 40, 69, 77, 120

Negative balance legislation, 153-45

Negro vote, 88

Neifert, Carson, 160
Neslen, Clarence C., 21-22
New Dealer, 38, 135
New Frontier, 194
Nisbet, Stephen S., 65
Nixon, Richard, 32, 92, 101, 106, 169, 213-15, 220-28
Novak, Robert D., 101, 104, 222
Nuisance taxes, 40
Nunn, Guy, 86-87

Oakley, Idaho, 17
O'Donnell, Gladys, 231
One-man-one-vote principle, 38
Operation Christmas, 168-69
Orlebeke, Charles J., 224

Payless payday, 41-47, 171
Pearl of Great Price, 13
Percy, Charles, 5, 11, 213, 221-22
Peterson, Elly, 152-53
Peterson, Vadal, 20-23
Polygamy, 16
Popa, Bob, 80, 170
Population growth and groupings, 33
Potomac fever, 207
Presidential primaries, 228-29
Pratt, Anna Amelia, 17, 23
Prendergast, William, 226
Priest (rank), 24
Principle of economic birth, 204-5

Quislings, 171

Race riot, 51
Rambler, 5, 57
Reagan, Ronald, 11, 141, 221-22, 229
Reapportionment, 120

Republican Coordinating Committee, 214-18, 227
Republican State Central Committee, 102, 229
Reuther, Walter, 51, 62, 71, 80, 86, 91, 149
Rexburg, Idaho, 18
Rhodes, James, 106
Rockefeller, Nelson, 11, 102, 106-8, 169, 213, 217, 221-26
Romney, Anna, 23
Romney, Amy, 18-19, 28
Romney, Charles W., 17-20, 24
Romney, Douglas Pratt, 17
Romney, Gaskell, 17-19
Romney, Gaskell M., 17, 19, 25
Romney, George Scott, 24, 50, 183
Romney, Jane LaFount (Mrs. Bruce Robinson), 50
Romney, Lawrence, 17
Romney, Lenore LaFount (Mrs. George Romney), 9-11, 22-24, 27, 46, 48, 78, 92, 181-84, 189, 231-32
Romney, Margo Lynn (Mrs. Larry Keenan), 50
Romney, Meryl, 19, 23
Romney, Miles Park, 16, 18-19, 27
Romney, Miles Pratt, 17, 24
Romney, Willard Mitt, 24, 50, 78
Romney Associates, 225
Romney for President Committee, 225
Romney Girls, 145
Romney Revolution, 8
Roosevelt, Franklin D., 30-31, 50, 201
Roosevelt, Theodore, 23, 226
Roosevelt Junior High School, 18

Saints, 14-17, 24-25
Sales Tax Diversion Amendment, 37
Sander, Al, 90, 160
Saxton, Isabel, 3
Scholle, August, 61-66, 80, 83, 89, 96, 122, 138, 149, 163-64, 185
Schlafly, Phyllis, 231
Scott, Hugh, 212, 216, 227
Scramble boys, 223
Scranton, William, 104-12, 169, 177, 216, 226
Seidman, William L., 223
Senate Campaign Committee, 230
Senior-citizens legislation, 156-57
Seven frontiers, 194
Smeekens, John P., 171
Smith, Gerald, 20, 27, 48
Smith, Joseph Jr., 13-15, 26
Smylie, Robert, 213
Spad, Carl, 226
Staebler, Neil, 42-43, 67, 69, 81, 96, 110-24, 176
State Administrative Board, 67, 74, 93
Straight-line depreciation bill, 154-55
Student Council, 22
Swainson, John B., 32, 39, 43-44, 63, 67-75, 144, 148-49, 176

Taft, William Howard, 201
Taft, Robert A., 226
Taylor, Harold C., 90
Teacher (rank), 24
Telescope (television program), 85
Ticket-splitting, 173
Toledo War, 29
Total American Progress, 6, 245
Total Michigan Progress, 163

Town-hall meetings, 55
Tracting, 25
Trade bridges, 205
Truman, Harry S., 53, 66, 141

United Auto Workers (UAW), 64, 86, 202
Utah War, 16

Volume Investment Fund, 56
VanDusen, Richard C., 223, 226, 237
Vestal, Bud, 157, 219
Veteran Trust Fund, 37, 42-44
Veto bloc, 67
Victory Council, 51-52
Vietnam, 169, 172, 212, 220, 236, 241-44
Vietnam address (April 7, 1967), 244
Vitiate the veto, 132
Voluntary Cooperation, 51, 169, 208

Wagner Act, 201
Wallace, George, 190
Walnut Hills Country Club, 96
Walsh, David, 46, 47, 53
Ward (of Mormon Church), 24
Washington Club, 49
Washington (grade school), 18
Ways, Max, 191
Williams, G. Mennen, 5-8, 32-39, 41-42, 71-84, 110-11, 129, 133-43, 154, 158, 171, 173, 237
Woodcock, Leonard, 62, 133

Young, Brigham, 15-16

Zhukov, Marshal, 198
Zion, 14-15